An Ethical Approach
to Practitioner Research

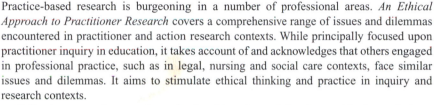
Practice-based research is burgeoning in a number of professional areas. *An Ethical Approach to Practitioner Research* covers a comprehensive range of issues and dilemmas encountered in practitioner and action research contexts. While principally focused upon practitioner inquiry in education, it takes account of and acknowledges that others engaged in professional practice, such as in legal, nursing and social care contexts, face similar issues and dilemmas. It aims to stimulate ethical thinking and practice in inquiry and research contexts.

Following moves to promote professional learning and development in the workplace, there is an increase in the number of practitioners engaging in action or inquiry-based learning in the workplace supported by university staff or consultants, as evidenced in the emergence of professional learning communities and learning networks. There are many tensions inherent in relationships between practitioners and academics in terms of the setting of the research agenda, the policy implications that may flow from it and the right to publish outcomes. Negotiating that relationship requires ethical probity where each party recognises, understands and respects mutual responsibilities. This book explores this through a wide variety of roles from those of academic researchers, consultants and teachers to professional practitioners as researchers and, importantly, students and children. It therefore illustrates a number of differing perspectives about ethics and research which are allied to those roles.

Drawing on the expertise of international researchers and academics from America, Australia and Europe, the book provides invaluable support to the novice researcher and illuminates some of the more intricate issues for the more experienced research practitioner. Packed with detailed and thought-provoking examples this book contains theoretical analyses of ethical matters and offers practical advice to practitioner and action researchers across the fields of schools, hospitals and community and family settings.

Anne Campbell was Professor of Education at Liverpool Hope University before moving to the Carnegie Faculty of Sport and Education at Leeds Metropolitan University in May 2007.

Susan Groundwater-Smith is Director of the Centre for Practitioner Research at the University of Sydney's Faculty of Education and Social Work, where she is an honorary professor.

An Ethical Approach to Practitioner Research

Dealing with issues and dilemmas in action research

Edited by Anne Campbell and Susan Groundwater-Smith

Routledge
Taylor & Francis Group

LONDON AND NEW YORK

First published 2007 by Routledge
2 Park Square, Milton Park, Abingdon, Oxon OX14 4RN

Simultaneously published in the USA and Canada
by Routledge
270 Madison Ave, New York, NY 10016

Routledge is an imprint of the Taylor & Francis Group, an informa business

© 2007 Anne Campbell and Susan Groundwater-Smith, selection and editorial matter; individual chapters, the contributors

Typeset in Times by
GreenGate Publishing Services, Tonbridge, Kent
Printed and bound in Great Britain by
T J International Ltd, Padstow, Cornwall

British Library Cataloguing in Publication Data
A catalogue record for this book is available from the British Library

Library of Congress Cataloging in Publication Data
A catalog record has been requested for this book

ISBN-10: 0 415 43087 9 (hbk)
ISBN-10: 0 415 43088 7 (pbk)
ISBN-10: 0 203 93927 1 (ebk)

ISBN-13: 978 0 415 43087 6 (hbk)
ISBN-13: 978 0 415 43088 3 (pbk)
ISBN-13: 978 0 203 93927 7 (ebk)

Contents

Notes on contributors

Anne Campbell was Professor of Education at Liverpool Hope University before moving to the Carnegie Faculty of Sport and Education at Leeds Metropolitan University in May 2007. She holds a Fellowship at the Moray House School of Education, Edinburgh University.

Campbell has a long history of both researching and supporting others in practitioner inquiry and research. She is the co-author of a major text in this area, *Practitioner Research for Professional Development in Education* (Sage, 2004), which is used widely in the UK by practitioner–researchers. Her interest in narrative research approaches in teachers' and students' stories of professional practice is evident in her book *School-based Teacher Education: Tales From a Fictional Primary School* (David Fulton, 1988).

She has directed and co-directed a number of government-sponsored evaluation and research projects in the field of teacher professional practice and learning including the practice of mentoring, teachers' perceptions of professional learning and partnership with schools in teacher education.

Campbell is currently a member of the Executive Council of the British Educational Research Association where she holds the portfolio for practitioner research. She is a member of the editorial boards of the journals *Teacher Development* and *Educational Action Research*.

With Susan Groundwater-Smith, Adjunct Professor at Liverpool Hope University, she convened the International Colloquium on Ethics in Practitioner Research in October 2005 in Liverpool, upon which this book is based.

Marilyn Cochran-Smith holds the John E. Cawthorne Millennium Chair in Teacher Education for Urban Schools and directs the doctoral programme in curriculum and instruction at Boston College's Lynch School of Education. Cochran-Smith earned her PhD in language and education from the University of Pennsylvania in 1982 where she was on the faculty of the Graduate School of Education until going to Boston College in 1996.

A nationally and internationally known scholar on issues related to teacher quality, teacher education and research on teaching, Cochran-Smith was President of the American Educational Research Association in 2004 –2005.

Cochran-Smith was the Co-Chair of AERA's National Panel on Research and Teacher Education. The report of the panel, *Studying Teacher Education*, edited by Cochran-Smith and Ken Zeichner, was published in 2005 and received AACTE's Best Publication award in 2006. Other recent books include *Walking the Road: Race, Diversity and Social Justice in Teacher Education* (Teachers College Press, 2004) and *Practice, Policy and Politics in Teacher Education* (Corwin Press, 2006). Dr Cochran-Smith was also editor of the *Journal of Teacher Education* from 2000 to 2006. She was appointed as a member of the National Research Council's committee on teacher education, which is sponsored by the National Academy of Sciences and was charged by Congress to study the state of teacher education in the US.

Christopher Day is Professor of Education and Co-Director of the Teacher and Leadership Research Centre (TLRC) in the University of Nottingham. Prior to this he worked as a teacher, lecturer and local authority schools adviser. He is founding editor of *Teachers and Teaching: Theory and Practice*; and co-editor of the *Educational Action Research Journal*.

His books have been published in several languages and include *Teachers Matter: Connecting Work, Lives and Effectiveness* (Open University Press, 2007); *Successful Principalship: International Perspectives* (co-edited, Springer, 2007); *A Passion for Teaching* (Routledge, 2004); and *Developing Teachers: The Challenges of Lifelong Learning* (Falmer Press, 1999).

He has recently completed directing a four-year DfES-funded research project on variations in teachers' work, lives and effectiveness, and is currently directing an eight-country project on successful school principalship, a nine-country European project on successful principalship in schools in challenging urban contexts; a national project on school leadership and pupil outcomes; and a national project on effective classroom teaching.

Danny Doyle started primary school teaching after studying as a mature student in Jersey, the Channel Islands. While working as a chef and as a part-time catering lecturer in adult education, he studied for an Open University degree. He then gained his teaching qualification as an articled teacher over two years. His interest in research began during that training while conducting action research to study interactive display. It was developed further when he researched the teaching of probability for an advanced diploma in Applied Studies in Mathematics Education. The focus of his master's degree was an action research project within the three core curriculum areas of English, mathematics and science to evaluate and develop personal professional practice. This was followed by research to determine head teachers' perspectives of the local Validated Schools Self-Evaluation (VSSE) process in Jersey.

He joined the National Teacher Research Panel after presenting the findings of his Doctor of Education research into pupils' perspectives of using one-to-one laptop access, 'Insider research into Microsoft's Anytime Anywhere

Learning: primary school children empowered in a constructivist classroom' at the panel's national conference in 2004. Danny Doyle is now deputy head teacher at Les Landes Primary School in St Ouen, Jersey.

Susanna Gorman (née Davis) is the University of Technology, Sydney (UTS) Research Ethics Manager. She has worked in the area of ethics since 1988 and has extensive experience in the University research sector. She has been responsible for the oversight of research ethics at UTS since the end of 1992, when the university's human research ethics committee was formed. She has witnessed the evolution of ethics and its incursion into research practice and governance in the Australian university sector. Gorman was the founding convenor of the network of NSW university ethics committees, which first met at UTS in 1994. The network, which meets annually, has since grown to encompass universities from other states and provides a forum for discussion of ethical issues in research as well as an opportunity for input into policy development by relevant government bodies.

Gorman studied moral philosophy in the early 1980s while studying for a Communications degree in South Australia. She has a Masters in Women's Studies from the University of New South Wales.

Gorman has an interest in the relationship between spirituality and ethics, in particular the spirituality of conversation, and was a convenor of Spirituality in the Pub (SIP) for over six years.

Susan Groundwater-Smith is Honorary Professor of Education in the Faculty of Education and Social Work at the University of Sydney. There she directs the Centre for Practitioner Research. She is also Adjunct Professor of Education at Liverpool Hope University where she works in partnership with Anne Campbell.

Groundwater-Smith has a long history of action research and evaluation that engages with the field of education in a number of ways and under a number of guises. As well as being a facilitator and consultant supporting the inquiry of others she has also investigated her own practice as a teacher–educator. In recent years her attention has been focused, in particular, upon the ways in which young people's voices can be foregrounded in practitioner research, such that they are not only data sources, but are active agents in constructing and interrogating research initiatives. She has undertaken this work in a number of settings, principally schools, but also environments where learning is conducted outside the classroom such as museums.

Groundwater-Smith is one of two international editors of the *Educational Action Research Journal* whose purpose is to disseminate and critique various action research initiatives. She contributes to a range of publications where she argues that matters of research quality must be governed by principles of ethical practice.

Caroline Leeson is Senior Lecturer in Early Childhood Studies at the University of Plymouth with particular interests in leadership, working relationships and children's participatory rights. She is currently studying for a PhD looking at the involvement of young children in decision-making processes when coming into care.

She worked for many years as a social worker, specialising in child protection, adoption and fostering and managed a family centre in an area of high ethnic diversity and poor integration. The development of community was a high priority, as was establishing resources where people could come together. These experiences taught her the value of working together, the importance of valuing the perspectives of others and the joy of working with young children.

Susan L. Lytle is Associate Professor of Education and Chair of the Language and Literacy in Education Division, Graduate School of Education, University of Pennsylvania, Director of the master's and doctoral programmes in reading/writing/literacy, and Founding Director of the 20-year-old Philadelphia Writing Project (PhilWP), a site of the National Writing Project and an urban school–university collaborative network focused on teacher-to-teacher professional development and fostering practice-based research on teaching, learning and schooling. Dr Lytle has worked closely with urban K-12 teachers, community college/university faculty staff, and adult educators to design and document a variety of inquiry-based collaborative research projects. She has published widely on topics related to literacy education, teacher learning and leadership, school–university partnerships, teacher research/practitioner inquiry, and urban education. Her co-authored book (with Cochran-Smith), *Inside/Outside: Teacher Research and Knowledge* (Teachers College Press, 1993) received the AACTE Outstanding Professional Writing Award in 1995. Lytle is co-editor of the Practitioner Inquiry Series of Teachers College Press as well as a past president of the National Conference on Research in Language and Literacy (NCRLL) and the NCTE Assembly on Research. Her recent work looks at the epistemology and ethics of practice-based inquiry conducted by educational leaders.

Olwen McNamara is a Professor of Teacher Education and Development at the University of Manchester. Her research interests are professionally focused and practitioner-oriented, with a particular emphasis on the initial and continuing education of teachers and mathematics education. She publishes widely in these fields; recent books being *New Teacher Identity and Regulative Government: Discursive Formation of Primary Mathematics Teacher Education* (Brown and McNamara: Springer, 2005); *Practitioner Research and Professional Development in Education* (Campbell, McNamara, Gilroy: Sage, 2004) and *Becoming an Evidence-based Practitioner* (RoutledgeFalmer, 2002). She is a member of the British Educational Research Association Council, where she chairs the Conference Committee.

Nicole Mockler is an Australian teacher–educator and education consultant who works with teachers and schools in practitioner research and pedagogy and curriculum reform. Mockler is also a PhD candidate in the Faculty of Education and Social Work at the University of Sydney where she is investigating the development and formation of teacher professional identity. She has published in the areas of teacher professional development, practitioner inquiry and transformative pedagogies, and along with Susan Groundwater-Smith and Jane Mitchell is author of *Learning in the Middle Years: More than a Transition* (Thomson Learning, 2007).

Lin Norton is Professor of Pedagogical Research and Dean of Learning and Teaching at Liverpool Hope University where she has worked for the last 20 years. In her present role, she leads the Centre for Learning and Teaching (www.hope.ac.uk/learningandteaching), whose aim is to encourage continuing professional development through reflective practice and through choice. A chartered psychologist and psychology lecturer for many years, her research interests include pedagogical action research, student assessment, meta-learning and lecturers' beliefs and practices. She has published extensively in journals and books. She currently holds the position of research director in the collaborative Centre for Excellence in Teaching and Learning on writing for assessment (www.writenow.ac.uk) and is Editor of Psychology Teaching Review.

Petra Ponte was awarded an MA with distinction in Special Education at the Amsterdam University, with Educational Innovation and Educational Psychology as subsidiary subjects. Before studying for her degree she had worked as teacher, head teacher and consultant in various settings. During and after her studies she worked as a lecturer, programme leader and researcher, first at the Amsterdam University and later at the Amsterdam University of Professional Education. She has published in the field of special education, pupil guidance, cross-cultural collaboration and action research. She completed her PhD thesis on a research into action research by teachers and the facilitation of that research in theory and practice. At the moment she combines her professorship at Fontys University of Applied Sciences, Department of Inclusive and Special Education, with a research post at Leiden University, Graduate School of Teaching. Finally she is an active participant in international networks in the fields of action research.

Lesley Saunders joined the General Teaching Council (England) as Policy Adviser for Research at its inception in September 2000 and has been engaged in developing and implementing a research strategy which draws on high quality scholarship and evidence to reflect the breadth of the GTC's remit and aspirations.

Saunders also holds a visiting professorship at the Institute of Education, London: her professorial lecture, given in March 2004, was titled 'Grounding the democratic imagination? Developing the relationship between research and policy in education'. Her previous career was as Principal Research Officer at the National Foundation for Educational Research where she headed the School Improvement Research Centre. Prior to that, she taught in the primary, secondary and adult sectors.

Saunders serves on the education sub-panel for the Research Assessment Exercise 2008. In her spare time, she is a published poet.

Andrew Townsend is Assistant Professor in Educational Enquiry at the University of Warwick, a post principally concerned with supporting the enquiry work of education professionals studying for accredited programmes. Before taking up his current post he worked as an educational consultant researching, conducting, supporting and evaluating action research. This was preceded by ten years of experience as a teacher of science in secondary schools, during which he developed his initial interest in action research and alternative strategies for change. His recent work has included studying the process and outcomes of collaborative and networked enquiry and supporting student research groups.

Foreword: In search of better times

Judyth Sachs

In a recent article in the *British Medical Journal* (Wade, 2005) it was argued that ethical considerations should apply to all forms of practice – in that case, medical practice – but that many people 'act as if they apply only to research' (p. 468). In this book it is clear that educational practices in many forms and manifestations should be conducted in an ethical manner; that is, one that satisfies the primary moral purpose of doing good and minimising harm. At the same time the contributors to the book, covering many facets of ethical practice, recognise that meeting such an injunction is highly problematic. Good for whom? Harmful to whom and in what way? Is what benefits a practitioner inquiring into a particular practice also of benefit to the consequential stakeholders who are using that practice or service? Is enhancing a particular practice, for some, undertaken at the expense of others? These are fundamental but often neglected questions. This book responds to these questions in various ways and in so doing provides a 'road map' for ethical practice. Marilyn Cochran-Smith and Susan Lytle indicate the terrain of the landscape in their chapter 'Everything's ethics'.

I do not intend, in this preface, to enumerate all of the contents of the book; this is covered in the opening chapter. Instead I wish to turn to a particular problem facing us in these challenging times – that is, how to engage in ethical inquiry in the context of an audit culture. Returning to the Wade article for a moment, there is a contrast between audit and research. For the author 'audit' is seen to be an inquiry process that investigates what is being done and if not, why not? Whereas 'research' has a more comprehensive and inclusive brief. For the purposes of this book audit culture is the managerial environment in which the research is conducted.

As I have argued elsewhere along with one of the editors of this volume (Groundwater-Smith and Sachs, 2002) public-sector reform in the field of education has been ongoing and relentless where the major concern has been in relation to public accountability by 'making practices and processes more transparent as well as efficient, effective and economic' (p. 341). Increasingly education bureaucracies conduct what amount to audits of professional performance. But such audits are conducted in the absence of trust in the professional judgement of practitioners.

Practitioner inquiry has at its heart a desire to know and act on specific circumstances in the interests of improving practice in an environment of mutual trust and respect. The given situation is analysed and potential actions and their implications identified and considered. Simultaneously, both in terms of the current practice and the intended actions, the ethical dimensions are addressed. What is morally acceptable? What is most compatible with overall social values as well as with those of the participants? Each chapter in this book argues, in one way or another, that every investigation should be examined for its ethical issues and dilemmas and the attendant risks and benefits.

Importantly, the role of those managing human research ethics from a university perspective is taken into account. Even in those circumstances, it is clear that much depends upon human judgment and is not a matter of ticking off the boxes on some kind of oversimplified checklist. As is made clear by Susanna Gorman, writing in her capacity as a manager of a human research ethics committee, the intention of the committee's work is to assist in identifying concerns that may not have been immediately apparent and thus the work of the committee can be seen to be contributing to the improvement of the overall investigation.

The range of papers in the book does bring to mind the matter of ethical literacy and how it might be addressed – both at institutional and individual levels. Much practitioner inquiry is carried out in partnership arrangements between academic and field-based operatives. Not all of these will be alert to the ethical dimensions of their work. Take, for example, the matter of employing student voice in a school-based inquiry. Has informed consent been sought? Who is being consulted and under what conditions? Typically, schools are places where teachers are accustomed to making a number of decisions on behalf of their students. They may not have taken account of the ethical dimensions of such taken-for-granted practices. The conscious stepping back and reflecting upon the moral purpose of teachers' work is not necessarily an expectation in a busy world. This book will act as an important resource in such circumstances, but more widely also. Ethical literacy is not some kind of tack-on skill that can be covered in a lecture or two; it is central to developing research competency for field-based and academic practitioners.

There can be no question that the quality of practitioner research rests upon the quality of the ethical dimensions that are understood and employed. This book makes a distinctive contribution to enhancing research quality and with it the possibilities of improvements in practice.

In closing this brief preface I turn to the opening words of Charles Dickens' *A Tale of Two Cities*:

> It was the best of times, it was the worst of times, it was the age of wisdom, it was the age of foolishness, it was the epoch of belief, it was the epoch of incredulity, it was the season of Light, it was the season of Darkness, it was the spring of hope, it was the winter of despair, we had everything before us, we had nothing before us, we were all going direct to heaven, we were all doing direct the other way – in short, the period was so far like the present

period, that some of its noisiest authorities insisted on its being received, for good or for evil, in the superlative degree of comparison only.

Our present period is indeed one that is bedevilled by the best and the worst. By attending, most seriously, to ethical considerations in relation to practice, this book, I believe, contributes new and important insights into the many debates such that we might, at least, move towards better times. And in these better times, better and more transparent practices.

Judyth Sachs

Deputy Vice Chancellor and Provost

Macquarie University, NSW, Australia

References

Groundwater-Smith, S. and Sachs, J. (2002) 'The activist professional and the reinstatement of trust', *Cambridge Journal of Education*, 32(3): 341–358.

Wade, D. (2005) 'Ethics, audit and research: all shades of grey', *British Medical Journal*, 26 February, pp. 468–471.

Acknowledgements

The editors would like to express their thanks to Ian Kane for his extensive help with the editing of the book and to Christina Anderson for her support in the preparation of the manuscript. Both have been patient and quietly assertive in the face of the editors' and authors' foibles.

Chapter 1

Introduction

Anne Campbell and Susan Groundwater-Smith

The origins of this book are located in the professional relationships between the editors and authors and their quest to investigate ethical issues in practice-based research and inquiry. In October 2005 the editors convened an international gathering in Liverpool, UK, the International Colloquium on Ethics in Practitioner Research: An International Conversation, to which all but one of the authors of this book contributed a paper. Caroline Leeson's chapter was based on a paper presented at the International Practitioner Research Conference at Utrecht in the Netherlands in November 2005 from which the editors identified her work as essential to the book. It is hoped that the book will make a contribution to what is now an increasingly important area of discussion and debate in the practitioner research communities of education, health and social care.

During the period of the International Colloquium in Liverpool in 2005, the authors demonstrated their commitment and passion to ethical issues and dilemmas by engaging in serious debate and questioning a number of important concerns such as: whether anonymity for respondents and participants is always necessary; the sensitivities involved in working with young children or vulnerable young people or adults; the benefits and problems of collaborative research with participants; roles, relationships and power in research; stakeholders, accountability and responsibility within research ventures and projects, especially within commissioned research projects; and the complex issues involved in informed consent. The group developed shared understandings and learned much from each other's differing contexts, as described below.

The foci in the book move through policy and practice and consider a variety of roles: academic researchers; consultants; teachers; professional practitioners as researchers and, importantly, students and children. It therefore illustrates a number of differing perspectives about ethics and research which are allied to those roles. It is distinctive in that it brings together issues and ideas about practice-based research from a wide-ranging international context in a substantial book.

Practice-based research is burgeoning in a number of professional areas. While this book is principally focused upon practitioner inquiry in education, it takes account of and acknowledges that others engaged in professional practice, such as in legal, nursing and social care contexts, face similar issues. Although not all practice-based research, often characterised as action research or action learning, is qualitative in nature, the dominant methods adopted by practitioners do fall into that category. There already exist many texts that guide practitioner inquiry in the use of a range of research methods, and which address ethical issues, often in relation to validity, robustness and trustworthiness questions. However, such works do not take ethics as their central or major theme and do not relate them to practitioner inquiry. The purpose of this book is to draw practitioner–researchers' attention to the many ethical challenges and dilemmas that they will face when undertaking their investigations.

Of significance is the relationship between the field-based practitioner–researcher and the academic researcher who may be acting as a research mentor and critical friend under the auspices of award-bearing courses or engagement in government-initiated projects. Following moves to promote professional learning and development in the workplace, there is also an increase in the number of practitioners engaging in action or inquiry-based learning in the workplace supported by university staff or consultants, as evidenced by the emergence of professional learning communities and learning networks. There are many tensions inherent in relationships between practitioners and academics in terms of the setting of the research agenda, the policy implications that may flow from it and the right to publish outcomes. Negotiating that relationship requires ethical probity where each party recognises, understands and respects mutual responsibilities. Not only that, but each may be governed by research ethics standards determined by their institutions. These may not always be compatible or serve the mutual interests of both parties. Furthermore each may be accountable to their institutions in different ways; the academic researcher is expected to contribute new knowledge to the field of study or discipline, while the practitioner–researcher is seeking to contribute to the practical knowledge of the profession. These may not necessarily be mutually exclusive, but institutional mores and norms will influence the aims and purposes of each. The boundaries may become even more blurred when the academic researcher is engaged in investigating his or her academic practice either internally or in conjunction with the professional field, or where the academic researcher is formally engaged as a consultant in a practice-based research project.

Within practice-based research there are also many issues that concern the consequential stakeholders, for example students in schools or patients in hospitals and clinics. How vulnerable are they? How well informed are they of the research and its purposes? To what extent has informed consent for the study been sought? How accountable are the practitioner–researchers to them? Are they themselves able to become partners in the research enterprise? These are but a few of the questions deserving consideration.

Of course practitioner–researchers will also have an audience that goes beyond their colleagues and those consequential stakeholders. Increasingly, practice-based research is making a contribution to the development of service-related policy in areas such as health and education. The ways in which results are published and disseminated have ethical implications in terms of access. Different writing genres, including reports, narratives, vignettes, case studies, all have their own conventions, many of which are not immediately explicit.

These are but a few of the practical issues. But there are also difficult epistemological issues regarding what counts as research and what may be the varying and competing knowledge interests.

This book is not primarily intended as a 'how to' text, but it will both provide invaluable support to the novice researcher and illuminate some of the more intricate issues for the more experienced research practitioner. It seriously addresses and makes problematic many issues that those engaged in practitioner inquiry will need to consider in their various contexts. One strength of the book is its capacity to draw upon the knowledge and experience of a range of well-recognised academic and practice-based researchers from the USA, the UK, Europe and Australia. It contains both theoretical analyses of ethical matters and offers practical and illustrative case studies.

Following this introductory chapter is Susanna Gorman's chapter on managing research ethics. She reminds us that the governance of human research ethics in universities should be directed to harm minimisation ahead of institutional risk management and highlights how research ethics is in danger of being reduced to a way of managing institutional risk in the complex, cutting-edge activity of today's research context. She provides a particular Australian perspective on the role and conduct of ethics committees and their relationship to researchers. Challenges for practice-based researchers are identified in the application of ethical principles. She also perceives the challenges for ethics committees of being 'ethical' themselves. Partnerships between researchers and research ethics committees can contribute positively to research design and enactment and she concludes with a consideration of the benefits for all of mutual, educational dialogue between partners.

Marilyn Cochran-Smith and Susan L. Lytle, in Chapter 3, have a wealth of experience of American practice-based research and they use this to illustrate dilemmas and tensions in the different positions of those in universities and schools with regard to a broad interpretation of practitioner inquiry. They justify practitioner inquiry as an 'umbrella' term for a number of inquiry formats. They argue for practitioner inquiry as a means of challenging a range of assumptions regarding learning and schooling. Necessarily such challenges produce complex tensions and dilemmas that have ethical consequences and as they put it, 'When it comes to practitioner inquiry and university culture, "everything is ethics"'.

Importantly, the chapter also clarifies the various terms employed by the authors of the chapters. Coming as they do from different language groups and traditions necessarily they employ a range of terms and labels; thus those require explication. The chapter, by providing insights into specific cases, illuminates those tensions and dilemmas referred to earlier. Finally the writers challenge some of the norms that govern the role of researchers, teachers, writers and partners when inquiry is conducted as a joint enterprise within the field of practice.

It seems appropriate at this point, as editors, to allude to the variety of linguistic styles in this international collection of chapters. We have decided to retain individual, national terms and to be consistent within each chapter. For example the American spelling of 'conceptualize' will be used in Chapter 3 but the word will appear elsewhere as 'conceptualise'. In this way we hope to accentuate and promote diversity as part of international collaboration. Having had the opportunity for extended conversations at the Liverpool colloquium we have engaged in serious debates and discussions about the ideas and terminology in the chapters and feel comfortable about not standardising spellings and terms. We hope it enriches the reading process and reminds us of the need for understanding each other's cultures and contexts in a global research community.

Chapter 4, 'Ethical issues for consultants in complex collaborative action research settings: tensions and dilemmas', moves to look at an extended case study example from a large, innovative initiative promoting networked learning communities. The initiative, sponsored by the English government's National College for School Leadership (NCSL), is the vehicle to discuss and explore issues for action researchers who work as consultants with schools over a sustained but temporary period of time. Chris Day and Andy Townsend contextualise the work in relation to the ethical roles and responsibilities of the research consultant inquiring with practitioners in the field.

The changing roles in partnerships between school and university personnel form the background for an exploration of five tensions in collaborative action research as follow: individual vs group; individual and school inquiry group vs networked learning community (NLC); school vs national policy initiatives; individual vs higher education (HE); and finally NLC vs the agenda of HE. The authors also identify eight dilemmas for consultants including power differentials, organisational and occupational professionalism and managing competing agendas. This is a lively chapter depicting some recent developments in England and the authors conclude that 'consultancy, like teaching, is an inherently moral and ethical activity'.

Lesley Saunders in Chapter 5, writing in her capacity as Visiting Professor at the Institute of Education, University of London, England, responds to the overall theme of ethics in practice-based research with regard to the generic values intrinsic to teaching and research, respectively. She argues that research and teaching share the same fundamental values, purposes and processes, whilst acknowledging that there are deep-seated differences and divergences between teaching and research as professional practices. She uses two sets of principles to elaborate her argument: the professional values of teaching from the General Teaching Council for England (GTCe) and the professional values of research from the USA's National Research Council. She provides an illustration of ideal typological contrasts between teaching and research in a useful table presenting teaching as activism and research as scepticism which relates to the discussion in Chapter 3 of the positioning of inquirers in schools and universities. However, in the end these positions are not offered as binaries, but as a tool for considering the overlapping contribution of each. She concludes that practitioner inquiry provides a site for the exploration and development of pedagogy as the constitutive professional practice of teaching.

Of particular appeal in relation to Chapter 6, 'Transdisciplinary enquiry: researching *with* rather than *on*', is the voice of the practitioner. Danny Doyle is a member of the National Teacher Research Panel in England (NTRP). This valuable perspective, drawing on the experience of a group of teacher–researchers, pays particular attention to the ethical demands of their work. A number of short scenarios is presented which highlight ethical challenges and dilemmas for practitioner–researchers such as: informed consent from children; the right to withdraw from a research project; and the thorny issues involved in confidentiality of respondents. He stresses researching 'with' rather than 'on' and suggests the use of 'participant' rather than 'subject' as an ethical stance with regard to recognising pupils' and teachers' contributions to research. He highlights sound and well-defended practices and poses questions that the teacher–researcher should consider. He concludes with the words of Lawrence Stenhouse: 'Communication is less effective than community in the utilisation of knowledge'.

In Chapter 7, 'Ethics in practitioner research: dilemmas from the field', Nicole Mockler argues that the path to teacher emancipation through practitioner research does not come without considerable ethical challenges and dilemmas. She sees her chapter as a simple example of second-order action research and examines these dilemmas through the eyes of one who supports practitioner research. The writer adopts the notion of 'critical incidents' to make her case. She continues to develop perspectives raised by Day and Townsend in Chapter 4 and asks questions about the stories told in practitioner research. As with the chapter which follows, the lens being employed is that of storying. She asks, 'Whose story is told? Who has the right to tell it? Are some stories privileged over others and whose stories make history?'. She continues by providing a section on theorising ethical dilemmas with a view to learning from dilemmas. She advocates moving from a 'project' approach to embedding an inquiry approach within teaching practice, towards 'inquiry as stance', as Cochran-Smith and Lytle in Chapter 3 argue. She also agrees that 'everything's ethics' and promotes an holistic approach. She concludes, in tune with Saunders in Chapter 5, that the implications of ethical dilemmas are much broader than the context in which they emerge and that the work of teaching is 'ethical work' and urges conversation and critique.

Anne Campbell and Olwen McNamara take the notion of storying one step further and expand into using practitioners' stories as stimuli for investigating and developing ethical issues in professional practice. Chapter 8 tackles a number of types of stories, fictional and hypothetical and positive and negative. It also discusses the use of fictionalised pen portraits to illustrate teachers' professional lives and their attitudes towards professional learning. Campbell and McNamara raise ethical concerns regarding teachers' experiences of teaching. They ask us to consider ways in which stories can act as provocations for academics and field-based practitioners alike to consider the ethical dilemmas inherent in the practice of fictionalising professional issues and experience. Issues raised in this chapter range from the power of narrative, biography and storytelling in depicting ethical dilemmas; anonymity or visibility of participants in research; and alternative ways of presenting data about professional identity. The authors advocate that theory and practice are brought together in an emancipatory fusion to promote ethical engagement in research.

While the preceding chapters have focused on the experiences of the academic and field-based practitioners, the two that follow draw our attention to the consequential stakeholders in inquiry, the students or pupils. Both Chapters 9 and 10 address the important perspectives of young people in practitioner research and the ethical challenges and dilemmas facing researchers. Susan Groundwater-Smith, in Chapter 9, considers the case for consultation with students and reminds us that listening to students is not a discovery of the twenty-first century by referring to Blishen's 1967 competition asking children about the school they would like to attend. Two powerful case studies are offered, each one raising a set of ethical challenges that come about when young people become part of the inquiry rather than apart from it. She uses the experience of working with a coalition of schools to illustrate how students' voices were central to the investigation of bullying in a girls' school and how boys' and girls' perceptions of their teachers as learners could inform professional learning plans and advise school policy.

While young people are positioned as powerful voices, they are also paradoxically seen to be vulnerable in the ways in which their voices may be heard and used in relation to the various and competing accountabilities. She identifies a number of challenges and dilemmas: students' right to say no; sustaining student voice and the need for dissemination and action. She advocates power *with* students not *on* students, a similar call to Doyle's in Chapter 6.

Most chapters in this book have explored practitioner research in the context of education. Chapter 10 takes us on a somewhat different trajectory as it considers the ethical sensitivities associated with children in state care. Caroline Leeson in her chapter entitled 'Going round in circles: key issues in the development of an effective ethical protocol for research involving young children' urges us to promote sensitivity and robust ethical consideration in research with children. She traces a personal journey towards effective, ethical protocols for research looking at the levels of participation of children and young people in the decision-making processes of the care system. Her approaches demand a child-centred approach from the researcher and she details how she constructs ethical codes and protocols as she structures her research to facilitate the authentic voice of the younger child.

Leeson discusses the ethical dilemmas she faced in raising what could be called traumatic and distressing issues for young children in her investigation. Similar to previous chapters – and a dominant theme of this book – the thorny issues of consent and confidentiality are raised. She argues that young children should be involved in research into difficult areas and should be active participants with a real voice that is listened to by researchers. These issues resonate with the arguments in Chapter 2 and suggest that ethical codes must be developed that permit action rather than stifle initiative.

The ethics of practitioner inquiry transcend national boundaries. Chapters in this book have highlighted concerns to be found as far afield as the USA, England

and Australia. Coming from a European perspective in the Netherlands, Petra Ponte in Chapter 11 addresses praxis as the development of knowledge through independent and purposeful action, and links the ideological, the technical and the empirical areas of knowledge. She contends that action research in education is based on social theories and could be enriched by pedagogical theories. Ponte refers to 'pedagogy as human science'. In developing praxis as an ethical frame-work for action research she identifies the following: the ethic of justice; the ethic of critique; the ethic of professionalism and the ethic of pedagogy. Ponte develops her idea of the pedagogical ethic through reference to thinking before and after the Perestroika period in Russia in the early 1990s. She concludes with a model for knowledge construction by teachers doing research but reminds us that the benefits should include the development of the relationship between the child, the school and society. Questions such as 'What is a good society? And what is the place of young people in such a society?' are raised in this chapter. The ultimate goal is seen to be to develop education that has a place for all pupils regardless of their social background or personal qualities.

In the penultimate chapter in this book attention shifts to practitioner inquiry in the tertiary setting. Lin Norton has long researched research upon teaching and learning in universities and the moral duty of the researcher to maintain ethical balance. The chapter raises questions of power and authority, control and disclo-sure within pedagogical action research in higher education. Questions of fairness and opportunity costs are raised and ways in which students that are at risk may be exposed. In addition there are matters associated with vulnerable academics who may be experiencing transition difficulties as they move into the higher education sector. It is not that these challenges are so very different to those raised earlier in the book but the change of setting serves to highlight their complexity. Norton also asks what happens when her research shows her institution or a student or a teacher in a 'bad light'. She analyses research articles in her field to identify how ethical issues are dealt with in the literature and also describes how her research into improving essay writing can illuminate difficult issues involved in feedback to students.

In the concluding chapter to the book the major themes raised by its various authors are revisited. Some particular concerns regarding the changing environ-ment in relation to the burgeoning of information and communication technologies are also considered.

It is our belief that this collective work arising from the Liverpool Hope University Colloquium is an important contribution to the ongoing conversation regarding ethics and practitioner inquiry around the globe.

Chapter 2

Managing research ethics

A head-on collision?

Susanna Gorman

In an increasingly nervous and litigious society, research ethics is in danger of being reduced to an easy means of managing institutional risk rather than something that is intrinsically valuable to the research process.

Ethics is not about simplistic solutions. It provides a framework for asking meaningful questions – and this, after all, is at the very heart of good scholarship.

Areas that have not traditionally been involved in academic pursuits have become part of modern universities rather than 'trades' or apprentice/cadet models of learning as in the past. These areas include, but are not limited to, nursing, journalism and the creative arts. Other areas, such as law, have had a different professional understanding of what constitutes 'research', and may have to reinterpret their existing codes to cater for academic research. Additionally, new areas are emerging in the fields of information technology, which lead research practitioners into previously uncharted territory.

Today's research practitioners are engaged in cutting-edge activity – juggling the demands of academia, of teaching and responding to students, of researching, of coping with new technology and increased accountability, while maintaining their own professional practice.

All these areas exert their own demands – they often have their own codes, cultures and practice, which can be in conflict with institutional and research ethics guidelines which are increasingly bound by external legislation, such as in the area of privacy.

In spite of this apparent conflict, an opportunity exists for researchers and ethics committees to navigate successfully a course in partnership, rather than conflict, with one another. In order to achieve this, they need to be able to overcome mutual suspicion and see the benefit of collaboration and dialogue.

Historical overview

It is useful to look back at the origins of ethics committees in order to understand why they might be tempted to view researchers negatively.

Ethics committees emerged from an international response to the horrors of some of the research conducted up to and during the Second World War. Evidence of unethical research shocked society and increased the demand for stronger regulatory processes. For example, during the Second World War, the Australian government conducted mustard gas experiments on university students and its own soldiers (McNeill, 1994: 26). In the United States, the infamous Tuskegee syphilis case involved monitoring but not treating 400 black men with syphilis over a 30-year period, during which time this publicly funded research was regularly reported in peer review journals (McNeill, 1994: 61).

The fact that such research could take place in democratic societies rather than totalitarian regimes led to a perception that researchers were not to be trusted – and it was the job of ethics committees to ensure that they did the right thing.

The Nuremburg Trials (1946) held after the Second World War resulted in the development of a code of conduct relating to research. The Nuremburg Code emphasised the importance of voluntary consent, the benefit of the research, and consideration of the degree of risk for subjects. This was followed in 1948 by the Declaration of Geneva, a Physician's Oath, which was also a response to Nazi medical atrocities. Since then, ethics codes have proliferated both internationally and in various countries as in the Declaration of Helsinki (1964) and the Belmont Report (1978).

An Australian perspective

Originally, research ethics guidelines were seen as applying only to medical research. In Australia, a system of formal ethics review began in the 1960s with the release by the National Health and Medical Research Council (NHMRC) of the *Statement on Human Experimentation* which could be traced directly back to the Nuremburg Code.

Australian research institutions were encouraged to adhere to this new approach by the linking of funding to proof of ethics approval. Institutions such as universities and hospitals agreed to abide by these guidelines in order to receive funding from relevant government agencies.

Since then, the original document has been refined and expanded to include all kinds of research, not just medical, and in 1999 the current *National Statement on the Ethical Conduct of Research Involving Humans* was released.

The *National Statement* was a breakthrough. Not only did it attempt to address other kinds of research, particularly qualitative and social, but it had been developed in consultation with other, non-medical areas, and was endorsed by the:

- Australian Vice-Chancellors' Committee
- Australian Research Council
- Australian Academy of the Humanities
- Australian Academy of Science
- Academy of the Social Sciences in Australia

and supported by the:

- Academy of Technological Sciences and Engineering.

Although still heavily medical in origin and focus, it gave ethics committees much more room to consider other types of research. Nonetheless, it was still heavily criticised by many qualitative researchers for failing to address their particular needs. At the time of writing the *National Statement* is undergoing extensive and exhaustive review in an attempt to address earlier criticism. Certainly anyone at all familiar with research in Australia will have heard many anecdotal reports of medically oriented ethics committees creating impenetrable obstacles for social researchers, and indeed health-related but non-medical research practitioners such as, *inter alia*, nurses, social workers and chiropractors.

The problem

Writing from the perspective of 14 years of research ethics management at an Australian university, I would say that in many cases problems arise not so much from a deliberate intention to act unethically, but, perhaps more worryingly, from a lack of awareness or thought as to what constitutes ethical behaviour. This is not limited to the arena of research. Society is littered with examples of what one age did not consider an ethical issue, but which is roundly condemned by the next. For example, in Australia, the term 'stolen generation' was coined in hindsight to describe indigenous children forcibly removed from their families 'for their own good'. Future generations will doubtless look back in judgement at our current attitude and practice in many areas, from our addiction to private transport, our waste of water, our erosion of social capital, and treatment of refugees.

Ethics committees

When ethics committees concentrate on assuming that researchers are incompetent or unethical, they lose an opportunity to work with researchers to find a way through that illuminates research practice, and encourages considerations of ethics across a wider spectrum. And worse, it can encourage researchers not to examine their own practice, and can make ethics appear unhelpful. Institutions can exacerbate the problem by treating ethics committees as a convenient risk management mechanism, increasing resentment on the part of researchers who understandably see them as a hindrance rather than an important part of the research framework.

Researchers

Similarly, when researchers take the easy way of blaming ethics committees for delays to their own research rather than accepting responsibility or attempting to engage in dialogue, they miss an opportunity for improving their own research and assuring society that they take seriously their obligation to act ethically. Researchers can view ethics committees as an impediment to academic freedom, and another bureaucratic hurdle that they have to overcome in order to conduct their research. However, this attitude is ignoring the fact that when researchers receive public money to conduct their research, they are publicly accountable for it. Even when researchers are privately funded, they are still required to abide by societal expectations and legislative requirements.

Role of ethics committees

Ideally, research ethics committees act to preserve the interests of researchers, institutions and society at large. It can be too easy for ethics committees to forget that were it not for researchers, they would not even exist. At the same time as recognising that they do serve the interests of researchers, they also serve the interests of institutions and research participants. An institution or researcher might pressure an ethics committee to fast-track approval so as to access funding, for example. But if the ethics committee does so at the expense of any concerns it might have, it does not do that institution or researcher any favours. Scandal arising from a failure to ensure that the highest ethical standards are met undermines the entire credibility of the institution and the researchers, not to mention the ethics committee itself. Ethics committees must have sufficient strength and independence to say 'no' when necessary.

Increasing dependence upon external commercial funding can undermine the ability of researchers and institutions to say 'no' unless they actively cultivate the ethics committee as an ally. Far from seeing ethics committees as a threat to academic independence, they are an important safeguard.

Generally, however, refusal of approval should be the last resort for ethics committees. If researchers genuinely engage in the ethics review process, such problems are unlikely to occur and should ideally be ironed out before the research proposal even reaches the ethics committee.

Options for ethics committees

When an ethics committee considers an application for ethics approval, it has a number of options:

- to approve without change
- to approve with minor changes
- to approve with major changes
- to negotiate with the researcher to enable the research to be undertaken
- to refuse approval.

The ideal would be to invite researchers to attend all ethics committee meetings, but this is clearly impractical. However, it is a useful option in the case of either refusal or a request for major amendments, and establishes a dialogue between the committee and researchers. Committees may also encourage dialogue through other mechanisms, such as the training and appointment of academic staff to act as ethics advisers in their institution. This model has been adopted by Griffith University, Queensland.

Such initiatives are of great importance to the effectiveness of the ethics committee. A committee can all too easily earn a reputation for being unreasonably bureaucratic or capricious. Institutions seem to thrive on gossip and bad news stories, and people remember negative experiences for years. It is therefore important for a committee to be very sure when it says 'no' that it has good, defensible and transparent reasons for doing so, and is able to communicate those reasons effectively.

Relationship of ethics codes to medicine

The concept of ethics in medicine can be traced back to Hippocrates in the fifth century BC (although the point has been made that the Hippocratic Oath is as much about professional standards and etiquette as it is about ethics: Siggins, 1996). The Nuremburg Code and the Declaration of Geneva, referred to above, specifically relate to medicine, and served as the model for many research ethics codes, such as the Belmont Report.

Medicine and health professionals became accustomed to the requirement for ethics approval for research, but only after shocking examples, such as those mentioned above, which were by no means limited to Nazi Germany.

These abuses are more obvious in areas such as medicine and nursing, where there is a well established and recognised tradition of a duty of care between health practitioner and patient. The results of unethical health and medical treatment can be immediate and unmistakable, although there are still examples, even today, of such instances of abuse. In Australia a recent medical scandal related to a Dr Jayant Patel, dubbed 'Dr Death' by the local press (Kron, 2005).

So even in areas such as medicine, where there is a history of ethical codes and an awareness of the need for ethics, unethical behaviour continues to occur. This results in a greater level of scrutiny and concern.

Research ethics in other professions

Medicine is often referred to as the second oldest profession. What lessons can the more recent professions draw from medicine? What are the similarities and the differences? And what opportunities exist for ethics committees and ethics professionals to assist them?

Professional practice

Originally, the professions were considered to be law, medicine and divinity. This has since been expanded to include many other areas, including nursing, journalism and education. It is not necessary to define exhaustively what makes a profession a profession, except to state that it involves tertiary education, research, responsibility to clients and fellow members of the profession, including students, and competency.

It might be useful to compare aspects of medicine and journalism as examples of established and recent academic professions, to illustrate some of the ethical issues involved.

Difficulties for 'professional' researchers

Complicating matters for journalists is the relative newness of their becoming a member of a 'profession' in the accepted sense. Previously journalists learnt their trade on the job, as cadets or apprentices, similar to the way nurses were trained.

For many professionals, entering into academia can be unnerving. They can feel out of their depth, and if they are insecure, may resent the ethics committee commenting upon their research.

There is often a different understanding of what constitutes research in a professional as opposed to an academic context. Lawyers and journalists commonly engage in 'research' in the pursuit of their profession. But this is quite different to an academic understanding of research, which occurs within a theoretical and critical framework.

The situation is further complicated because research practitioners need to focus on professional requirements and relationships as well as research issues that arise from the research. Relationships within a professional context may include clients, fellow professionals, government and regulatory bodies, and possibly the supervision of students. When the professional is engaged in research, these relationships may expand to include research participants (who may be clients and/or students), students, employer institutions, funding bodies, and of course, ethics committees.

In those professions where there is a clear responsibility to one's client, such as medicine, the duty of care remains primary. In other areas, such as the creative arts, journalism or criminology, where there are no corresponding primary relationships with individuals, the situation can be even more complex.

Traditionally, doctors have had a relationship with, and an obligation to, an individual patient. When doctors engage in practice-based research, their responsibility to their patients must remain paramount, at least in theory. In reality, this is not always simple, especially in some of the research for drug companies, but the notion of a relationship based on trust between doctor and patient persists.

In contrast, journalists have not so much a relationship with an individual as one to society as a whole, except in the case of protection of sources. Freedom of the press is recognised as being of vital importance to the health of a democratic system, and even protection of sources is seen as being an important pillar of that freedom.

Relationships central to quality research

In research involving direct interaction with humans, the quality of the research will stand or fall upon the quality of the relationships. Within medicine, the relationship will be affected by a number of factors, including the type of the research, any pre-existing relationship between the medical practitioner and patient, the severity of the risk, the health or illness of the patient/participant, the ability to consent, and so forth. A surgeon or anaesthetist will tend to see a patient only once or twice, for a specific and limited purpose, whereas the family doctor will be more likely to have a relationship that is established over a long period of time.

Different relationships also exist in journalism. Journalists may well consider that they have an obligation to protect a source, and journalists have been jailed for refusing to reveal the identities of informants. In the area of investigative journalism, however, the relationship may well be combative and quite hostile, even aggressive. Journalists might not even identify themselves as journalists in certain circumstances, for example, going under cover to expose a particular practice in an organisation. In such cases, the notion of consent, which has become central to medicine, is not possible in the same way.

It is generally accepted that it is improper to use force or coercion to ensure participation in research. However, some journalists might try to bully and/or coerce cooperation, either subtly or not so subtly. 'I'm going to run with this story anyway, so you may as well put your side of it ...'

Journalists might argue that they have an obligation to society rather than to an individual, and express concern at the dangers of limiting their ability to be unfettered in their investigations and articles.

Importance of research

Research is of vital importance to professional groups as well as to individual professionals. It enhances knowledge and improves practice across an entire profession, and can increase the knowledge, standing and possible earning potential of an individual member of a profession. An incompetent or unethical professional might cause harm to an individual because of poor practice, and the capacity for such harm expands when research enters the equation. Unethical research may harm the individual, the institution, and the profession as a whole, and impact upon the future willingness of potential participants to engage in research.

Just as doctors were forced to accept that they were not the sole arbiters of their practice both as professionals and researchers, so all researchers need to accept a greater degree of scrutiny due to increased legislation and societal expectations. The point has been made that this is reflected in the change of language from the term 'research subject' to 'research participant' (Allen, 2006).

Challenges for practice-based research practitioners

There are many pressures on academics today: to research, to produce outcomes, write papers, obtain funding, and so on. Areas that are relatively new to academia and research, such as law, nursing, the fine arts, marketing, accountancy, criminology and journalism, often lack a great deal of experience in conducting academic research, and their professional practice has a different understanding of what constitutes research. A lawyer or a journalist, for example, will consider that 'research' forms a part of their normal professional practice, and as such it is governed by professional codes of conduct. However, as mentioned previously, what might be acceptable in the context of professional research (such as engaging in deception to obtain information) can be in contravention of research ethics guidelines and expectations. This clearly has the potential to create conflict between researchers and ethics committees.

Critical reflection on one's own practice is part of being a professional in any field. It is how professionals work out if what they are doing is effective, whether their practice is in the best interests of their clients. This has always been the case in medical research. It is not unusual for doctors to experiment on their patients, try things out without knowing if they will work, or test new drugs and treatment regimes.

In educational research, the 'research practitioner' will have varying relationships and corresponding responsibilities that can be difficult to reconcile. Which relationship should take precedence: that to students, parents, colleagues, employers – even one's self?

In journalism, for example, what interests would the professional be responsible for protecting? Journalists have often justified their actions as being for the benefit of society at large. But one of the underpinning ethical principles, that of respect for persons, derives from the view that someone cannot be used as a means to an end, especially if they have no choice in the matter. The practice of informed consent flows from this, but clearly in the case of investigative journalism, this creates problems.

In medical research, the effects of intervention, whether research related or not, are likely to be obvious and immediate. Sometimes they can lead to a dramatic improvement in outcome for the individual patient; sometimes the outcome can be equally dramatic but less than favourable, even fatal.

In all practice-based research, complications can arise if there are any conflicts between one's roles and responsibilities. When anyone is engaged in researching their own practice or institution, further difficulties can arise when it comes to determining whose interests he or she is primarily responsible for. What of the teacher who becomes aware that the school is impacting negatively on students? Is a teacher primarily responsible to teaching colleagues, to parents, to students? What does a nurse do if their research highlights conflicts in interests for their nursing colleagues, other health professionals, or patients? To whom is a nurse primarily responsible?

The process of ethics approval will hopefully highlight these and other issues before they become problems, at least in relation to research. The approval process will not eliminate all such problems, but should minimise them. Further, even with the best preparation, unlooked-for problems can arise. However, the process of critical ethical reflection will itself increase the researcher's ability to deal with the problems as and when they arise. If a researcher is unprepared, then they may not only cause harm to others, but could endanger the future of their own research and in some cases, their career.

Regardless of the area of practice-based research one is engaged in, it stands to reason that if there is a capacity for benefit to occur as a result of the research, there is also the capacity for risk and harm. The degree of harm or benefit will vary greatly depending upon the type of research, the degree of invasiveness, the level of intervention, and the vulnerability and interests of the groups involved.

Respect for persons

However much a researcher and ethics committee might disagree on conclusions, it would be hard to disagree on the importance of the principle of 'respect for persons'.

Section 1.2 of the Australian *National Statement* (1999: 11) defines the principle of respect for persons as 'regard for the welfare, rights, beliefs, perceptions, customs and cultural heritage, both individual and collective, of persons involved in research'.

This means that researchers and ethics committees must consider research in view of:

- risk/harm
- benefit
- consent

and the degree to which the design of the research places respect for the beliefs, rights and welfare of the potential participants ahead of academic objectives.

Risk/harm

Even where risk might be minimal, it must be considered. The very act of considering the risk of harm will reduce the likelihood of it occurring, as well as improving the ability of researchers to deal with it positively, should it arise in the course of their research or afterwards following publication.

Benefit

Benefit can be difficult to measure. It can be easier to see in medical research, where the lofty aim might be to cure cancer or blindness. In other kinds of research and academic activity, benefit might be harder to quantify, and may be mainly the obtaining of qualifications and/or experience on the part of the researcher. Even this is itself a legitimate benefit, as long as it is clear to participants and the researcher.

In the case of the creative arts, benefit is even more nebulous, as is risk. Art, by its very nature, can challenge and shock. There are many examples of art which are revered today but were reviled or ignored at the time of their creation (and vice versa). Some artworks are deliberately intended to shock and even offend – witness the controversy in Australia from the exhibition of a painting known as the 'Piss Christ' by Andres Serrano. Others, such as the Impressionist artists, might just have been ahead of their time. Van Gogh sold only one painting in his lifetime.

For many experienced researchers, the comments and input of the ethics committee are a welcome resource, particularly for their students. They recognise the importance of critical appraisal in relation to their own work, and accept that it will increase the robustness of their research, as well as reducing the potential for problems.

Consent

Consent is of great importance and cannot be overemphasised. It is at the heart of the notion of respect for persons, and we overlook it at our peril. History has demonstrated too often that those people who decide that consent is unnecessary are often likely to underestimate risk and overemphasise benefit. This is often the case in times of war or national crisis, and many examples exist, not just in Nazi Germany, of doubtful research in such times.

Whilst a degree of risk is inevitable, the requirement that participants are fully informed as to the nature and degree of risk before they consent makes it much more likely that researchers will do their best to minimise the risk and maximise benefit.

Pre-existing relationships can complicate consent, particularly when the researcher is in a position of power over the potential participant.

Balance of risk, benefit and consent

In all research, there must be an accepted balance between risk and benefit. It may even be that an individual might accept a degree of risk, knowing that they themselves might not benefit, but in the hope and belief that it will contribute overall to society. Providing that the participants are competent to consent freely, that the benefit has been demonstrated, and the risk minimised, ethics committees must learn to accept this, otherwise they themselves fail to demonstrate respect for persons.

This is where the application of ethical principles can be of great benefit to both researchers and ethics committees.

Application of ethical principles

In spite of criticisms of research ethics processes being too closely attuned to medical research, there are many useful areas of overlap, particularly in relation to the application of ethical principles. The following common ethical principles form the basis of bioethics:

- autonomy
- beneficence
- non-maleficence
- justice.

These principles apply equally to all types of research, not just medical. Problems arise for researchers and ethics committees when they are distracted by the type of research, rather than looking at the research in the context of ethics.

The principle of *autonomy* and the notion of *respect for persons* would make us ask questions relating to consent. Have people consented? Have they fully understood what they are consenting to? Can they withdraw at any time?

In considering *beneficence* (meaning to do good) and *non-maleficence* (meaning not to do harm) we would question the balance of potential benefit with that of potential harm and risk, and ask how that potential harm is minimised. What are the interests of the parties involved? Who could be harmed and how? Who could benefit, and how might they?

In looking at the principle of *justice*, we would look at how risk and benefit are shared and the possible impact of the research across a wider spectrum.

These principles provide a framework for both researchers and ethics committees to ask the following critical questions.

- Who will benefit?
- Who might be harmed?
- How might they be harmed?
- Does the potential harm outweigh the potential benefit?
- How can the possibility of harm be reduced?
- Are there any conflicts of interests for the researcher?
- Have participants consented fully?
- What does the research involve for participants?
- Are they aware of the risks?

Clearly there are more questions that may be asked, depending upon the type of research, and any local or legislative requirements, such as research involving children, but these questions provide a basis for consideration of risk.

Regardless of the context, whether in a classroom or a clinic, the questions remain the same. It is our response that may differ, for it may be argued that what is unacceptable in one circumstance may be acceptable in another, if the justification is sufficient, and if certain mechanisms are put in place to address the ethical concerns that have been identified. For example, in most situations, an ethics committee might adopt the view that it is not ethically desirable to focus on one's own students because of the pre-existing power relationship and associated difficulties in obtaining free consent. However, the committee might accept a researcher's argument that they can only conduct this research on their own students, because it is the only class teaching this particular subject, or because they are focusing on their own practice.

The question then shifts from whether or not the research *should* be done, to *how* such research can be conducted ethically. Additional questions will be identifying the issues, including potential risk and harm, and developing strategies for minimising the potential for negative impact on participants.

The vexed question of risk

In order for ethics committees to be effective, they need to recognise the delicate balance between risk and benefit, and to accept that all research involves a degree of inherent risk, however minimal. The unfortunate origin of research ethics can lead to an overemphasis by ethics committees on risk, and an almost unconscious assumption that researchers are not to be trusted. Similarly, it is easy for researchers to underestimate risk and overestimate benefit. Either attitude undermines the relationship between researchers and ethics committees.

Generally, however, the capacity for harm in much non-medical research is not always very high, and ethics committees need to be realistic when assessing the degree of potential harm against the likelihood of it occurring.

There are some instances where, of course, the potential risk is greater. Researching with vulnerable populations, such as refugees, or people in dependent relationships, including one's own clients, students, employees or patients, creates particular problems, especially in relation to consent. This will always be the case where there is a situation of unequal power.

Whilst the likelihood and degree of harm are important to consider, they must be balanced with potential benefit. Where the risk has been justified, ethics committees may find it more helpful to emphasise strategies for minimising risk, than to assume that risk can be done away with altogether.

Where an ethics committee is overly focused on risk to the exclusion of benefit, this creates a different kind of risk – that of over-regulation and strangling of research itself. If we accept that research is beneficial to society as a whole, then society has a vested interest in research taking place. Thus the role of an ethics committee is not merely to minimise risk, but to promote and support ethical research.

This is undoubtedly a challenge for ethics committees. On the one hand, a committee that is too lenient and insufficiently rigorous in its consideration of research ethics might lead to researchers' treating the process as a joke. The ethics committee could be guilty of condoning and approving unethical or incompetent research. On the other hand, an overly risk-averse ethics committee might make life so hard for researchers that they either avoid it altogether, or become deterred from doing research.

Not all risk is unacceptable, and whilst it is also the role of the ethics committee to ensure that risk is minimised as much as possible, it could be argued that it is the role of potential participants to choose whether or not to assume that risk, because as members of a society that benefits from research, everyone has a vested interest in supporting it.

Participants, if fully informed, may accept a degree of risk because they believe in the hoped-for outcome of the research. Again, this can be easier to see in a medical context. A person with cancer might be willing to trial a drug, because it can give them hope that even if they don't benefit directly, their experience will help others in the future.

Risk is an inevitable part of life, and an inevitable part of research. The risk might be negligible, but it will be there, and must be considered. And it stands to reason that the more a piece of research is likely to have an impact, the greater the likelihood there will be risk associated with it. This is more difficult when we are making those decisions on behalf of someone else. Children, for example, may not fully comprehend the implications, and are not legally able to consent.

Challenges for ethics committees

It is important for ethics committees themselves to be ethical. In the same way that researchers can sometimes fail to see the consequences of what they propose for participants, ethics committees can fail to see the consequences of their comments and decisions for researchers, and to realise the impact they can have on them.

Ethics committees have an obligation to demonstrate respect for persons, not just in consideration of potential risk for participants, but in their relationships with researchers. The actions of ethics committees impact significantly on researchers as well as the researched.

If ethics committees see their role as being adversarial, or purely as gatekeepers, then they run the danger of driving researchers underground. Researchers will have a vested interest in giving as little information as possible to ethics committees.

If ethics committees look for problems, the chances are that they will find them. But the question is how important these 'problems' really are, and whether or not they merely reflect the prejudice or preoccupation of particular committee members. Some members might fixate on the grammar of the consent form, for example, while completely missing the potential for harm, or indeed good, from the research.

If researchers are discouraged from conducting valuable research, then not only do they suffer, but society loses out on a potential benefit, and the ethics committee has failed to fulfil its obligation to promote ethical research.

The role of an ethics committee, no matter what the context of the research, is to ensure that due consideration has been given to the ethical consequences of the proposed research, and that the researcher has ensured that risk is minimised.

Benefits for researchers

One of the most obvious benefits for researchers is that ethics approval may be necessary for publication or to access funding. Additional benefits include the fact that they are protected by the institution, and are less likely to make mistakes that might negatively impact on their reputation. Going through the ethics application process will involve greater consideration of research beforehand, and it stands to reason that the more thought-out and planned research is, the better it will be. This is of particular value to research degree students, who can be either overwhelmed by the sheer size of the task confronting them, or can plunge in before they have thought through their approach.

Benefits for ethics committees

Ethics committees clearly benefit from engaging positively with researchers, because otherwise they run the risk of gaining a poor reputation, of being treated with contempt and avoidance, of having complaints made against them, but most importantly, of failing to achieve their aim of promoting ethical research. By engaging with researchers, they are more likely to find creative solutions rather than taking the easy way out, that of just refusing research.

Benefits for institutions

Institutions obviously need ethics committees to meet their own regulatory and governance requirements. Research cannot take place (in theory at least) unless it has had appropriate scrutiny and approval. Funding is dependent upon having regulatory mechanisms in place. And reputation requires the avoidance of scandal and the assurance that the staff and students of an institution can be trusted to act ethically.

Benefits for society

Society also has a clearly vested interest in the continuance of research, and in being assured that sufficient protections are in place for them to repose trust in the institutions and individual researchers.

Relationship between researchers and ethics committees

When ethics committees engage in a mutually educational dialogue with research practitioners, everyone benefits. Ethics committees can inform researchers of the ethical considerations, including how the research might be perceived by others. Researchers in their turn are able to inform ethics committees of the requirements of their profession, and ensure that committees are aware of the impact of their deliberations.

Any group, whether it is the ethics committee or the researchers, which is too narrowly focused on itself as its own reference point, courts disaster. The balance is to know when and where to draw the line. Having that external view is invaluable, not only in enriching the research itself, but ensuring that the research is ethical.

Well known in Australia and New Zealand is the case of the National Women's Hospital in Auckland, where one doctor's research over a decade from the mid-1960s led to the deaths of a number of women from cervical cancers that may otherwise have been successfully treated (Women's Health Action, 2005). The research was considered by an ethics committee which was later criticised by a Royal Commission for being overly medical in focus (McNeill, 1994: 77), with little or no protection for participants.

The lack of an external view is dangerous, because it can lead to 'groupthink', where everyone shares the same values and outlooks. This is why ethics committees should be established carefully to ensure that they have not only a variety of members from different backgrounds, but that they have a mixture of internal and external representation. In Japan in the Second World War, Unit 731 was established to conduct biological warfare experiments. In this instance, the Unit was deliberately isolated, as were the staff and prisoners, to ensure that there was no other view possible. The prisoners who were the subjects of the experiments were referred to as maruta, or 'log of wood' (McNeill, 1994: 24), which discouraged any consideration of the impact of the research.

Tips for ethics committees

An ethics committee should always remember to:

- listen to researchers
- invite researchers to be part of the committee
- rotate researchers on the committee
- invite researchers to meet with and give input to the committee
- learn from researchers about their needs and professional field and any concerns they may have
- be fair
- be transparent
- be flexible
- be positive and encouraging in its response
- always justify comments and decisions and link to ethical principles and guidelines
- differentiate between ethical and administrative/methodological comments
- be aware of the potential impact of comments and requirements on researchers

- always offer a way forward
- never close off dialogue
- ensure ongoing critical reflection of their own practice.

Tips for researchers

Researchers in their turn should:

- not be afraid to challenge ethics committees
- be open to critical appraisal and comment
- seek advice beforehand
- view the ethics process positively, not negatively
- educate ethics committees as to the issues and needs of researchers in the field
- learn from ethics committees about ethical issues
- recognise that ethical research will lead to better quality research
- remember that the ethics process reduces risk for researchers of problems arising that may negatively impact on their careers
- allow sufficient time.

Conclusion

If we accept that good research benefits society, then it follows that the work of ethics committees also benefits society and researchers. The primary focus of ethics committees ought always to be the protection of research participants, researchers, institutions, and indeed research itself. Good research is necessary for an open society to flourish.

A degree of humility is needed by ethics committees in particular. Ethics committees would not even exist if it were not for researchers. And researchers in their turn need to recognise the value of ethics committees. Positively engaged with, the ethics review process will enhance rather than detract from research.

References

Allen, G. (2006) Personal communication.

Commonwealth of Australia (1999) *National Statement on Ethical Conduct in Research Involving Humans*, Government Publication: p.11.

Kron, J. (2005) 'Blowing the whistle – Australian Doctor', Editorial, *Sydney Morning Herald*, 26 April 2005.

McNeill, P. M. (1994) *The Ethics and Politics of Human Experimentation*, Cambridge: Cambridge University Press.

Siggins, I. (1996) 'Some historical antecedents', in M. Coady and S. Bloch (eds) *Codes of Ethics and the Professions*, Melbourne: Melbourne University Press.

Women's Health Action (2005) www.womens-health.org.nz/cartwright/cartwright. htm#unfinished (accessed 12 October 2005).

Chapter 3

Everything's ethics

Practitioner inquiry
and university culture

Marilyn Cochran-Smith and Susan L. Lytle

For two decades, we have worked with each other and with a wide array of students, inquiry communities, and school-, program- and university-based colleagues in order to conceptualize and engage in research about teaching, learning and schooling. We use 'practitioner inquiry' as an umbrella term that encompasses a number of inquiry approaches and genres. Over the years, we have learned that when practitioners do research, they dramatically realign their relationships to the brokers of knowledge and power. Along these lines, we have argued that, when taken seriously, practitioner inquiry represents a radical challenge to the cultures of schools and universities, questioning fundamental assumptions about: the knowledge needed to improve teaching, learning and schooling; how knowledge is produced, interpreted, exchanged, and used; and the tendency of those who work at universities to call for school transformation without parallel self-examination and restructuring.

In this chapter, we make a different, but complementary point. We suggest that when the premises of practitioner inquiry are taken seriously over a long period of time, by those who are differently positioned in universities and schools or other educational settings, it is inevitable that complex dilemmas and tensions emerge. Although the particulars vary, most of these dilemmas have to do with ownership, authorship, presentation and representation, priorities and purposes, voice, critique, collaboration, value and evaluation, accountability, frames of reference, language and culture, and the traditions and conventions of university-dominated research. Our argument, which we elaborate in this chapter, is that all of these issues are ethical issues and thus, when it comes to practitioner inquiry and university culture, 'everything's ethics.' The chapter begins with a brief discussion of 'practitioner inquiry' as an umbrella term for describing a number of inquiry formats and genres as well as the features and assumptions that most versions and variants share. Then we consider the role of practitioner inquiry in the university and the major ethical dilemmas that emerge from this work. To do so, we draw on our own experiences working with teacher research and other inquiry communities within the contexts of large research universities, over a period of more than 20 years. We focus explicitly on the ethical, political, and practical dilemmas and contradictions that are created when practitioner inquiry and its underlying premises are taken seriously over a long period of time and within the culture of the university.

Practitioner inquiry

In this chapter, we use 'practitioner inquiry' as a conceptual and linguistic umbrella to refer to a wide array of educational research modes, forms, genres, and purposes. It is not our intention to suggest that the terms encompassed by the general phrase are synonymous nor do we want to blur the important ideological, epistemological, and historical differences that exist between and among them. Rather we hope to illuminate the differences across these forms of inquiry at the same time that we clarify some of their commonalities.

Versions and variants

Arguably, the most common terms for practitioner inquiry that occur in the current discourse of educational research are: action research, teacher research, self-study, narrative inquiry, the scholarship of teaching and learning, and the use of teaching as a context for research. 'Action research' is commonly used to describe collaborations among school, university, and community-based activists to alter curriculum, challenge common school practices, and work for social change through a process of problem posing, data gathering, analysis, and action. The roots of action research are in the social action traditions of Kurt Lewin and Stephen Corey in the 1940s and 1950s in the US, the teacher-as-researcher curriculum development movement in the UK, spearheaded by Lawrence Stenhouse, John Elliott, Jean Rudduck, and others, and the Australian participatory and critical action research movement, led by Wilfred Carr and Stephen Kemmis (Noffke, 1997; Zeichner and Noffke, 2001). The phrase 'teacher research' is now commonly used to refer to the North American renewal of interest in teacher inquiry that emerged in the late 1980s (Anderson and Herr, 1999; Cochran-Smith and Lytle, 1993, 1999). Generally, 'teacher research' refers to the inquiries of K-12 teachers and other educators who work in inquiry communities to examine their own assumptions, develop local knowledge by posing questions and gathering data, and – in some versions of teacher research – work for social justice.

The term 'self-study,' is used almost exclusively to refer to inquiries at the higher education level by academics involved in the practice of teacher education, broadly construed. Self-study has been conceptualized by members of the AERA Self-Study Special Interest Group as a way to reinvent teacher education by continuously interrogating one's own practice and all of its underlying assumptions (see, for example, Cole and Knowles, 1995; Hamilton, 1998; Loughran and Northfield, 1998; Russell and Korthagen, 1995). Closely related to and sometimes overlapping with self-study, 'narrative inquiry' and/or 'autobiographical inquiry' refer to the narratives produced through systematic reflections by prospective and experienced teachers and/or by teacher–educators that contain knowledge within them. Narrative inquiry has been conceptualized by Jean

Clandinin and Michael Connelly (Clandinin and Connelly, 1995, 1996) and by Nona Lyons and Vicki LaBoskey (Lyons and LaBoskey, 2002) as a way to uncover and represent teachers' personal practical knowledge.

Another form of practitioner inquiry is 'the scholarship of teaching and learning,' derived from a term originally coined by Ernest Boyer (1990), then President of the Carnegie Foundation, as part of special report on the priorities of the professoriate. Making a distinction between Boyer's notion, which emphasizes 'scholarly teaching,' Lee Shulman, and his current colleagues at the Carnegie Foundation (Hutchings, 1998; Shulman, 2001; Shulman *et al.* 1999) have conceptualized 'the scholarship of teaching and learning' as studying, understanding, and enhancing teaching and learning across disciplinary areas and at both K-12 and higher education levels by making the scholarship of teaching public, accessible to critique by others, and exchangeable in the professional community. The final mode we include under the practitioner inquiry umbrella is research carried out by university-based researchers who take on the role of teacher in K-12 settings in order to conduct research on the intricate complexities involved in the problems of practice. The best known examples of this kind of inquiry are the work of Magdalene Lampert, Deborah Ball, and their colleagues and students (e.g. Lampert, 1990, 2001; Lampert and Ball, 1998) who conceptualize 'pedagogical inquiry' as a way for teachers to learn from very experienced and expert teachers' records of practice.

Shared features

Although there are differences in emphasis and intention, several shared features of practitioner inquiry cut across versions and variants. In all forms of practitioner inquiry, the practitioner himself or herself takes on the role of researcher. This is quite different from what is usually the case with research on teaching and schooling where practitioners are the topics of study, the objects of someone else's inquiry, or the informants and subjects of research conducted by those outside the situation. In addition, in most versions of practitioner inquiry, collaboration is key, and the local community is the context in which knowledge is constructed and made public to the scrutiny and consideration of others.

A second shared feature of practitioner inquiry is the assumption that the knowledge needed to understand, analyze, and ultimately improve educational situations cannot be generated primarily outside of those contexts and then transported from 'outside to inside' (Cochran-Smith and Lytle, 1993) for direct implementation and use. Rather practitioner inquiry is built on the assumptions that practitioners are knowers, that the relationships of knowledge and practice are complex and distinctly non-linear, and that the knowledge needed to improve practice is influenced by the contexts and relations of power that structure the daily work of teaching and learning.

A third common feature is that the professional context is taken as the site for inquiry, and problems and issues that arise from professional practice are taken up as topics of study. When the practitioner is engaged in inquiry about his or her own professional context, the questions emerge from the day-to-day experiences of practice and, often, from discrepancies between what is intended and what occurs. The unique feature of the questions that prompt practitioners' inquiry is that they emanate from neither theory nor practice alone but from critical reflection on the intersections of the two.

The boundaries between inquiry and practice blur when the practitioner is a researcher and a knower and when the professional context is a site for the study of problems of practice. Most of the modes of practitioner inquiry described above also share the assumption that inquiry is an integral, not separate, part of practice and that learning from practice is an essential task of practitioners across the professional lifespan.

Issues about generalizability and validity have often been used to discount the value of practitioner inquiry, which, by definition, is prompted by the questions of individuals or local groups of practitioners, and is often conducted in the context of a single classroom, course, school, or program. However, an important feature is that notions of validity and generalizability are quite different from the traditional criteria of transferability and application of findings (often, the identification of causes and effects) to other populations and contexts.

All forms of practitioner inquiry share the features of systematicity and intentionality. Stenhouse's (1985) emphasis on research as 'systematic' and 'self critical' inquiry emphasized this idea early on. In some forms of practitioner inquiry, systematic documentation of issues related to teaching, learning, and schooling resembles the forms of documentation (observation, interviews, and document/artifact collection) used in ethnographic research, grounded theory, and other forms of qualitative and interpretive study. Part of what distinguishes the inquiries of practitioners from those of outside researchers who rely on similar forms of data collection is that in addition to documenting students' learning, practitioner–researchers also systematically document their own teaching and learning – their own thinking, planning, and evaluation processes as well as their questions, interpretive frameworks, changes in views over time, issues they see as dilemmas, and themes that recur.

Finally, although the focus of practitioner inquiry is, by definition, the work of practitioners in their own professional contexts, most forms of practitioner inquiry are characterized by their emphasis on making the work public and open to the critique of a larger community. Along these lines, Stenhouse (1985) defined research as systematic inquiry 'made public' to others, and much of the current North American teacher research movement is distinguished by the work of K-12 teachers, teacher–educators, and others working together to generate 'knowledge of practice' within inquiry communities (Cochran-Smith and Lytle, 1999). Although some descriptions of practitioner inquiry suggest that it generates practical knowledge that is quite distinct from formal knowledge, which is generalizable and widely usable (Richardson, 1996), many of the forms of practitioner inquiry are characterized by their efforts to break with the traditional epistemological distinction between formal and practical knowledge.

The above analysis of key shared features of practitioner inquiry not only reveals the general ways that divergent forms of practitioner inquiry are united, but also points to many of the issues that divide practitioner inquiry from more traditional university-based research. For example, the discrepancies between practitioner inquiry where roles and boundaries are blurred, on the one hand, and traditional forms of research that makes sharp demarcations between researcher and that which is being researched, on the other, are clear in many of the critiques that have emerged about practitioner inquiry over the years. We elaborate these and other tensions and ethical dilemmas that are inherent in the work of practitioner inquiry in university culture in the remainder of this chapter.

Practitioner inquiry and university culture

Our argument in this chapter is that all of the dilemmas and tensions involved with taking practitioner inquiry seriously within university culture are in a certain sense ethical issues. This point is somewhat akin to James Gee's (2005) comments about the National Research Council's (NRC) report, *Scientific Research in Education* (2001), which prompted a great deal of critique and commentary. Gee argued that the principles of inquiry formulated by the NRC panel in an attempt to define scientific research in education were 'relatively vacuous' outside of the specific theories of specific domains, which he pointed out were considerably smaller than whole disciplines (like education). Gee captured this point in his title, 'It's theories all the way down,' arguing that discussions about the 'science' of educational research were inseparable from particular theoretical frameworks of specific disciplines, such as linguistics. Gee's argument is similar in valence to the argument crystallized in our title, 'Everything's ethics.' In short, we are arguing that meaningful discussions about practitioner inquiry within the culture of universities cannot be separated from discussions about ethics, and that whenever practitioner inquiry is conceptualized, conducted, supported, used, referred to, or evaluated by those working within the cultures of universities, all issues are in a certain sense ethical issues. We make this argument by first tracing our own roots as university-based educators who 'worked the dialectic' of conceptualizing and conducting practitioner inquiry and then focusing explicitly on several key ethical dilemmas.

Tracing our roots

We trace our interest in practitioner inquiry to an increasing dissatisfaction with business as usual at the university – particularly with the way practitioners were positioned in teacher education and professional development, and with the way university-generated knowledge was assumed to encompass everything there was to know about teachers and teaching. From the beginning, we worked closely with new and experienced urban teachers at the University of Pennsylvania to develop innovative pre-service and professional development projects and programs, particularly the pre-service program, Project START (Student Teachers as

Researching Teachers), and the school–university collaborative, PhilWP (the Philadelphia Writing Project), an urban site of the National Writing Project. Throughout our time at Penn, and elsewhere, we were never solely practitioners nor solely researchers. Rather we saw ourselves as negotiating the uncertain borders of educational practice and scholarship by simultaneously wrestling with the daily dilemmas of practice and at the same time contributing to conceptual frameworks for the emerging domain of teacher research.

From the beginning we regarded our projects as strategic sites for both research and practice, positioned to prompt the rethinking of fundamental assumptions about the intellectual project of teaching and to explore the prospects for reconstructing practice as inquiry across the professional lifespan. It was our close work with teachers that heightened our awareness of the gap between university discourse and the reality of daily life in schools and made us reject the claim that universities could take the major responsibility for creating enduring change in schools and classrooms. Early on, we realized that it was not just university scholars who took a critical perspective on the social and political arrangements of schools and schooling. Rather many of the urban teachers with whom we were collaborating (particularly those who were members of the Philadelphia Teachers' Learning Cooperative, Teacher Educators for Social Responsibility, and those who worked with Patricia Carini and others at the Prospect School and the North Dakota Study Group) had a long history of documenting, and taking critical perspectives on, their work with students and the larger sociopolitical contexts of school and society.

Jointly with these and many other teachers and student teachers, we explored teacher research as a way to rethink practice, question our own assumptions, and challenge the status quo – not only in schools but also in the university. Over time, we came to use the term 'teacher research' (and later, to be more inclusive of the range of practitioners involved, 'practitioner inquiry') as a kind of shorthand for a larger set of premises about: teachers as knowers, reciprocal school–university relationships, teaching as both an intellectual and political activity, learning to teach as a process that occurs within inquiry communities throughout the professional lifespan, schooling as deeply influenced by culture and history, and the need for parallel transformation of universities and schools.

We trace the roots of our interest in teacher research to a time long before these projects, however. Both of us began our work at the university having been K–12 teachers, and then we were part-time instructors and/or supervisors of student teachers and lecturers for a number of years. Later, after we completed our doctorates at Penn in the early 1980s, we continued as lecturers or adjunct faculty for a number of years until there was an opportunity to 'apply for our own jobs' as tenure-track assistant professors.

Throughout this time period, we were actively involved in all aspects of the academic programs at the university and also engaged in scholarly and professional work, both before and after we were 'officially' faculty members. Despite the important opportunities these positions gave us to teach and to learn, it is also clear that during the early years, like some women at schools of education at many other research universities, we were marginalized as members of the faculty. In addition, because of our close work with teachers and student teachers, some university colleagues identified us with practitioner-oriented issues rather than with 'real' research. At many schools of education at research universities at that time in the early 1980s, an individual's status roughly mapped to her closeness to or distance from the daily practice of schools and other educational programs. This kind of hierarchy distinguished those who did social science (i.e. they engaged in scholarship about education broadly construed and/or closely identified with the concerns of a particular discipline, such as psychology, history, or economics) on the one hand, from those, on the other hand, who identified themselves as educators working in the field of education, typically teacher–educators and others whose work was directly focused on curriculum, teaching, learning, and schooling.

In retrospect, we realize that our reluctance to privilege neither scholarship nor practice contributed not only to our early marginalization as faculty members but also to our need to construct a kind of critical integration that connected our more grassroots work with teachers to our teaching and research at the university. This desire to locate our work at the intersection of two worlds deeply informed and continuously called into question our perspectives on collaboration and power, voice and representation, culture and difference, and the interrelationships of inquiry, knowledge, and practice.

Part of the reason we were able to work at this intersection at a major research university was the relatively small size of our programs in pre-service teacher education and in reading, writing, and literacy. In addition, in those early days, both of us had a great deal of autonomy and what we now realize were unusually rich opportunities to invent new program structures, imagine new relationships with school-based colleagues, and figure out how to make our projects critical sites for inquiry. Commenting on our apparent freedom to pursue these ideas, one of our colleagues from another university once pointed out that many administrators and faculty at Penn appeared for the most part 'mercifully uninterested' in what was going on in our programs, even though we were by then writing about them and beginning to draw attention to this work.

Our ideas about teacher research were also in sync with the growing interest at Penn's Graduate School of Education in qualitative research. Beginning in the mid-1970s, the University of Pennsylvania was at the forefront of exploring and fostering qualitative research as a legitimate mode of inquiry into educational problems and issues. Led over the years by well-known researchers from anthropology, linguistics, and literacy, including Dell Hymens, David Smith, Shirley Heath, Frederick Erickson, Bambi Schieffelin, and Nancy Hornberger, Penn was among the first to offer an array of courses in qualitative research methodology and to permit and indeed encourage doctoral dissertations that relied on qualitative approaches to data collection and analysis. Much of this work explored the cultures of schools and classrooms and attempted to represent teachers' knowledge from their perspectives inside schools. Efforts of this kind were intensified and made public via the university's Ethnography and Education Forum, which began in the late 1970s and continues annually. This conference, in which we participated from the beginning, has been known over time for promoting conversations about qualitative research among an unusually wide range of participants, both local and national, including graduate students, school- and program-based teachers and administrators, and university faculty.

Ours and many others' ideas about teacher research were first made public at 'Teacher Research Day,' a special event we initiated with teachers and student teachers at the Forum in 1986. Since that time, Teacher Research Day has attracted teacher researchers and inquiry communities locally and from around the world as well as featured speakers who helped to conceptualize and disseminate the notion of practitioner inquiry as a mode for knowledge generation, professional development, and activism for school change. As co-authors, we used the forum as a context for sharing our emerging ideas about what it meant to make inquiry central to teaching and learning to teach. Over the years, we had the privilege to present more than a dozen keynote talks that introduced Teacher Research Day by positing conceptual frameworks at once firmly rooted in our ongoing projects and programs, and also intended to suggest generative questions and issues for the larger field. All of these were eventually published in one form or another in educational journals and in some cases in professional newsletters and in-house publications. Over these same years, our student teachers and our school- and program-based teacher colleagues also presented their work at the forum and at a growing number of regional and national conferences related to teacher education, language and literacy, and urban education. Over time, engaging in research on our own practice became the central way of knowing for our growing inquiry community in the Philadelphia area.

Working the dialectic

As this discussion about our roots suggests, we have worked over time to conceptualize and take seriously the concept of teacher research – and its underlying premises about knowledge, teaching, schooling, and power – and to instantiate and act on those premises in our daily university work, in various partnerships and collaborative contexts, in K-12 schools, and in community-based adult program literacy and other settings. We think of these efforts collectively as 'working the dialectic.' By 'dialectic,' we refer to the reciprocal, recursive, and symbiotic relationships of research and practice, analysis and action, inquiry and experience, theorizing and doing, and being researchers and practitioners, as well as the dialectic of generating local knowledge of practice while making that knowledge accessible and usable in other contexts and thus helping to transform it into public knowledge. When we 'work the dialectic,' there are not distinct moments when we are only researchers or only practitioners. Rather these activities and roles are intentionally blurred.

By 'working' we mean capitalizing on, learning from, and mining the dialectic as a particularly rich resource for new knowledge. Clearly, this occurs when we study and theorize our practice as university-based faculty members and teacher–educators. But in our teaching and program evaluation efforts, we highlight and learn from the work of those who have engaged in teacher research and other practitioner inquiries. Thus, for example, in the construction of reading lists for courses or in the synthesis of research literature for scholarly publications, we recognize practitioners as legitimate knowledge generators and thus include in our reviews the inquiries of school-based teachers and university-based teacher–educators. We also 'work' the dialectic by collaborating with others to develop the contexts that support the inquiries of student teachers, new and experienced school-based teachers and administrators, university-based fieldwork supervisors and teacher–educators, community program-based educators, and many other educational colleagues and collaborators.

As university faculty members working the dialectic, we have explored the ways we and our students and colleagues co-construct knowledge; we have investigated issues of language, culture and literacy; and, we have analyzed the contexts that support inquiry communities and teacher learning across the professional lifespan. Drawing on data collected periodically over two decades from a number of sites – pre-service teacher education programs, urban professional development projects, and other university or field-based programs – we have explored the complex relationships of inquiry, knowledge, and professional practice. Within this program of research, we have tried to understand how teachers raise questions, collect classroom and school data, generate analyses and interpretations, and alter students' learning opportunities. We have looked at how prospective teachers reconcile the issues of race, culture, and diversity with issues of high standards, content coverage, and accountability as they learn to teach. We have looked at how experienced teachers understand race, culture, and diversity as dimensions of leadership in an urban school district undergoing dramatic change. We have compared the literacies of women in a university program, women in a community college, and women who are homeless, in order to explore how individuals, differently positioned in terms of gender and schooling, construct their learning 'herstories'. We have traced the attempts of a large teacher education faculty group from very different disciplinary and methodological backgrounds, to grapple with the question of what it means to do teacher education for social justice. We have explored the characteristics of pre-service and in-service teacher inquiry communities as environments that support ongoing learning in the face of continuous societal and educational change. All these strands of our research program have informed and are informed by our evolving theories of the interrelationships among inquiry, knowledge, and practice.

Although many of these questions could be explored by researchers outside of their own professional contexts, something different results when one's own professional work is the research site and one's own emerging issues and dilemmas are the grist for systematic study. When university-based faculty intentionally work the dialectic of research and practice, it makes possible a genre of scholarship in which rich new ways to 'theorize practice' and, at the same time, 'practicize theory' are developed.

In our case, as university-based faculty members, working the dialectic has been an especially productive way to invent and direct teacher education and professional development projects and, at the same time, theorize and analyze many aspects of those projects. Based on this work, we have tried to conceptualize teacher research through a series of essays presented and published over a period of some 20 years. In each conceptual essay we wrote about teacher research, we tried to address a particular question or set of questions that had been problematic in our daily work as teachers, teacher–educators, and researchers. Thus, in a very real sense, the contradictions in our own practice oriented our research just as much as did our reading of the wider literature related to teacher learning, inquiry, school change, and language and literacy. At the same time, the distinctions we made in our writing provided new lenses on our practice and on our interpretation of the theoretical and empirical literature. An early essay on the genres of teacher research, for example, grew out of our extensive reading of the varied forms in which teachers wrote about their daily work, and also out of our participation with teachers in a range of oral documentary processes. These experiences contributed to our growing discontent with the assumption that research by school-based teachers should be expected to follow the conventions of method and presentation developed in the university. The conceptual framework we developed influenced us to formalize and rethink the kinds of inquiry opportunities available in our programs and projects. Working the dialectic is a decidedly non-linear process. For us, it has been more like improvising a dance than climbing a set of stairs. As we theorized the relationships of inquiry, knowledge and practice, based on critical analysis of others' work, as well as systematic inquiry into our own practice, we saw many ways to reinvent practice, which prompted further nuances in our theoretical frameworks and posed new questions to analyze; these, in turn, suggested new interpretive frameworks and strategies.

Over the years, working the dialectic changed our work, changed who we are, changed what we do and how we do it. We have found that inquiry changes the people who do it, and for us, in our location at the university, it also challenged many of the formal and informal rules universities live by. It has been our experience that taking teacher research seriously at the university creates ethical issues and tensions that are at once difficult and generative. These have to do with positions and relationships, research conventions and practices, and the broader meanings of scholarly activity. As long as dealing with these ethical issues does not make working within the university context impossible (as they have for some of those involved in practitioner inquiry at research universities), they can be generative – suggesting new questions and prompting further critique about school–university relationships.

The ethics of practitioner inquiry within university culture

Although there is now a substantial literature about the role of practitioner inquiry in schools and in school–university partnerships, there is much less that focuses on the university, particularly on the contradictions that are generated when practitioner inquiry brushes up against, and sometimes collides with, what has traditionally been valued and rewarded in university culture. Some of the most interesting and provocative work along these lines has been written by teacher–educators who are active in the self-study of teacher education practices community, particularly Ardra Cole and Gary Knowles, Jack Whitehead, and Tom Russell and Fred Korthagen (see, for example, Cole and Knowles, 1996, 1998; Russell and Korthagen, 1995; Whitehead, 1995). Their work has exposed some of the raw underbelly of university culture, exploring what happens when those who engage in alternative forms of research and inquiry work in universities where this work is not only not valued, but – much worse – is regarded as improper, subversive, and worthy of censure. More recently, and along quite different but related lines, some arts and sciences faculty members who have engaged in the scholarship of teaching have begun also to acknowledge the ethical issues that are raised when university teachers engage in research about their own practice and their own students' learning. These involve questions of privacy and respect as well as negotiation of policies regulating human subjects research, such as institutional review board regulations and exemptions (e.g. Hutchings, 2002a, 2002b), which often simply do not fit well with practitioner inquiry.

In a certain sense, it is not surprising that there has been relatively little work about the ethics of practitioner inquiry within research universities to date. The idea of university-based scholars engaging in research about their own work as practitioners is, after all, relatively new. But it is also the case that examining the culture of universities is in and of itself rather inconsistent with the culture of universities, which have long had a tendency to call for school transformation without parallel self-examination and restructuring. Anderson and Herr (1999) make this point about university-based educators who work closely with school-based educators: 'Academics who form alliances with practitioners or who send practitioners out into their schools to generate knowledge about practice should be equally willing to submit their own institutions and practices to the same level of investigative scrutiny' (p. 17). Similarly, Wisniewski (2000) suggests that ethnographic studies of change in the academy are needed, but avoided, by university researchers who prefer to direct their 'gaze' at K-12 school change rather than at their own settings and interactions with students, administrators, and colleagues.

Below we discuss some of the key tensions and contradictions that have arisen from our own experience as university-based teachers and researchers trying to take seriously and act on the concepts and premises of teacher research. As our title indicates, we see all of these issues as centrally involved with ethics.

The ethics of inquiry as stance

As teacher–educators, we treat inquiry as a stance on teaching, learning, and schooling (Cochran-Smith and Lytle, 1993, 1999) rather than as a bounded activity or project. This means that the central tenets of inquiry structure and inform every dimension of our work, and nearly all of the courses, seminars, and institutes with which we are involved have in common posing, not just answering, questions, taking practice as the site for inquiry, interrogating one's own and others' practices and assumptions, and learning from and about practice by collecting and analyzing the 'data' of daily work.

This stance is incongruent with the role that many teacher–educators, as well as new and experienced teachers, have been socialized to expect the university to play in teachers' learning. For many years – and especially now in the current era of accountability – university experts have been expected to offer the latest theories (although often considered too abstract and thus irrelevant to 'real' school) or to provide training and coaching in 'best practices' to be immediately applied in classrooms. In either case, the assumption is that outside experts had knowledge that needed to be 'injected' into school practice. Inquiry as a stance disrupts this idea by controverting the expert–novice conception, challenging the knowledge transmission model, and questioning the assumption that learning to teach is accomplished in the early years of teaching and then needs only periodic updating.

There are a number of ethical dilemmas involved with making inquiry a stance, however. For example, in our enthusiasm for the idea of inquiry as a primary pedagogy of teacher education, we urge and in some ways impose this perspective. Of course, in a certain way, all teaching is imposition. And yet, there is a fine line between inviting practitioners to engage in inquiry, on the one hand, and, on the other, requiring them to do it in order to obtain a degree or earn credit for an in-service course. There is a fine line between collaboratively constructing an agenda within an inquiry community, on the one hand, and, on the other, pre-determining content, processes, and outcomes. The contradiction between inquiry and imposition is especially visible in discussions of the questions that emerge from inquiry. In our writing about practitioner inquiry, we have argued many times that practitioners' questions come from their own felt needs and thus are different in important ways from those of university researchers. We have pointed out that these questions come from unique perspectives on classroom and school life and reflect the interpretive frameworks that practitioners have developed, based on their work inside schools and other educational contexts.

Nonetheless, sometimes we hear ourselves reframing or evaluating practitioners' questions – casting them in our own language and images and subtly, or not so subtly, promoting adherence to certain university conventions. Sometimes this is motivated by our desire to 'help' the questioner locate her question within a wider conversation, sometimes it involves distinguishing a 'researchable' question from one that is more like product-testing, and sometimes it reflects the consensus of a group not to avoid the hard issues of schooling. Whatever prompts our responses, our experience is that two basically contradictory things can occur simultaneously when inquiry is a stance in the university context: genuinely inviting practitioner inquiry to challenge the hegemony of university knowledge, on the one hand, and 'front-loading' our own agenda as university scholars in ways that may actually discourage opposing viewpoints. The result is a set of ethical oxymorons in connection to the concept of inquiry as stance – 'imposed felt need' or 'transmitted inquiry' or 'coerced critique'.

The ethics of inquiry as collaboration

To make inquiry genuinely collaborative, we have tried to develop close and equitable working relationships with student teachers, teachers and many other practitioners. We have also collaborated with field-based educators whose positions fit neatly into none of the traditional school or university categories, such as teachers who divide their time between school leadership and university teaching roles. These collaborations have made possible the design, governance, and assessment of inquiry activities at every organizational level and across a wide range of formats such as courses, institutes, on-site teacher research groups, steering committees, and so on.

Obviously these efforts to share power and leadership are intended to disrupt the culture of the university in that policy-making is more inclusive, decisions are more widely negotiated, and responsibilities are shifted. But there are ethical issues and contradictions here as well. One set of ethical issues occurs when collaborative relationships are nested within degree programs – here students are invited to 'collaborate' with faculty who also grade them, and fieldwork supervisors or adjunct faculty are invited to 'collaborate' with those who may participate in hiring, firing, and evaluating them. Other issues occur in school–university partnerships where the power relationships are more ambiguous – here collaborative relationships may in fact perpetuate privilege in more (and less) subtle ways or, in quite the opposite direction, may be interpreted by teachers as abdication of responsibility.

Unfortunately, instances of silencing and control seem to come with the territory of inquiry as collaboration. In addition, in both degree programs and partnerships, there are almost always ethical issues related to critique. Who can critique whom? When is critique appropriate, and when is it destructive of the fragile strands of collaborative relationships? Are private contexts for critique more appropriate than public ones, or do these simply force underground a discourse that could make visible the very issues with which the group most needs to engage? These ethical issues around critique are complexly related to the alliances and loyalties that structure the lives of practitioners in both universities and schools – the culture of silence about the work of one's colleagues, the culture of social groups based on bonds of gender, race, class background, and ethnicity, and the culture of seniority and experience that makes longevity in a group – and sometimes age, rank, or other markers of prior status – the passports for full participation for some, while at the same time inhibiting the contributions of others.

The ethics of inquiry made public and accessible

As noted above, we have for a long time now focused some of the research we do on our work with others in various inquiry communities, including at times the learning communities we try to create in each of our courses. These communities, which become the contexts for important inquiries about many issues related to schooling, also function as sites for research about inquiry. By studying the communities we are part of, we have the opportunity to explore the ways we and our students and colleagues co-construct knowledge; we can investigate issues of language, culture and literacy; and, we have a chance to analyze the contexts that support the work of inquiry communities and the professional development of teachers across the life span.

Organizing our teaching and research lives in these ways not only alters the content of what can be researched but also intentionally violates a number of research conventions that are part of university culture. Researching our own teaching, researching the research of others, and researching our experiences as participants in inquiry communities deviate dramatically from the more distanced topics that many consider the proper concern of scholarly educators. In addition, this kind of inquiry violates expectations in the research community about the most useful research regarding programs and projects – the norm is more toward evaluation or outcome studies based on data gathered by a researcher who is outside the setting itself. In that we draw on feminist, critical, and interpretive research traditions, we make the relationships of researcher and researched problematic in our work. But because the participants in our projects are in so many complicated ways already both researchers and researched, it is almost ludicrous to fit some of this work into the university's categories. Who indeed are the 'human subjects' in this kind of research? Who 'signs off' on whom? Who's entitled to write about whom, and who 'owns' the data?

The ethical issues involved in making inquiry public and accessible to others have primarily to do with authorship, ownership, representation, and co-optation. For example, for many years, we have written together looking broadly and synoptically at the Philadelphia inquiry community, theorizing teacher research and professional development by drawing on projects that involved enormous efforts by many other people over many years. We have built our own understandings and arguments out of the work of communities and have explicitly used many examples of the writing of others. In our co-authored work, we have often chosen to represent the work of the community through our perspectives as university-based teachers and researchers. Of course we always had the appropriate permissions, acknowledgements, and disclaimers about not speaking for others. None of these, however, really altered the reality that we, as university-based faculty, got a generous amount of the credit for this work within the educational community. In addition, partly because of 'what counts' within the culture of the university, we committed most of our time and resources to writing for academic journals and handbooks, rather than for more practice-oriented and/or local outlets. The trade-off here has been that we have not learned what we surely would have learned by writing explicitly for a wider, more inclusive audience.

On the other hand, when we try to address some of these issues by representing the work of communities through collaborative writing with others involved in these projects, there are additional ethical dilemmas. What conventions of writing, what audiences, and what modes of data collection and analysis are ultimately privileged, even when the explicit intention is not to perpetuate the dominance of the university? How are the different roles in writing opted for, designated, and/or valued, even when the intention of the group is to make these decisions jointly? How do the various collaborators participate in conceptualizing, drafting, revising, and editing, and what does collaboration really mean, when often – in the final product – we retain for ourselves the 'last word'?

At the heart of many of these decisions is how collaborative groups – in which we as university educators are simply members, though, in a certain sense, never simply members – negotiate priorities in purposes and goals for making their joint work public and accessible. Some of the most significant moments in these negotiations are those when we realize that even deciding what to disclose and what to obscure or omit is an ethical issue in that it entails very different risks and consequences for the differently positioned writers in the group. What is troubling is that, as university researchers, we tend to argue for pushing boundaries, for opening up and writing about unsettling subjects. But, as university researchers, we are also much more likely to get credit for doing this and much less likely than some of our school-based colleagues to have to deal directly in our professional lives with the fall out of our choices.

A particularly dicey ethical dilemma along these lines is how, when, and whether it is appropriate to make public examples from inquiry communities that may reflect negatively on the participants, or on the group as a whole, or on the students who are being represented. Further, the culture of the university depends on sharp and even excoriating critique of others' research, and indeed we have been chastised by some university-based colleagues for not being appropriately critical in our analyses of the teacher research that we include in our writing, and not making public the full range of the problems inherent in the work of inquiry communities. We realize, of course, that including more of the messiness is probably essential to furthering the wider social, political and intellectual agendas of the practitioner inquiry movement. Finding ways to do this that do not undermine the very relationships that make the work possible and do not yet again reinforce the hegemony of the university, however, is daunting. These may require that teacher–educators and teachers together rethink and reinvent approaches to critique that are more congruent with the politics of this movement.

Conclusion: everything's ethics

Among the consequences of taking practitioner inquiry seriously over the last 20 years has been the rewriting of our own job descriptions at the university and the blurring of our roles as researchers, teachers, writers, and partners in university–field networks and collaboratives. As many of our colleagues involved in similar work know, refusing to privilege the role of researcher over all others clearly disrupts university norms and its neat demarcations – for each individual faculty member – of contributions to research, teaching, and service, the stuff of which tenure, promotions, and merit pay raises are made. When one chooses to do this kind of work, much of which is invisible through the lenses of the university, one also agrees to accept the fact that 'everything's ethics' and thus, in a certain sense, chooses to take on a number of complex ethical issues and dilemmas.

In her 1992 AERA presidential address, entitled 'The meaning of scholarly activity and the building of community,' Ann Lieberman (1992) suggested an expanded view of scholarly activity:

> I use the phrase, 'scholarly activity,' despite its seeming to be a marriage of contraries or contradictions ... an embrace of what appear to be two ideas that do not fit comfortably together: scholarship, defined as 'a quality of knowledge and learning ... which is systematic, attempting accuracy, critical ability and thoroughness,' and activity, 'requiring action, producing real effects as opposed to theoretical, ideal, or speculative' ... . The development of a synthesis from these seeming contradictions has important implications for scholarly work: the kinds of relationships we develop, how we frame and carry out our work, and how we give voice to both activism and knowledge building.
>
> (p.8)

In making this point, Lieberman recognized and clearly valued activism, asserting that it ought to be an integral part of the work of scholarship in schools of education and that it was one of the ways to resolve the contradictions in our professional lives. She also implicitly acknowledged the inevitability of dealing with contraries and contradictions, many of which are related to serious ethical issues.

In conclusion, we wish to point out that building professional lives that are founded on the premises of practitioner inquiry challenges many aspects of university culture and carries with it multiple – and tricky – ethical dilemmas. We believe that these are by and large constructive – even generative – dilemmas in that they get at many of the issues that are at the heart of practitioner inquiry, especially issues related to knowledge construction and use and issues related to the purposes or ends of engaging in inquiry. In looking closely and systematically at our own experiences with practitioner inquiry, it is evident that there are many ethical contradictions, tensions, and dilemmas that come with this territory and are not easily resolved or explained away. Even as we identify and explore these issues in this chapter, we are acutely conscious that the next task is not finding ways to fix or resolve these issues, but rather ways to think and talk about the ethics of practitioner inquiry differently and more openly, so that they continue to feed (not stymie) the work and support (not interfere with) the commitment of inquiry communities to interrogate even our most cherished assumptions and practices.

References

Anderson, G., and Herr, K. (1999) 'The new paradigm wars: is there room for rigorous practitioner knowledge in schools and universities?', *Educational Researcher*, 28(5): 12–21.

Boyer, E.L. (1990) *Scholarship Reconsidered*, San Francisco, CA: Carnegie Foundation for Advancedment of Teaching.

Clandinin, D.J., and Connelly, F.M. (eds) (1995) *Teachers' Professional Knowledge Landscapes*, Vol. 15, New York, NY: Teachers College Press.

Clandinin, D.J., and Connelly, F.M. (1996) 'A storied landscape as a context for teacher knowledge', in M. Kompf, M. Bond, D. Dworet and T. Boak (eds) *Changing Research and Practice: Teachers' Professionalism, Identities and Knowledge,* Washington, DC: Falmer Press, pp. 137–148.

Cochran-Smith, M., and Lytle, S. (1993) *Inside/outside: Teacher Research and Knowledge*, New York, NY: Teachers College Press.

Cochran-Smith, M., and Lytle, S. (1999) 'Relationship of knowledge and practice: teacher learning in communities', in A. Iran-Nejad and C. Pearson (eds) *Review of Research in Education*, Vol. 24, Washington, DC: American Educational Research Association, pp. 249–306.

Cole, A.L., and Knowles, J.G. (1995) 'A life history approach to self-study: methods and issues', in R. Russell and F. Korthagen (eds), *Teachers who Teach Teachers: Reflections on Teacher Education*, London: Falmer Press.

Cole, A.L., and Knowles, J.G. (1996) 'Reform and "being true to oneself": pedagogy, professional practice, and the promotional process', *Teacher Education Quarterly*, 23(3): 109–126.

Cole, A.L., and Knowles, J.G. (1998) 'The self-study of teacher education practices and the reform of teacher education', In M.L. Hamilton (ed.) *Reconceptualizing Teaching Practice: Self-study in Teacher Education*, London: Falmer Press, pp. 224–234.

Gee, J.P. (2005) 'It's theories all the way down: a response to *Scientific Research in Education'*, *Teachers College Record*, 107(1): 19–29.

Hamilton, M. (1998) 'Case studies of individual self-study: introduction', in M. Hamilton, S. Pinnegar, T. Russell, J. Loughran and V. LaBoskey (eds) *Reconceptualizing Teaching Practice: Self-study in Teacher Education*, Bristol, PA: Falmer Press, pp. 111–112.

Hutchings, P. (ed.) (1998) *The Course Portfolio: How Faculty can Examine their Teaching to Advance Practice and Improve Student Learning*, Washington, DC: American Association for Higher Education.

Hutchings, P. (ed.) (2002a) *Ethics of Inquiry, Issues in the Scholarship of Teaching and Learn*, Menlo Park, CA: Carnegie Foundation for the Advancement of Teaching.

Hutchings, P. (2002b) 'Ethics and aspiration in the scholarship of teaching and learning, introduction to ethics of inquiry', in P. Hutchings (ed.) *Ethics of Inquiry, Issues in the Scholarship of Teaching and Learning*, Menlo Park, CA: Carnegie Foundation for the Advancement of Teaching.

Lampert, M. (1990) 'When the problem is not the question and the solution is not the answer: mathematical knowing and teaching', *American Educational Research Journal*, 27(1): 29–63.

Lampert, M. (2001) *Teaching Problems and the Problems of Teaching*, New Haven, CT: Yale University Press.

Lampert, M. and Ball, D. (1998) *Teaching, Multimedia, and Mathematics: Investigations of Real Practice*, New York, NY: Teachers College Press.

Lieberman, A. (1992) 'The meaning of scholarly activity and the building of community', *Educational Researcher*, 21(6): 5–12.

Loughran, J. and Northfield, J. (1998) 'A framework for the development of self-study practice', in M. L. Hamilton (ed.) *Reconceptualizing Teaching Practice: Self-study in Teacher Education*, London: Falmer Press, pp. 7–18.

Lyons, N. and LaBoskey, V.K. (eds) (2002) *Narrative Inquiry in Practice, Advancing the Knowledge of Teaching*, New York: Teachers College Press.

National Research Council (2001) *Scientific Research in Education*, Washington, DC: National Academy Press.

Noffke, S. (1997) 'Professional, personal, and political dimensions of action research', in M. Apple (ed.) *Review of Research in Education*, Vol. 22, pp. 305–343.

Richardson, V. (1996) 'The case for formal research and practical inquiry in teacher education', in F. Murray (ed.) *The Teacher Educator's Handbook*, San Francisco, CA: Jossey-Bass, pp. 715–737.

Russell, T. and Korthagen, F. (eds) (1995) *Teachers who Teach Teachers: Reflections on Teacher Education*. London: Falmer Press.

Shulman, L. (2001) *Report of the President from the 96th Annual Report: The Scholarship of Teaching and Learning, a Perspective after Four Years*, Palo Alto, CA: Carnegie Foundation for the Advancement of Teaching.

Shulman, L., Lieberman, A., Hatch, T. and Lew, M. (1999) 'The Carnegie Foundation builds the scholarship of teaching with K-12 teachers and teacher educators', *Teaching and Teacher Education: Division K Newsletter, American Educational Research Association*, 1–5.

Stenhouse, L. (1985) *Research as a Basis for Teaching*, London: Heinemann.

Whitehead, J. (1995) 'Educative relationships with the writings of others', in T. Russell and F. Korthagen (eds) *Teachers who Teach Teachers: Reflections on Teacher Education*, London: Falmer Press.

Wisniewski, R. (2000) 'The averted gaze', *Anthropology and Education Quarterly*, 31(1): 5–23.

Zeichner, K. and Noffke, S. (2001) 'Practitioner research', in V. Richardson (ed.) *Teaching* (4th edn), New York, NY: Macmillan.

Chapter 4

Ethical issues for consultants in complex collaborative action research settings

Tensions and dilemmas

Christopher Day and Andrew Townsend

Introduction

This chapter explores issues for action research consultants who work with a range of clients over a sustained period of time but whose interventions are relatively brief and temporary in relation to their working lives. Whilst each of these clients may have a common purpose (i.e. improvement of practice), they may also have different notions of how this may be achieved. The clients in this case are teachers, teaching assistants and head teachers engaged in inquiry-focused work within schools which is part funded by a government agency. They thus have multiple accountabilities for their work, i.e. to pupils, parents, colleague professionals and the network funding agency. These multiple accountabilities, together with the additional commitments and work caused by their (voluntary) participation produce inevitable tensions and dilemmas. The role of the consultant is, therefore, more complex than would be the case in a more normal consultant–client relationship. Whilst, as in more normal relationships, the consultants must be trusted by all their clients, appreciate the complexity of context for the action research and exercise a range of skills, they must also hold and display a clear set of ethical principles within a particularly complex accountability setting.

This chapter discusses the consultancy process over a period of three years with teachers and head teachers in ten schools which were formally linked in a 'Networked Learning Community' which was funded in equal parts by the National College for School Leadership and the schools themselves. Its success was reliant on the establishment of a range of partnerships between professionals from a variety of backgrounds (including ourselves as external consultants). It is the tensions within and between these partnerships which form the focus of this chapter. Discussion of the ethical dimension of the consultancy roles is informed throughout by Campbell's definition of professional ethics:

> Professional ethics is conceived of broadly as elements of human virtue, in all its complexity, as expressed through the nuances of attitudes, intentions, words and actions ...

> (Campbell, 2003a: 9)

We also adapt Campbell's writing about ethical principles in teachers' work with students and apply these to our work as consultants, using consultants as the substitute for teachers and teachers as substitute for students.

- Consultants must be aware that their actions and beliefs have a fundamentally moral and ethical influence on teachers and, therefore, they must be able to distinguish between good and bad effects on the basis of a sound understanding of right and wrong.
- Consultants must conduct themselves as responsible professionals at all times – with honesty, integrity, fairness, impartiality and kindness.
- A consultant's first moral responsibility is to the teachers in his or her care.

The increased complexity of consultants' work has its origins in the new market-driven economy of the public services in England, the so-called culture of 'performativity' (Lyotard, 1984). In essence, teachers' roles and accountabilities have become more intense and diverse in educational climates which, for many, are now characterised as less values driven and more instrumental than previously. Essentially then, the nature of inquiry-based work, intended to stimulate the growth of schools as learning communities, is itself problematic, since it produces tensions between the desire for more democratic practices which focus on teaching and learning and the need to produce measurable value-added pupil attainments through batteries of national tests in important (but still narrow) areas of the curriculum. The general effects of this and its impact on schools in England have been well documented (Ball, 2003; Jeffrey, 2002; Pollard, 2005).

Networked learning communities contexts: continuities and contradictions

The Networked Learning Communities Programme operated in England between September 2002 and September 2006. This policy initiative championed collaboration, supporting networks of six or more schools working together towards common inquiry foci. During its existence, over 1000 schools, in 77 local education authorities (LEAs) were members of a total of 104 funded networked learning communities (NLCs). Many of these communities existed before the advent of the NLC initiative, and some continue to exist now, after the formal end of the partial funding and programmes of support provided by the National College for School Leadership of England (NCSL); and it should be remembered that, important as this initiative was, it applied only to 10–15% of all schools in England.

Each community received matched funding by the NCSL for a minimum of £50,000 per network annually, for up to three years. Schools themselves provided the equivalent of a further £50,000. In order to gain networked learning community status each group submitted a bid to the NCSL outlining a core network focus, their plans for the implementation and establishment of the network and their anticipated impact on the following six different levels of learning as below:

- pupil learning (linked to pedagogic focus and to raising achievement)
- staff learning and professional development (emphasising practitioner inquiry, innovation and collaborative adult learning)
- leadership for learning and leadership development (at all levels, particularly collaborative head teacher learning)
- school-wide learning (supporting the development of schools as professional learning communities)
- school-to-school learning (creating dynamic new learning partnerships with a wide diversity of partners)
- network-to-network learning (spreading learning across the whole education system).

(NCSL, 2002a: 6)

These levels of learning described the anticipated outcomes of networking, and they were intended to be achieved through a series of innovations underpinned by what was termed 'practitioner inquiry' (NCSL, 2002a). The networked learning communities team identified inquiry as 'evidence and data informed learning' and described itself as 'committed to developing collaborative, capacity-building and sustainable learning programmes' through inquiry (NCSL, 2002b). Indeed, the design of these networks and their inquiry element have been directly related to action research in general (Jackson, 2002) and specifically to the work of Kurt Lewin (1946) whose pioneering work on community action and participation projects in the USA is regarded as a significant, if not solitary, foundation for action research (Adelman, 1993; Noffke, 1994). This espoused value by the initiator of the NLC's initiative produced tensions with the results-driven expectations of the government on schools in general and, as was quickly to emerge in the documentation of the NLC initiative itself and its subsequent accountability demands, tensions between the teachers, schools and the NLC leaders at national and regional levels.

The form of practitioner inquiry advocated and supported by the networked learning communities had a number of different facets. These included: commissioning teachers to conduct pieces of research; advocating collaboratively planned, implemented and evaluated innovations in classroom teaching practices; and encouraging networked learning walks, where pairs or groups of teachers from different schools across a network would visit and observe each other's work. The networks were thus intended to be:

- driven by inquiry, emphasising knowledge creation and evidence-based practice
- led by participants, promoting high degrees of ownership

- rich in data, for example establishing baseline surveys and other data sources for all participants, and to model innovation in data management for network schools
- underpinned by strategies to stimulate and support the diffusion of knowledge and capacity across networks, rather than defining effective practice and disseminating it through vertical channels of support and accountability
- contributory to school-wide growth.

(NCSL, 2002a)

In addition these networks were seen as mechanisms which could lead to improvements in pupil performance results, for example through enhancing teaching and learning processes and a way of providing a mechanism for sharing these (Desforges, 2005). Through these means, policy and practice were intended to be more closely matched (Chapman and Aspin, 2005). At the core of the work was a series of partnerships between external consultants (academic researchers and others) who acted as facilitators of action research and providers of support for teacher researchers in the pursuit of generating practice-relevant knowledge.

Partnerships in knowledge generation: changing roles

Partnerships between individual university tutors and school teachers are not new. Many teacher–educators have their roots in schools; most teachers have been trained in universities and there is a complementarity of moral purpose in their work (Cuban, 1992; Day, 1997). Partnerships are often located in:

(i)   the supervisory/mentoring relationships between tutors and teachers in pre-service programmes

(ii) 'provider-led' relationships in which universities offer a 'smorgasbord' of modularised award and non-award-bearing in-service development programmes to teachers

(iii) research and development relationships between university tutors and the education community. These may be subdivided as (a) pure research in which university scholars alone are deemed to have the technical expertise necessary to generate knowledge about teachers, teaching, learning and schools; (b) applied research in which university scholars lead others in curriculum and staff development projects; and (c) collaborative research in which university researchers work alongside teachers in order to generate 'grounded' knowledge alongside needs identified by the teacher participants themselves.

(Day, 1997)

Such partnerships are concerned with the development of schools and practices of individuals within them, in ways that are meaningful to those individuals.

Networked learning communities utilise such partnerships. The role of the higher education consultant in that process of development has been described as providing 'guidance on the process of inquiry and reflection' but not extending to 'advising teachers on curricular, pedagogical or management matters' (Frost *et al.*, 2000: 23).

The nature of these university–school 'partnerships' in general has been changing over the last decade, partly as a direct result of educational reforms which have altered the balance of power between those who traditionally produce knowledge (universities) and those who traditionally disseminate it (schools). The usefulness, rigour and relevance of university research have been called into question and universities have been forced to compete for custom as their own standards of research and teaching have come under close finance-led, ideologically determined, public scrutiny (for example see: Hammersley, 1997, 2002; Hargreaves 1997, 1999; Hillage *et al.*, 1998). Gibbons *et al.* (1994) discuss this change in the perceptions of knowledge and its application; and they identify a transition from a position where knowledge is generated externally to the context of its use through processes governed by a limited community, to one where knowledge 'is created in the context of application' (Day, 1999). These forms of knowledge, described as 'Mode 1' and 'Mode 2' respectively (Gibbons *et al.*, 1994), further reflect a greater emphasis on research which is conducted in, and relevant to, practitioners' working contexts.

These changes have caused a crisis of identity for many teacher–educators, who have had to reassess their roles. No longer regarded as having the right to hold a monopoly on legitimate knowledge production or dissemination, they have been forced to acknowledge and encourage other stakeholders' rights (e.g. teachers) to participate in the generation of knowledge about schools, teaching and learning. School-focused and school-led partnerships have become the norm in initial teacher training and education; and in in-service school- and classroom-focused inquiry work, where university personnel have had to renegotiate contracts in a world of purchasers (schools) and providers of services (universities). Moreover, university tutors have had to learn to cope with such reform-driven imperatives alongside continuing scepticism by school teachers of the theory-bound esoteric world of the academic, which contrasts with the perceived practice-bound action worlds in which they work. As identities have become deconstructed and reconstructed, so roles have changed, with teacher–employers and teachers as 'clients' now participating indirectly and directly in shaping the content and process agendas of their own development programmes, often dictating the timing, duration and location. It is as well to remember, however, that in England over the last 20 years it has been government that has shaped school curricula, pupil assessment and standards for school inspection. These central dictates have provided clear boundaries in which teachers' generation of Mode 2 knowledge can take place.

Leadership and control of even the 'applied' research agenda, too, is being strongly contested. Governments are increasingly targeting development or evaluation of particular programmes and focusing available funding upon issues of their choice. These do not always correspond to or complement those identified by schools themselves and thus compliance of the latter with the former itself causes tensions. Furthermore, governments throughout the world are demanding that educational research results contribute more visibly and more directly to measurable improvements in teaching, learning and achievement in schools. Collaborative-inquiry led research of the kind which was the basis of the networked learning communities survives partly because it is part of the government's rhetoric of lifelong learning and partly because it was, and is, based upon the consonance of individual value systems of teachers, which is seen as having direct practical benefit to the well-being, health and sustenance of individuals and organisations.

Consultancy support for action research

The support that we provide in our role as consultants to these networked learning communities of action researchers has two main elements. The first is advising on the most appropriate school and network structures and systems to support the research conducted by groups of staff within and across schools. The second is in directly advising staff on the planning and conduct of their action research, including on the ethical aspects of this work. The advice we provide in both instances is informed by our views and experiences of the principles and practices of action research and their relationship with the issues being addressed by action researchers.

Our relationships with the practices of the individuals with whom we work are less direct than those of other educational consultants, who are directly concerned with influencing the teaching and learning practices within schools. Schein (1998) identifies three models for consultancy: the 'process' model, the 'doctor–patient' model and the 'purchase of expertise' model. The focus of change and the nature of the relationship between consultant and client differ between these models. Of these three, it is the process consultant model which is most akin to our role in supporting networks of action researchers. Indeed, Schein also identifies the connection between action research and process consultancy (1998). This is in contrast, for example, with consultants who advocate particular changes to teaching and learning practices, and guide clients through changes to their practice in which the consultants are knowledgeable, e.g. coaching. In that model, consultants would be operating more along the principles of the purchase of expertise or doctor–patient models.

Consultancy, in the context of the work discussed in this chapter is, therefore, focused upon assisting the thinkings of practitioners (often teachers) as action researchers about their work, not only about actions specific to their roles as action researchers but also, more fundamentally, in terms of their professional identities – in this case as teacher–researchers whose work is closely aligned to core educational values which inform their practices. Thus, it is expertise in adult learning and change processes that are the primary parts of the process consultant's make-up. This does not mean that consultants do not possess other, particular, knowledge and skills, but rather that these are put at the disposal of the client(s) when sought and in response to need. The success with which an external consultant can influence the development of the client's values and practices, however, is also dependent both on their own self-knowledge (of values and beliefs) and their willingness and ability to place those of the staff with whom they work ahead of their own. The role of the process consultant is to 'understand, and act on the process events that occur in the client's internal and external environment in order to improve the situation as defined by the client' (Schein, 1999: 20) and which 'starts ... with the needs of the client, is client driven and involves the researcher in the client's issues' (Schein, 1995: 15).

Thus, a clear sense of professional identity is important, also, for the external consultants if they are to succeed in their role of process facilitators. The essence of the consultant's role is in supporting others to do work which they perceive as important, and for which the consultant is not directly responsible:

> ... any form of providing help on the content, process or structure of a task or series of tasks, where the consultant is not actually responsible for doing the task (i.e. anything a person, group or organisation is trying to do) itself but is helping those who are. The two critical aspects are that help is being given, and that the helper is not directly responsible within the system ... for what is produced ...
>
> (Steele, 1975)

Our work with action research networks is, like the process model of consultancy, to support clients through processes of reflection and change on topics of interest to them.

There are three key challenges for external consultants in action research settings. Firstly, they need to support the review and renewal of educational beliefs, values and practices and secondly, to support individuals and groups in processes which enable them to achieve their practice aspirations. Thirdly, they need to manage collaboration within the contexts of competing tensions, i.e. to assist those who must manage the tensions of meeting the demands of policy imperatives whilst also promoting individual and collaborative practitioner inquiries, the outcomes of which are not always predictable and which may not, therefore, result in improvement in the terms in which improvements are defined by such policy imperatives. External consultants in these contexts are likely to find themselves working at the nexus of inquiries which may often be intended to democratise decision-making processes within and across schools and thus do not sit comfortably in the broader results-driven agendas and in schools which may not have a history of staff participation, democratic leadership, or cultures of inquiry.

Five tensions of collaborative action research in competing contexts

During the period that we have been working as consultants in this networked learning community we have identified five tensions. These tensions, outlined below, are derived from the complex relationships between the values and practices of different stakeholders and stakeholder groups and from their sometimes uneasy relationships (and, therefore, indirectly, ours) with school and external agendas which are not always perceived as unproblematic.

Individual vs group

The network is composed of individual and groups of teacher–researchers working within and across schools. The in-school groups of teacher–researchers are known as school inquiry groups (SIGs). We use this term deliberately to differentiate our thinking from that which underpins school improvement groups since our experience is that focus on inquiry is a necessary precondition for this. The first tension we identified exists between the differing agendas of individuals and of the school inquiry groups to which they belong. In this case the agendas of individual practitioners were mediated by the SIG of which they were a part:

> In a way the agenda is set higher up, I [as SIG coordinator] work with [the head teacher] and then I open it up to the SIG and ask for ideas but the ideas that come through have been ones that I've put in their minds, as it were.
>
> (SIG coordinator)

Arranging inquirers into groups within schools has many benefits for both the school and the inquirers themselves. School inquiry groups may be able to achieve changes in the school beyond the scope of any one individual and they also provide a supportive forum for individual inquirers to share progress, successes and challenges. However, working in a group creates a tension between the interests of individual inquirers and the shared focus and work of the group. This creates a dilemma for the consultants who must decide to what extent they should be advocating a shared focus for inquiry or a collective of inquirers concerned with different issues. Taking a view which espouses the benefit to the whole school might suppress the interests and ownership of individual inquirers, and hence compromise the democratic aspirations of inquiry, whilst advocating the creation of a group in which inquirers are working towards their own, separate, interests might lead to inquirers becoming isolated and losing the support of their colleagues. Such a position can only be taken through consideration of the context, school and network, and decided through dialogue with the inquiry group itself. The decision of the consultant to advocate a particular approach can be informed by the articulated interests of group members, but their advocacy could also be informed by questions such as:

- To what extent is there commonality (explicitly and implicitly) in the interests of different members of the SIG?
- How representative is the SIG of the school staff as a whole?
- What differences are there in the status of SIG members and, hence, could these differences in status influence the extent to which they can contribute equally to the work of the SIG?
- Are inquirers members of other support networks within or beyond the school? For example, are individual inquirers working with inquirers from other network schools?

Individual and SIG vs NLC

Just as the agendas of individuals were mediated by the agenda of the SIG to which they belong, so those SIGs competed with those of the network as a whole. In this case we identified three aspects to this form of competing agendas.

(i)   The agendas of individual practitioners were also mediated by the influence of the NLC.
(ii) The agendas of individual schools were mediated by the demands of the NLC for cross-school collaboration.
(iii) The agenda of the NLC, whilst primarily concerned with the development of relationships within and between networks, also included the promotion of certain preferred forms of development, e.g. research lessons, in which groups, or pairs of teachers collaboratively plan, implement and evaluate a lesson; and related the success of the work to improving the measurable outcomes of pupils.

> It is hugely complicated to take on a huge project which is research based because it is optional. It's an extra to all of the things we have to do and it's really difficult to fit in all the things we need to do ... and the pressure then to take on a new big research project and to keep with the network and other people because you don't want to let people down.
>
> (Head teacher)

During the application process to become networked learning communities, potential networks had to identify an overriding topic for their work. This was a change for some networks which, until that point, shared the common commitment to developing practices through the process of action research, but with no unified topic for that action research. Although the establishment of a shared focus for change provides a common area for dialogue within the network, it also restricts the freedom that individual and groups of inquirers have, or feel that they have, over identifying their own areas for inquiry. This tension, between the individual nature of action research and the need for a collective focus across the network, operates both in terms of the focus for inquiry and the nature of inquiry itself. The NCSL, through its support of inquiry-based net-working, also advocated approaches to inquiry which differed from the initial intentions of the network.

In addition, the agendas of individual schools within the network may not match those of the network itself, or even of the staff that are a part of their SIG. This is especially pronounced in schools under close scrutiny from Ofsted inspectors or whose remit requires them to work in other collaborative partnerships. The issue for the consultant is to question the extent to which the focus and process of inquiry have relevance and meaning for the inquirers and then to consider how the selection of a particular focus and the proposed approach for addressing it relate to the school in which the inquirer works and the network as a whole. It may be, for example, that the selection of a particular focus for inquiry might be contrary to the position of the school, or network, and that by pursuing it the ability of inquirers to pursue their legitimate agendas and the support they receive from the network may be compromised. In addition, in deciding on how best to support inquiry throughout the network, the consultant needs to consider how the conduct of inquiry would be viewed by the funding body and, therefore, how likely they would be to continue supporting the work of the network, and to ensure that such issues are discussed within the network. At all times, however, it will be the 'good' of the network itself that will have primacy.

School vs national policy

The members of school inquiry groups need to balance not only the needs of the individual group and the network but those of the school itself. These needs are sometimes in contrast to the requirements of national policy. In this respect we have identified two forms of competing interests, one referring to the influence of national education initiatives and the other resulting from school reporting and associated accountability measures.

(i) The influence of national assessment, an emphasis on teaching methods at Key Stage 3, affecting teachers of children aged between 11 and 14, and an increasing emphasis on personalised learning in primary school teaching which affects teachers of pupils aged up to 11.

(ii) The school management agenda, e.g. (a) to measure and evaluate school developments against targets, (b) to lead on the measurement of the quality of schools themselves in terms of value for money and (c) to judge the worth of individuals wishing to advance their careers against whole school targets relating to a combination of results- and value-driven agendas.

I think what I've found is that [the head teacher] likes initiatives, so sometimes, I find, it's [me] trying to say [to her], we're already doing that or we could tie that in to our [inquiry] work. An example of that is the building learning power, and I got the work of the SIG onto the school improvement plan with that attached, because, to a certain extent, that is what we're doing, building learning power.

(SIG coordinator)

The challenge for consultants supporting inquiry, in contexts influenced by policy and under close scrutiny from a variety of forms of inspection, is to consider how any topics and processes for inquiry relate to those processes of scrutiny and influence. For example the selection of a focus which is directly related to a policy initiative may not necessarily be contrary to the beliefs and interests of the inquirer, but the question remains, to what extent, other than its relevance as a policy initiative, this focus is a current and relevant concern of the inquirer.

In addition, the requirement of schools to provide evidence of their work for public and private scrutiny influences the selection of methods and topics which can support the school's claims for success. In this case, the role of the consultant is to consider the nature of evaluation in inquiry, and to champion forms and methods of evaluation which not only assist the inquirer in understanding their work, but also provide evidence for others of the process and outcomes of change. This requires developing broader definitions of evidence, including collecting data referring to personal growth and development, and consideration of evidence beyond those used in reporting school performance.

Individual vs HE

Our work has also highlighted differences between the perceptions of inquirers, and of representatives of HE (including ourselves), of what constitute appropriate foci for, and process of, action research. This concerns the conflicting perceptions of particular initiatives held by inquirers and consultants and the differing value individuals place on the worth of action research, in particular between the action researchers themselves and individuals dismissive of action research.

(i) The promotion of agendas of other education-driven research, e.g. enhancing 'student voice', 'emotional intelligence' and 'teaching and learning styles', which profess to offer advances in teaching and learning, but which might be contrary to existing beliefs and practices of teachers in schools.
(ii) The expectations of HE of the nature of research, its validity, reliability and ethical conduct. The cynicism displayed by some in HE which, in certain cases, can be used to dismiss the work of practitioner–action-researchers.

I think, probably, I felt [at a conference] that I have academics telling me how to do my job and telling you that you should do it this way, and knocking teachers, and I was quite … if I hadn't done the research myself, I would have said 'ok yes that's fine' but having done the research myself, I was able to say, how dare you tell me what to do, because I've done research and this is what this research has told me … it was the use of the academic language, and I was thinking 'I'm not really sure what you're asking about that' and it was in other sessions also, the knocking of teachers, of my profession, by people who were standing outside.

(SIG coordinator)

Development programmes initiated externally to the working context of the inquirer represent a similar challenge to the consultant as policy initiatives. Whilst there is more choice over the selection of such development programmes than there is in imposed policy-initiated developments, such developments raise the same problem, i.e. of the extent to which the chosen development programme addresses personal and professional issues for the inquirers and their practice. In addition, when being consulted on these developments, the consultant needs to consider the influence that championing such approaches to developing practice might have on the members of an inquiry network, i.e. how many are excluded by such a selection?

In acting as an advocate for inquiry in schools, the consultant must also champion the work of inquirers beyond the school community. The questions raised about the relevance and rigour of action research can separate the education community as a whole into separate communities of research and practice. The responsibility for a consultant championing action research is to attempt to break down these barriers, to identify opportunities for sharing this work and to support inquirers in engaging in a wider debate around the purpose and practice of educational research.

The agenda of networked learning communities vs the agenda of higher education

Finally, we identified a contrast between the interests and beliefs of the networked learning communities as a national policy and funding initiative and higher education. In particular the problem posing 'lifelong learning agenda' of HE tends to problematise and raise alternative ways of understanding which acted at times against the networked learning communities which sought time-limited solutions to pressing problems:

The review process that we have to go through, was asking for information, but it wasn't that we don't have it, but it was just a perception that we should have got to [a certain point] and then the expectation that we are going to provide them with writing, like their enquiry … and even though we're very positive about what has been going on they're small steps that we've been taking, and you get the feeling that it's got to be a sudden outcome and I sense a tension between [consultants] and [policy pressures]. All that's happening here is that we're doing something that is more about lifelong learning than their sudden influx of, 'you could try this …' and everything is going to be hunky-dory and it's a quick fix, but it isn't like that!

(Network coordinator)

This tension exists between the pressing need to present the outcomes of network developments and the processes of inquiry which can not be easily predicted and which, therefore, require working with doubt and uncertainties about the outcomes of inquiry and the time that it takes to run its course. The dilemma for the consultant, therefore, is advising on processes which preserve the uncertainty of inquiry, but which also identify the outcomes and consequences of inquiry and networking processes. Approaches to this differ, but network events, at which SIGs present and share their work, provide opportunities not only for inquirers to reflect on the progress and effects of their own work, but also for the consultant and network personnel to gain appreciation of changes resulting from inquiry work across the network. Once again, one element of the consultant's role is in advocating a view of change in which the growth and development of inquirers, and the part that the network has played in that, are considered as being just as relevant to any judgment of the success of inquiry as the contextual outcomes of the inquiry themselves, such as any changes in pupil attainment or attitude.

Each of these tensions will challenge the capacities of those different individuals and groups who are engaged in practitioner research to achieve their goals; and it is the ethical conduct of the external consultant(s) which will contribute – positively or negatively – to the scope, direction, pace and harmony of their work.

What are tensions for participants create dilemmas for consultants.[1] To manage this dynamic requires consultants not only to have and to exercise a multiplicity of cognitive and emotional qualities and skills necessary to support collaborative practitioner research in complex settings but also to have and exercise a consistent ethical stance within moral purposes.

Ethical consultancy and moral purposes in practitioner-led advocacy research

Whilst consultants are not responsible for outcomes of research within the systems they are supporting, they, nevertheless, carry moral responsibilities for ensuring that their clients do experience success. Because in networked learning communities there are a number of clients with potentially conflicting and certainly disparate agendas, they need to work within a clear set of ethical principles. Consultancy in these settings requires the establishment and maintenance of particular ethical relationships between consultants and action researchers within and between schools which may not always have the same inquiry focus over a period of time. Fullan (2000: 225) states that 'most research shows that external consultants are effective only when they are in an internal … team that supports their activities … [and so consultants] … should establish some ongoing relationship with [staff] who will act collectively to follow through change'. Whilst this statement is undoubtedly true, it is the unpacking of the meaning-in-practice of 'some' which is key to understanding the nature of the ethical contract which itself informs the nature of such ongoing client–consultant relationships. Such relationships (i.e. between consultant and teacher, consultant and head teacher, consultant and groups of teachers and head teachers within and across schools) are bound to be located within existing webs of interests, relationships, practices and aspirations which will not always be convergent. Thus, the establishment of an ethical contract has been at the heart of our work in being able to understand the contexts in which the action research is set and in sustaining the support for different individuals and stakeholder groups throughout the duration of teacher inquiries.

Fundamental to action research is reflection in, on and upon practice and the personal, situational and broader policy and societal contexts which moderate and mediate practice are necessary to teachers' continued learning. In terms of this, a key role of the action research consultant (whether or not a co-researcher) is to act as a catalyst for reflection not only on educational practices and policies but also, 'what is ethically as well as instrumentally, appropriate to achieve them' (Carr, 1993: 265). They must assist teachers and others with whom they work in reflecting upon, for example, the 'relative importance of conflicting factors ... in order to deal effectively with messy and imprecise problems which defy a formulaic response' (cited in Campbell, 2003a: 60).

Most ethical protocols address three main themes.

- No harm should be done to respondents. This, the basis of the ethical practice of research, is elaborated in the other key principles.
- The informed consent of respondents is a '*sine qua non*'. Respondents must be able to choose to be involved in the research from a position of having been given sufficient information about the focus and conduct of research. They retain the right to withdraw from the research for any reason.
- Respondents' identities must be protected. Throughout the conduct and reporting of research the identities of respondents are concealed and records of their actions or words are identifiable only to the researcher and themselves.

The conduct of any piece of research should adhere to these principles. A failure to address them is a failure to ensure that research does not compromise the human relationships upon which it is based. Indeed without the ethical practice of research 'we cannot rely on our discipline's stock of knowledge – in which case the collective enterprise of research collapses' (Payne and Payne, 2004). And so the conduct of research and our dependence on the outcomes of ethical research practice in general are predicated on its ethical conduct.

However, these general principles do not readily relate to action research because it is predicated on the choice of the participant to participate actively in self-inquiry, which is designed to enhance their understanding of aspects of their own professional practice and the personal, professional, organisational and policy contexts in which it occurs, and consequently to enable them to take decisions about change as a result of systematic inquiries designed to increase understanding of the micro, meso and macro contexts in which they work.

Nor do the principles easily relate to the role of the 'consultant' or 'facilitator' in action research settings. The involvement of a consultant in support of action research is by invitation only. Action researchers are not 'respondents' but 'lead participants' and 'clients' rather than 'subjects' or 'informants'. Those who facilitate or otherwise support action researchers in the process of action research will be in different kinds of partnerships in what is essentially practitioner-led research, and will, therefore, engage in a different order of responsibilities and accountabilities than the traditional researcher who, in educational settings, usually seeks to co-opt others to their agendas.

As Elliott noted:

> Action research cannot be undertaken properly in the absence of trust established by fidelity to a mutually agreed ethical framework governing the collection, use and release of data.
>
> (Elliott, 1978: 12)

Essentially, consultants in action research must take an 'advocacy' role and this implies being partial rather than neutral, continuously reconciling the standpoints of impartiality and partiality:

> More precisely, advocacy entails a willingness not just to adopt the 'big picture', not to act entirely impartially, but to exercise socially sanctioned (and reasonable) partiality to one's client.
>
> (Cribb, 2005: 6)

Whether acting as facilitator, co-researcher, expert, partner, mentor, resource provider or critical friend, the central function of the consultant to a networked learning community consisting of a variety of professionals with diverse agendas and relationships is that of broker:

> Brokers must often avoid two opposite tendencies: being pulled in to become full members and being rejected as intruders. Indeed, their contributions lie precisely in being neither in nor out. Brokering, therefore, requires an ability to manage carefully the coexistence of membership and non-membership, yielding enough distance to bring a different perspective, but also enough legitimacy to be listened to.
>
> (Wenger, 1998: 75)

These advocacy and brokering roles inevitably present personal and professional tensions and dilemmas for the 'process' consultant in building and sustaining trust across a range of clients. Clients will be ends in themselves, rather than means to ends. All the more important, then, that they are aware of the need for consistency within a variety of practices in their ethical stance and ethical standards. In each situation, they will ask:

   (i)   Are my principles (of honesty, fairness, integrity) clear to all?
   (ii)   What are the possible problems in relationships; their causes and consequences?
   (iii) Who comes first here?
   (iv) Do I always need to give an opinion?

The consultant in this kind of work must work in the middle of a web of complex social and political relationships. Below are eight examples of dilemmas.

Problem clarification

This could involve dealing with clients in many different phases of personal and professional development, with differing capacities/opportunities for critical reflection and in widely differing organisational cultures. Consultants may be torn between wishing to support and affirm the client (as part of his/her negotiated and ethical relationship) as they strive to prepare for change. They also know that the analysis and complexity of the problem is unlikely to be sufficient for sound change processes to follow. Consultants have limited opportunity to encourage, challenge and support clients in their problem identification phase ensuring that it is fully explored and that there is a considered emotional/rational basis on which change is to be negotiated.

Change

An example is working with clients whose value system may be at odds with the deeper moral purposes of the consultant, e.g. in such areas as pupil behaviour management. The implementation of change (e.g. a new discipline policy) may be one (easy) solution to the problems identified but may conflict with that of the consultant. However, they may have to support developments about which they find it difficult to be enthusiastic and which involve consequences for others at a distance (e.g. pupils).

Espoused theory vs theory in practice

There may be political and personal tensions between developing democratic decision-making (grass-roots knowledge generation) and the top-down standards agenda/school improvement. The need to show results as a consultant within a funded environment may conflict with educational ideals.

Power differentials

These may be apparent in managing tensions between wishing to encourage collaboration within/between schools where significant power differentials are operating. There may be tensions in supporting the development of the thinking of the individual against the pressures of other dominant individuals/groups. The choice of focus and planned changes resulting from action research may also have implications for the action researcher within this power context. The consultant should be aware of how the choices affect their client's position and what the likely repercussions are.

Ethical conduct by proxy

Consultants need to be confident that clients distinguish between normal professional practice and research practice. There may be difficulties in ensuring that clients (teachers) are fully responsible to, and careful of, ethical research conduct with among others, pupils, colleagues, parents, governors and that these ethical principals relate both to the conduct of research and to the ethical expectations of the context in which this practice is based.

Managing the knowledge–power dilemma

Practitioner action researchers are recognised to have knowledge and the position to exercise their knowledge in practice. The dilemma is in when and how the consultants uses their own expert knowledge as part of the cooperative learning and change dialogue.

Organisational and occupational professionalism

The consultant needs to be clear about the kinds of professionalism which the action research process is promoting but within the context of experience in which the clients are working.

Managing competing agendas

Examples of these include those between the expressed needs and interests of individuals with low power and those with high power in organisations, i.e. who knows what their needs are? Whose choice counts?

Conclusion

Teachers' moral agency in classrooms is grounded in ethical principles which advance definitions of core objective virtues such as honesty, justice and fairness, courage, integrity, kindness, and seen through another lens, social justice.

External consultants who seek to assist teachers in their own learning and change must also have moral as well as instrumental purposes and so they must themselves hold similar ethical principles. Sockett (1993: 62) suggests five virtues which are central to understanding the practice of teaching: courage, honesty, care, fairness and practical wisdom. Others identify justice, integrity, trust, truth, respect for others, compassion, consistency of treatment, responsibility, civility, commitment, honour and balance (in Campbell, 2003b: 111).

As Weston (1997: 4) notes, 'The real point of ethics is to offer some tools for thinking about difficult matters, recognising from the start … that the world is seldom so simple or clear-cut'. Struggle and uncertainty are a part of ethics, as they are a part of life! Ethics cannot account for specific contexts.

> Professional ethics cannot be improved, for by their nature they must be internalised to become part of the collective consciousness and the individual conscience.
>
> (Thompson, 1997: 1, in Campbell, 2003b: 108)

We have suggested in this chapter that consultancy, like teaching, is an inherently moral and ethical activity and that the primary responsibility of the consultant is for the educational well-being and advancement of the client. Struggle and uncertainty are key components in which consultants are 'bound by a sense of ethical dimensions of the relations among professionals and clients, the public, the employing institution and fellow professions' (MacMillan, 1993: 11, in Campbell, 2003b: 189). Thus, since the responsibilities of the consultant are both functional and personal, formalised codes of practice are an insufficient means of establishing authentic professional relationships and ways of working. These must – if trust is to be built, and influence be reciprocal – be rooted in core principles or ethical virtues if the core emancipatory and democratic purposes of action research are to be realised. These virtues should be developed through a sustained period of support during which the consultant develops a better understanding of the working context of the client and so is better able to appreciate the competing agendas influencing their work and the resulting implications in the conduct of and outcomes from their action research.

Note

1 Dilemmas in this situation are situations which present at least two contradictory propositions. Whichever is chosen will not be entirely satisfactory. They underscore a continuing dynamic between core personal values, consultancy functions and client demands.

References

Adelman, C. (1993) 'Kurt Lewin and the origins of action research', *Educational Action Research*, 1: 7–24.

Ball, S.J. (2003) 'The teacher's soul and the terrors of performativity', *Journal of Education Policy*, 18(2): 215–228.

Campbell, E. (2003a) *The Ethical Teacher*, Maidenhead: Open University Press.

Campbell, E. (2003b) Let right be done: trying to put ethical standards into practice, in P.T. Begley and O. Johansson (eds) *The Ethical Dimensions of School Leadership*, Dordecht: Kluwer, pp.107–125.

Carr, D. (1993) 'Questions of competence', *British Journal of Educational Studies*, 41(3): 253–271.

Chapman, J. and Aspin, D. (2005) 'Why networks and why now?', in *International Perspectives on Networked Learning*, Nottingham: NCSL.

Cribb, A. (2005) 'Professional roles and the division of ethical labour', paper for the ESCR/TLRP seminar series on Changing Teacher Roles, Identities and Professionalism, Kings College, London, 19 October 2005.

Cuban, L. (1992) 'Managing dilemmas while building professional communities', *Educational Researcher*, 21(1): 4–11.

Day, C. (1997) 'Being a professional in schools and universities: limits, purposes and possibilities for development', *British Educational Research Journal*, 23(2): 193–208.

Day, C. (1999) *Developing Teachers: The Challenges of Lifelong Learning?* London: Falmer Press.

Desforges, C. (2005) *On Learning and Teaching*, Nottingham: NCSL.

Elliott, J. (1978) *Who Should Monitor School Performance?* Mimeo, Cambridge Institute of Education.

Frost, D., Durrant, J., Head, M. and Holden, G. (2000) *Teacher Led School Improvement*, London: RoutledgeFalmer.

Fullan, M. (2000) *The New Meaning of Educational Change* (2nd edn), London: Cassell.

Gibbons, M., Limoges, C., Nowotny, H., Schwartzman, S., Scott, P. and Trow, M. (1994) *The New Production of Knowledge: the Dynamics of Science and Research in Contemporary Societies*, London: Sage.

Hammersley, M. (1997) 'Educational research and teaching: a response to David Hargreaves' TTA lecture', *British Educational Research Journal*, 23: 141–161.

Hammersley, M. (2002) *Educational Research, Policy Making and Practice*, London: Paul Chapman.

Hargreaves, D. (1997) 'In defence of research for evidence based practice: a rejoinder to Martyn Hammersley', *British Educational Research Journal*, 23: 405–419.

Hargreaves, D. (1999) 'The knowledge creating school', *British Journal of Educational Studies*, 17: 122–141.

Hillage, J. R., Pearson, A., Andreson, A. and P. Tamkin (1998) *Excellence in Research on Schools*, London: DfEE.

Jackson, D. (2002) 'The creation of knowledge networks: collaborative enquiry for school and system improvement', paper presented to the CERI/OECD/DfES/QCA ESRC forum, Knowledge Management in Education and Learning, Oxford, 18–19 March.

Jeffrey, B. (2002) 'Performativity and primary teacher relations', *Journal of Education Policy*, 17(5): 531–546.

Lewin, K. (1946) 'Action research and minority problems', *Journal of Social Issues*, 2: 34–36.

Lyotard, J.F. (1984) *The Postmodern Condition: A Report on Knowledge*, Manchester: Manchester University Press.

MacMillan, C.J.B. (1993) 'Ethics and teacher professionalisation', in K.A. Strike, and P.L. Ternasky, (eds) *Ethics for Professionals in Education: Perspectives for Preparation and Practice*, New York: Teacher College Press, pp. 189–201.

NCSL (2002a) *Why Networked Learning Communities?*, Cranfield: National College for School Leadership.

NCSL (2002b) *Principles*, Cranfield: National College for School Leadership.

Noffke, S. (1994) 'Action research: towards the next generation', *Educational Action Research*, 2: 9–21.

Payne, G. and Payne, J. (2004) *Key Concepts in Social Research*, London: Sage.

Pollard, A. (2005) 'Explorations in teaching and learning: a biographical narrative and some enduring issues', *International Studies in Sociology of Education*, 15(1): 87–105.

Schein, E.H. (1995) 'Process consultation, action research and clinical inquiry: are they the same?', *Journal of Managerial Psychology*, 10(6): 14–19.

Schein, E.H. (1998) *Process Consultation, Vol. I: Its role in Organizational Development* (2nd edn), Reading, MA: Addison-Wesley.

Schein, E.H. (1999) *Process Consultation Revisited: Building the Helping Relationship*, Reading, MA: Addison-Wesley.

Sockett, H. (1993) *The Moral Base for Teacher Professionalism*, New York: Teachers College Press.

Steele, F. (1975) *Consulting for Organisational Change*, Amherst, MA: University of Massachusetts Press.

Thompson, M. (1997) *Professional Ethics and the Teacher: Towards a General Teaching Council*, Stoke on Trent: Trentham Books Ltd.

Wenger, E. (1998) *Communities of Practice: Learning, Meaning and Identity*, Cambridge: Cambridge University Press.

Weston, A. (1997) *A Practical Companion to Ethics*, New York: Oxford University Press.

Chapter 5

Professional values and research values

From dilemmas to diversity?

Lesley Saunders

Introduction

In this chapter, I respond to the book's overall theme in terms of the generic values that are declared to be intrinsic to teaching and to research respectively. To do so, I have selected two codes or sets of principles that are in the public domain and which exert symbolic power, the one particularly for teachers and the other for academic researchers. Discussing these codes allows me first to investigate whether there are significant disjunctions between conceptions of 'teaching' and conceptions of 'research' that may be especially significant for our thinking about 'practitioner research'; and secondly to suggest a way of thinking about the roles of research that might offer a way forward.[1]

Beyond the positions enshrined in the two sets of principles I have alighted upon, the relationship between research and education – or, more specifically, between enquiry and teaching – has been expounded and enacted in a wide variety of ways from a diversity of epistemological and ideological stances. It is often argued – including by this author elsewhere (see, for example, Saunders, 2004, 2006) – that research and teaching share the same fundamental values, purposes and processes, captured in the notion of 'passionate enquiry' (Dadds, 1995). Such a conceptualisation – much more fully elaborated by many educationalists, of course, beyond that single but evocative phrase – has a long, distinguished and still-vital provenance, and when I've spoken in that register myself I've usually felt that I'm standing on firm intellectual and ethical ground, believing in the capacity of research to deepen teachers' professional learning and individual practice.

On the other hand and at other times, I have also felt – not least by hearing how some teachers and researchers talk about each other at the group level – that there are deep-seated differences and divergences between teaching and research as professional practices. It's not just about casual conversations either: Hammersley's (2004) carefully expounded article proposes that the characteristics and aims of research and teaching may be so different as to make 'action research' a contradiction in terms.

I also think the view of research and teaching as differing in significant ways is reinforced, albeit unintentionally, by those who construe teachers' relationship with research primarily in terms of their 'use' of (others') research: what teachers most need, the argument goes, in order for the aspiration of a research-informed profession to be realised is simplified summaries of research evidence on which to base their practice, plus the capacity to use and interpret pupil performance data. If teachers are acknowledged as engaging in research themselves, it is often within a discourse which manages simultaneously to be both patronising (teachers' research not being expected to be anything other than 'small-scale' and localised) and over-ambitious (being asked to demonstrate a link with raised standards of pupil attainment) – I return to these points later.

So, I shall briefly explore whether and how far my impression of a disjunction between the values of teaching and research has any underlying force, through what I admit is the device of setting alongside each other particular codes or sets of principles that are declared to capture the aspirations for teaching and for research respectively. The texts I have chosen to discuss are as follows.

The values of the teaching profession have been codified for, and with, teachers in England through the General Teaching Council's *Statement of Practice and Values*. (The Training and Development Agency's Professional Standards Framework for Teaching is a different way of enshrining professional expectations and requirements, and one that has statutory leverage on teachers' lives as well as their careers – but the revised version of these was not published at the time of writing.)

The values of research, by contrast, are encapsulated or implied in a multitude of different kinds of documents, including but not restricted to the ethical guidelines of professional associations and learned societies. For the purposes of this chapter, I am choosing to use the 'scientific principles of educational research' set out by the National Research Council in the US (2002), which has also excited much interest in the UK. The NRC example is contentious because of its apparent preference for an empiricist (some would also say positivist and reductionist) model of research. Nonetheless, it is an attempt to say something general about the character and the values of research in education, and for that reason I find it useful.

Elaboration

In repeating that I have chosen to interpret the notion of 'ethics' in the book's title rather broadly, in terms of general aspirational statements, let me add some further clarification. The sets of principles I have selected do not attempt to encapsulate specific criteria, minimum standards or detailed procedural requirements and thus they do not function as disciplinary codes or gatekeeping mechanisms, important though those may be for the public standing and regulation of a profession. The particular statements of principle I have chosen are each also the subject of some dispute, and although that is not the reason I have selected them, it is no accident that they are in that sort of space. Whilst ethical codes are often, in essence, concerned with mediating, managing and mitigating, through procedural protocols, the power relationships between participant parties, statements of values on behalf of an entire professional community are a high-profile, high-stakes way of laying claim to important public territory that others may think they have a better reason to occupy.

I next present an overview of the two sets of principles themselves before moving on to discussing some of their possible implications.

The professional values of teaching: the General Teaching Council for England

The General Teaching Council (GTC) is the independent professional body for teaching in England. The GTC was created by the 1998 Teaching and Higher Education Act, and came into being in September 2000. The GTC is mandated to maintain and guarantee high standards of teaching and learning in the interests of pupils, parents and employers, and to enhance the standing of the profession.

The 1998 Act gave the GTC three principal functions:

- to maintain a register of qualified teachers in England
- to regulate the teaching profession
- to advise the Secretary of State for Education and Skills on matters pertaining to the profession.

As with other professional bodies, the GTC is governed by a Member Council of – at the time of writing – 64 members, representing a coalition of the teaching profession and education stakeholders. There are currently 42 practising teachers, including head teachers, and 22 lay members representing the equality bodies, faith groups, parents, governors, teacher education, employers and business.

Since its inception, the GTC has drawn up and published various guidelines and frameworks which articulate and give guidance upon various aspects of professionalism. A relatively early codification of professional values was the *Code of Professional Values* which was agreed at a full meeting of the Council on 27 February 2002. The code was drawn up following extensive initial consultation with teachers, most of whom welcomed the idea of such a document as affirming the high standards – based on professional beliefs, values and attitudes – that exist in the profession; it was also thought that it could be helpful in raising morale. The code was re-named the *Statement of Professional Values and Practice for Teachers* and was widely distributed for formal consultation. Around 20,000 teachers (and others) responded, with the majority agreeing that it was appropriately aspirational, as well as helpful for guiding practice.

The *Statement* was revised in March 2006 to reflect changes in the policy and legislative environment, notably the Children Act of 2005 (see Box 5.1 or visit www.gtce.org.uk/standards/disc/StatementOfProfValues).

Readers may also like to know that, so far as 'minimum standards' for regulatory purposes are concerned, the GTC has also published a *Code of Conduct and Practice* which is complementary to the GTC's *Statement of Professional Values and Practice for Teachers* (visit www.gtce.org.uk/standards/regulation/CodeOf ConductAndPractice/). The *Code of Conduct and Practice* was agreed at a full meeting of Council on 30 June 2004 and came into effect on 1 November 2004. It is a codification of minimum standards for use in regulating the conduct and competence of registered teachers, and in particular in guiding the judgements that are made by the Council in individual cases of alleged misconduct, incompetence or conviction of a criminal offence.

Summarising the principles enshrined in the 2006 *Statement of Professional Values and Practice*, we could say that professional practice in teaching is characterised and indeed recognised as such by:

- being grounded in pedagogical knowledge and skills
- being client-focused and having a sense of personal vocation
- active conformity with legislative requirements, including those concerned with promoting equality of opportunity
- working in close partnership with other professionals, parents and young people themselves
- taking responsibility for improving practice through the continuing development of skills and knowledge at whatever stage of career.

The important thing in the context of this chapter, however, is that these are values concerned with moral purpose, and with realising intentions for the future, of individual young people and of society.

Box 5.1 The GTC's *Statement of Professional Values and Practice for Teachers*

The GTC's *Statement* underpins the Council's advisory and regulatory work. This version was agreed by Council in March 2006 in the light of changes to policy, legislation and the Professional Standards Framework. The GTC's *Statement* is kept under review to ensure it continues fully to reflect society's expectations of and aspirations for teachers, teachers' own values and aspirations, and the context in which teachers work.

General introduction: the high standards of the teaching profession

First and foremost, teachers are skilled practitioners.

They have insight into the learning needs of children and young people. They use professional judgment to meet these needs and to choose the best ways of motivating pupils to achieve success. They use assessment to inform and guide their work. They are highly skilled at dealing with the rigours and realities of teaching.

Teachers inspire and lead children and young people to learn, in and beyond the classroom. They enable them to get the most out of life and develop the knowledge, skills and attributes for adulthood – so that they can achieve their potential as fulfilled individuals and make a positive contribution to society – while staying safe and healthy.

Teaching is a vital, unique and far-reaching role requiring high levels of individual knowledge, skill and judgment, commitment, energy and enthusiasm. It is one of the most demanding and rewarding of professions.

Teachers work within a framework of legislation, statutory guidance and school policies, with different lines of accountability. Within this framework they place particular importance on promoting equality of opportunity – challenging stereotypes, opposing prejudice, and respecting individuals regardless of age, gender, disability, colour, race, ethnicity, class, religion, marital status or sexual orientation.

Teachers recognise the value and place of the school in the community and the importance of their own professional status. They understand that this requires judgment about appropriate standards of personal behaviour.

The professionalism of teachers in practice

Children and young people

Teachers place the learning and well-being of young people at the centre of their professional practice.

They use their expertise to create safe, secure and stimulating learning environments that take account of individual learning needs, encourage young people to engage actively in their own learning, and build their self-esteem. They have high expectations for all young people, are committed to addressing underachievement, and work to help young people progress regardless of their background and personal circumstances.

Teachers treat young people fairly and with respect, take their knowledge, views, opinions and feelings seriously, and value diversity and individuality. They model the characteristics they are trying to inspire in young people, including enthusiasm for learning, a spirit of intellectual enquiry, honesty, tolerance, social responsibility, patience, and a genuine concern for other people.

Parents and carers

Teachers respond sensitively to the differences in the home backgrounds and circumstances of young people, recognising the key role that parents and carers play in children's education.

They seek to work in partnership with parents and carers, respecting their views and promoting understanding and co-operation to support the young person's learning and well-being in and out of school.

Professional colleagues

Teachers see themselves as part of a team, in which fellow teachers, other professional colleagues and governors are partners in securing the learning and well-being of young people.

They recognise the importance of effective multi-agency working, are clear and confident about their own role and professional standards, and understand and respect the roles and standards of other colleagues. They are keen to learn from others' effective practice and always ready to share their own knowledge and expertise. They respect young people's and colleagues' confidentiality wherever appropriate.

Learning and development

Teachers entering the teaching profession in England have met a common professional standard.

Initial education has prepared them to be effective teachers, and they take responsibility for their continuing professional development.

They reflect on their own practice, develop their skills, knowledge and expertise, and adapt their teaching appropriately to take account of evidence about effective practice and new technology; they understand that all of these are vital if young people are to receive the best and most relevant education.

Teachers make use of opportunities to take part in mentoring and coaching, to evaluate and adapt their own and institutional practice, and to learn with and from colleagues in the wider children's and school workforce.

The professional values of research: the US National Research Council

In its report, *Scientific Research in Education*, the US National Research Council (2002) was concerned to make a strong case for the quality and rigour of educational research which have been challenged, as we are all well aware, on a number of fronts in the UK, the US and elsewhere. The report intends to show how and under what conditions 'scientific' research can illuminate 'the increasingly complex and performance-driven US education system' (p. 1). The report is so sanguine about the need for a scientific approach, which it defines as the capacity of knowledge to meet the test of conceptual and empirical adequacy over time, that it does not discuss alternative or postmodernist construals of knowledge creation. However, it defines scientific inquiry fairly broadly, as 'a continual process of rigorous reasoning supported by a dynamic interplay among methods, theories and findings. It builds understandings in the form of models or theories that can be tested' (p. 2).

To pre-empt detailed critiques of the report – critiques which are necessary but will be better served through other fora than this chapter [2] – I also want to point out that the report is clear that 'advances in scientific knowledge are achieved by the self-regulating norms of the scientific community over time, not, as sometimes believed, by the mechanistic application of a particular scientific method to a static set of questions. The accumulation of scientific knowledge over time is circuitous and indirect … and depends on a healthy community of researchers' (p. 2). By these two or three prominently placed sentences I take the authors to distance themselves from three of the 'bêtes noires' that enrage many educational researchers: firstly, the notion that there is a single methodological 'gold standard' such as random controlled trials or systematic research reviews; secondly, the narrow empiricism encapsulated in the demand to know 'what works'; and thirdly, the idea that so-called scientific methods can and should be enshrined in state or federal legislation governing educational research and evaluation.

Here is my summary of the National Research Council's definition of the six guiding principles of scientific research:

- Research should pose significant questions, in the form of one or more testable hypotheses, that can be investigated empirically; the questions should reflect an understanding of the relevant theoretical, methodological and empirical work that has come before.
- Research should be linked to relevant theory, which explicitly or implicitly underpins every scientific inquiry.
- Methods should be relevant to, and permit direct investigation of, the research questions – and usually this requires a variety of different methods to be deployed.
- Researchers should provide a coherent and explicit chain of reasoning: explanations, conclusions and predictions should be based on what is known and observed. The validity of inferences depends upon identifying limitations and biases, estimating uncertainty and error, and – crucially – ruling out plausible counter-explanations in a rational and compelling way.
- Knowledge is always provisional and partial; accumulation of knowledge is hard-won and proceeds when promising studies are replicated in different populations and settings, and – if possible – generalisations drawn from resulting studies carried out.

- Studies need to be disseminated and subjected to professional scrutiny by peers – the security of knowledge does not reside in the design features of particular studies, still less in the character traits of individuals, but in the publicly enforced norms of the professional community.

Plainly, there is an assumption here that scientific research represents the most rigorous mode of knowledge production and a further assumption that scientific enquiry is essentially an empirical undertaking. Neither of these assumptions has passed – or should pass – unchallenged. Nonetheless, the principles are useful for my purpose in their unequivocal advancement of the claim that the core professional values of research revolve around a concern with the quality of knowledge and knowledge creation.

Contrasting teaching and research as ideal types of activity

Well, if readers can agree that these two explications of the professional values of teaching and research are at least worth considering, then I will try to go a little further and set out the ways in which, as statements of principle, they might logically lead to some contrasts between teaching and research, especially with regard to the creation of knowledge. Table 5.1 expresses these contrasts in a shorthand way. I want to stress that these are abstractions, and not typical descriptors of teachers or researchers.

Table 5.1 Some ideal typological contrasts between teaching and research in relation to knowledge

Teaching as 'activism'	Research as 'scepticism'
Social–relational	Epistemological–scientific
Vested interest	Neutrality
Priority question: 'What use is this work?'	Priority question: 'How valid is this work?'
Looking for confirmation	Looking for refutation
Concerned to identify extent of applicability	Concerned to identify type/extent of error
Insights for action	Insights for understanding
Priority outcome: 'How will this knowledge enable me/my colleagues to take action(s) and/or make decisions?'	Priority outcome: 'How does this research enable new theory and/or knowledge to emerge?'
Management issues concerned with implementation	Management issues concerned with quality assurance

The drift of my argument then makes me wonder whether practitioner–researchers themselves think of teaching and research as having different values, in the way I have attempted to outline them above; whether they think these differences are sufficiently important to worry about; and how they manage the tensions in their own practice arising from the differences. Other and wiser educators than I have explored such issues, of course, and one solution offered is to turn practitioners into scholars: 'Labaree's (1998) notion of teachers moving from the normative to the analytical, from the personal to the intellectual, from the particular to the universal and from the experiential to the universal' (Turner-Bisset, 2005). But such a solution (and there are several variants of it) seems to assume that research values should predominate over teaching values, and thus begs the question rather than addressing it.

Another solution is to try to collapse the differences, pretend they do not exist – sometimes this has problematic consequences. I'd like to give you a concrete example, as follows. Hilary (not her real name) is doing some groundbreaking work in setting up and managing a multidisciplinary research institute based at a school for young people with severe autistic spectrum disorders. The school was recently adjudged by the official school inspectors to be an excellent school providing an outstanding quality of education. The research projects hosted by the school are intended to be pedagogically developmental as well as empirically grounded in biology, physiology and psychology. In order to provide a framework for the conduct of research with such vulnerable young people that respects their individual conditions, needs and wishes whilst acknowledging the need to gather, analyse and interpret data in the most rigorous way possible, Hilary has been engaged in writing some ethical guidelines. (It is interesting as an aside, that she found nothing 'off-the-shelf' that she felt was sufficiently elaborated and explicit for their circumstances.) In the first draft of the guidelines which she sent to me for comment, there were two or three requirements that seemed to me to sit at odds with each other, justifiable though each might be in its own terms. One was concerned with minimising the scale and perceived impact of interventions, given that these young people are likely to be averse to change in their routines; another requirement was concerned to ensure that sufficient data be gathered to give statistical significance, in order that decisions could be made with firm knowledge; a third was concerned to arrange that any interventions would have a positive impact, because it would be hard to persuade carers and the young people themselves to give informed consent if the interventions were not going to make a difference for the better.

One way of understanding these requirements and their dissonant relationship to each other is as an expression – in authentic and, I hope, sympathetic terms – of the tabular contrasts I presented above.

As I mentioned earlier, another more straightforward expression of a similar phenomenon – and often, I'm bound to say, initiated by grant-givers and policy-makers as much as by practitioners – is to be found in the encouragement, or even the requirement, to link interventions (changes in teaching styles or the curriculum, innovations in the organisation of the school day, particular professional development provision for teachers and so forth) causally to measurable changes in pupil learning outcomes – but without resourcing the kind of research design that is a prerequisite for such inferences, including ways of ruling out plausible counter-explanations. And sometimes there is encouragement to go even further and move towards a statement of generalisability without having gone through the necessary methodological and logical disciplines.

Contrasting research as 'evidence' and research as 'pedagogy'

Yet, as I have continued to reflect on these issues, I have started to develop a rather different pair of comparisons that may offer a way forward in explicating these discourses a little further. It is the contrast between research when it is understood and deployed as *evidence* with research when it is understood and enacted as something different, that I would wish to call *pedagogy*.

This is how I would put it: one set of expectations people – whether academic or practitioner–researchers – have of research, one way we have of talking about its quality and significance, can be encapsulated in the word 'evidence', the now-famous, or notorious, demand to know what works. I think this sense or function of research has some characteristic terms, concepts and activities clustered around it, such as:

- 'Mode 1' knowledge creation, in the sense described by Gibbons *et al.* (1994)
- an apparatus of systematic reviews, databases, portals
- an expectation that the knowledge produced will be generalisable, objective, public
- metaphorical turns of phrase that tend to the materialist: 'accumulation', 'building' an evidence-'base', and the like
- an intention that the knowledge created will be applied in some way to something
- and that it will be moved around the system through dissemination and communication (as a specialised form of information)
- because its main justification is about *use* – so the knowledge should be relevant, accessible and impactful.

In other situations or contexts, however, the same people may find themselves talking about research in a quite different register, and entertaining quite other expectations of what it can provide and achieve. I want to call this the discourse of research as pedagogy, which I would characterise like this:

- 'Mode 2' knowledge creation (Gibbons *et al.*, 1994)
- an apparatus of case studies, networks, collaborative enquiry and so forth
- an expectation that the process of creating knowledge will be heuristic (exploratory), hermeneutic (seeking to interpret and make sense), intersubjective (seeking to be in relationship to other minds) – even intimate

- metaphors of 'engaging', of 'catching' (as of fire or a virus)
- an intention that the knowledge created will be transformative of something or someone
- and that it will be moved around the system through active mediation and dialogue
- because its main drive is for *learning* – knowledge in this sense should be generative, meaningful and influential.

These are, nonetheless, not mutually exclusive categories or discourses: they are both, for example, rationalist and truth-seeking, rather than revelatory or theological, ways of knowing. And they both depend on deliberation and the exercise of professional or expert judgement. Another way of putting this is to say that it's important to be clear about whether it's what you're for or what you're against that matters most in stating your position. It could be argued that a fully realised practice of teaching needs both the 'evidential' and the 'pedagogical' affordances that research offers.

Coda

Well, and so what? Despite the impression I may have given in some places, I am really not interested in adding to the unhelpful distinctions that are made between academic and practitioner research – usually to the detriment of the latter – on the grounds, for example, that the one is 'big research' and the other is small-scale; or that the one is done by professionals and the other by amateurs – although it's not usually put that way, that's the implication. Distinctions that are made essentially on the basis of institutional location or allegiance are unsustainable in reality; and they also smack of producer interest on the part of universities. Nor am I concerned to differentiate between pure and applied educational research, or indeed to pursue any of the other distinctions that advocates and critics of evidence-based or research-informed practice have found it helpful to draw.

So I think the tentative conclusion I am drawing is something different and altogether less 'grand plan'. It is that, especially when designing programmes that aim to support teachers' creation of professional knowledge through research, it may be useful to consider more explicitly the underlying values of teaching and of research; and to plan carefully how to deploy the appropriate kinds of support and expertise that will help teachers to become even more aware of, and capable of engaging fully with, the demands of the enterprise they are engaged in. This means, amongst other things, developing a more fully articulated and widely shared conceptualisation of the pedagogy of teachers' engagement in and with research: in other words, an understanding of which forms and modes of professional learning are integral to the creation of professional knowledge.

We might then go on to ask ourselves how, in both conceptual and practical terms, we can work together across different initiatives explicitly to respect the diversity, whilst protecting the integrity, of practitioner research: diversity, in order that teachers at different stages of their careers can be supported with their teaching of widely varying subjects and skills over highly diverse social settings and learning contexts; integrity, in order that teachers can be supported in creating trustworthy professional knowledge that can justifiably lay claim to the major educational territories of the curriculum, pedagogy and assessment in a political environment where government and government agencies are exerting increasing control over such terrain in the name of raising standards.

For one of the dichotomies that has dominated the discourse of teaching in recent years in England is the idea that teaching is grounded in a kind of 'craft' or tacit knowledge (in contrast to the explicit and elaborated knowledge of academic research). One might view the political appropriation of professional practice – together with the rhetoric of 'what works' – in terms of having taken its justification from this notion. The discourse of pedagogy has become particularly impoverished and the thought I want to end with is this: that practitioner research is appealing, both in reality (as witness the number of teachers engaged in school-based research with no major streams of funding to support them) and in theory, precisely because it creates a site for the exploration and development of pedagogy as the constitutive professional practice of teaching.

Notes

1   My background means I have a vested interest in this issue: at different times in my life I have been a teacher, in primary and secondary state schools, and adult education, in England, and a researcher, at the National Foundation for Educational Research for England and Wales; and in my role at the General Teaching Council for England I have been responsible for a research strategy which, among other things, seeks to promote and encourage engagement in and with research by teachers.
2   For example, a project funded under the Economic and Social Research Council's (ESRC's) Teaching and Learning Research Programme and led by David Bridges is exploring the epistemological basis of educational research findings.

References

Dadds, M. (1995) *Passionate Enquiry and School Development: A Story about Teacher Action Research*, London: Falmer Press.

General Teaching Council For England (2006) *Statement of Professional Values and Practice*. Available online at http://www.gtce.org.uk/standards/disc/IntroductionToStatement

General Teaching Council For England (2004) *Code of Conduct and Practice*. Available online at http://www.gtce.org.uk/standards/ regulation/CodeOfConductAndPractice/)

Gibbons, M., Limoges, C., Nowotny, H. and Schwartzman, S. (1994) *The New Production of Knowledge: The Dynamics of Science and Research in Contemporary Societies*, London: Sage.

Hammersley, M. (2004) 'Action research: a contradiction in terms?', *Oxford Review of Education*, 30(2,): 165–181.

Labaree, D. (1998) 'Educational researchers: living with a lesser form of knowledge', *Educational Researcher*, 27: 4–12.

National Research Council (2002) *Scientific Research in Education*, Committee on Scientific Principles for Education Research, Washington, DC: National Academy Press.

Saunders, L. (2004) 'Doing things differently?' (Editorial), *Teacher Development Journal, Special Issue*, 8(2 and 3): 117–126.

Saunders, L. (2006) 'Teachers' engagement in and with research: supporting integrity and creativity in teaching', *Forum*, 48(2): 131–144.

Turner-Bisset, R. (2005) 'Understanding research capacity – a US view: two BERA seminars on the future of educational research in the UK', *Research Intelligence*, 92: 22–23.

Chapter 6

Transdisciplinary enquiry

Researching *with* rather than *on*

Danny Doyle

Introduction

'Teachers as researchers' took off in Britain in the mid-1970s. In 1975 Stenhouse led the way and published his ideas about curriculum research and development. He argued that there was a frustrating gap between the many exciting educational proposals and ideas student teachers experienced during teacher training and the reality of teaching in schools (Stenhouse, 1975). To close this gap, and extend the teachers' professionalism, Stenhouse advocated the teacher as researcher. Instead of implementing the theories of educationalists and outside researcher, in their classrooms, he called for teachers to become researchers and research their own teaching, either alone or in a group of cooperating colleagues. He argued for an evolving style of cooperative research by teachers and using full-time researchers to support the teachers in testing out theories and ideas in their classroom. Today, partnerships of universities and schools for teacher research empower teachers and facilitate collaboration and autonomy in professional development:

> Teachers researching their own contexts, sometimes alone, sometimes in collaboration with colleagues or even pupils from their own or other schools, debating their findings and working in partnership with universities and local authorities are a powerful force within the profession to frame a vision for the future. Teacher research is an idea whose time has come.
>
> (Campbell, 2002: 12)

In England the Training and Development Agency for Schools (TDA) has developed the Postgraduate Professional Development (PPD) progamme to ensure teachers' learning and development after initial teacher training. The TDA is providing funding for 31,000 training opportunities for teachers in England by 2008. Fifty-seven different providers/consortia will run programmes for the PPD. In order to receive funding from the TDA, there must be a research element to the award bearing courses at master's (M) level or above leading to postgraduate certificates, diplomas, masters' and doctorates. In addition, the General Teaching Council for England (GTCe) builds enquiry into all of its teacher learning academy work. The National Academy for Gifted and Talented Youth (NAGTY), the British Educational Communications and Technology Agency (BECTA), Creative Partnerships, and the National Centre for Excellence in Teaching Mathematics (NCETM) all offer research awards to teachers, thus seriously increasing the scale and status of teacher research beyond the PPD programme. With so many teachers researching, questions of ethics and ethical guidelines will arise including the importance and rights of the individuals involved. These individuals will include the researcher, colleagues and parents. Children will inevitably be participants in the research.

Educational research students in England have to satisfy their higher education institute's (HEI) ethical requirements. These vary between institutions. They can include submitting a research proposal to an ethics committee or adhering to the institution's guidelines under the supervision of the course supervisor. Some institutions, as part of their guidelines/rules/code of practice, refer students and school-based researchers to the guidelines of a professional research organisation such as those of the British Educational Research Association (BERA). HEI staff researchers usually need approval from their institution's ethics committees and quite often when conducting research funded by an external body the researchers need to obtain ethical approval before applying for the funding.

So what does ethics look like in practice? This chapter draws on the experiences of a group of members of the National Teacher Research Panel (NTRP) while participating in research with colleagues or academics, or while conducting practitioner enquiry themselves. The National Teacher Research Panel is a group of teachers with expertise in research, funded by the General Teaching Council, the Department for Education and Skills Innovation Unit, and the National College for School Leadership, to provide an expert teacher perspective on national research policies, initiatives, priorities and proposals; and to promote teaching as a research and evidence-informed practice. The experiences discussed are in the form of short scenarios that highlight ethical challenges and dilemmas for the practitioner–researchers when involved in research, as either researcher or participant, in their schools. The teachers portrayed in the scenarios are not necessarily NTRP members.

Informed consent

A fundamental requisite of research involving children is the care of those children and that care begins before the data collection starts, by obtaining informed consent. Covert research ignores the tenet of voluntary participation and is usually considered unethical even with adults. When used, the public's right to know usually justifies it and the researcher balances the potential benefit of a research project against the potential harm to the participants. It would be difficult for teachers researching in their classrooms to justify covert research and BERA guidelines call for the participants in educational research to give voluntary informed consent.

In the first scenario the teacher/researcher took it upon herself to gain consent from every parent for the research she was about to undertake. When the research was outlined to the parents many were unconvinced that their child would get any benefit from being withdrawn from class to be interviewed and they refused to allow the participation of their children. This threatened the research. The teacher found it difficult but did manage to persuade them in the end and consent from parents was obtained for every child.

The first point to make here is that while the research may be part of the teacher's professional development, the children are not there for the teacher's development. The opposite is the case. The teacher is there for the development of the children. Of course the two are linked because it is in the interest of the child that the teacher is a better teacher, but the child's participation should not be taken for granted. An analogy might be the learner driver in her one-hour driving lesson spending ten minutes of her time being interviewed for the instructor's research. The findings of the research could mean the instructor will be a more effective teacher and the learner will pass her test more quickly or be a more competent and safer driver. Knowing this the learner might well agree to the interview giving up some of her learning time when she knows the purpose and the benefits she might get. She is informed.

Following the initial refusal by parents for their children to take part in the research in the scenario above, the persuasion by the teacher changed the parents' minds resulting in unanimous consent. The refusal of most of the parents may have been because they considered time out of class would result in missed learning or being interviewed by the teacher in a place away from the classroom would have been intimidating for their childen. What did the teacher say to cause the parents to change their minds? Two possible reasons for the change are that the parents were not informed when asked for permission initially and, as in the driving analogy, after the purpose and benefits were explained, they agreed; or they were coerced into giving permission. If the teacher had fully informed the parents about the research initially then the response may have been better and the need to persuade could have been avoided.

The information given should include:

- what the research is for
- who will conduct the research and how
- how data will be collected and what will happen to the data including where it will be stored and who will see it
- whether there are any risks, physical or psychological
- how confidentiality will be dealt with; when the research is finished whether it will be published and who will read it; and finally
- the benefits participants will enjoy.

It can be assumed the teacher–researcher in the scenario hopes to develop professionally and so benefit from the research especially if the research is to be used to achieve a goal or an end such as a postgraduate certificate, diploma, master's or doctorate. But will the children benefit? If not, then they are being used as a means for that end. Of course there may be benefits to the child's being interviewed by the teacher that we cannot know from a brief scenario, such as a better understanding of the child's learning or any concerns the child might have. Indeed the benefits might not just be for the children taking part in the research. One result from the research may have been the development of more effective teaching methods that will have benefits not only for the children in that class but throughout the school or other schools.

It would have been unethical of the teacher to coerce the parents into giving permission. Teachers are in a powerful position. Students and parents may feel they have to give consent or upset the teacher if they withhold it. Teachers have the institutional powers to create curriculum, lesson content and what is learned. They decide groups, sets, forms, rules, punishments and they use teacher assessment to decide grades, and levels. The organisation of the curriculum, standardised testing and grading send messages to students about their worth and place in society (Shor, 1993, 1996). Teachers can decide if a student passes or fails. Teachers as researchers need to be aware of the differential power relationships between the teacher and student. These are social and historical and not personal; they already exist in the classroom before any teaching takes place (Shor and Freire, 1987).

Not all research in an education involves children as participants.

Gatekeeping

In 2005 teachers from different schools within one local authority (LA) went to a course organized by a famous university team for continual professional development on a new and popular national initiative, only to find themselves being interviewed individually and recorded on tape by a team of researchers. It was only after the interviews, when the teachers reassembled and discussed this, that they found out that the taped interviews were part of ongoing qualitative research. It appears the researchers had informed the teachers' head teachers but not the teachers. The head teachers assumed the teachers were informed and had given their own consent.

Surely professional people would not sit down with an interviewer, watch them turn on a tape recorder and then be interviewed if they did not want it to happen? In the scenario above that is exactly what happened. Foucault (1978) argues that power and knowledge are closely interwoven. When there is power, there is also knowledge and power increases through knowledge. When these teachers were put in a similar differential power relationship as teacher–student by attending a course for their professional development, they too felt pressure not to question the 'famous university team'. Professional researchers must adhere to some code of ethics. They sought permission from the head teachers. Can that be enough? Of course the detail from the scenario is brief but the interviewers may have sought 'implied consent' (Berg, 1989). This is used in interviews when the researcher (or the participant) does not want the participant's name recorded, for example on a consent form. Alternatively, if the researchers did not know who was going to attend the continuing professional development that day, and could not seek and receive permission from each individual before the course, implied consent could have been sought. The important point here is that the process of informing the participant be not by-passed. Before the interview the researchers must explain the purpose of the interview, as well as the potential benefits and risks. The potential participant should be properly informed and not feel obligated to take part and the researchers must not take advantage of the power differential outlined above. The researchers should be aware of the power constituted in the relationships they have with their research participants and their ethical responsibility. Completed interviews imply consent. In the scenario above, it appears the informing happened after the interviews; therefore the basic notion of informed consent outlined earlier was disregarded. The participants had no information about the research prior to the data being recorded. There may have been communication problems between the head teacher and the participating teachers, which is unfortunate, but the ethics of the research and the duty to obtain informed consent are the researcher's responsibility. The role of the head teacher in this scenario is that of gatekeeper. Other gatekeepers could be parents or guardians, or teachers. They give access to researchers, insider or outsider, to conduct research in the school. In this scenario, having received the head teachers' consent, the researchers assumed the teachers' consent (Heath *et al.*, 2004).

In the UK people under the age of 18 are legally considered to be children and in some cases the consent from the child is all that is needed to carry out research. Parents need not be asked or informed but this does not depend on chronological age. The precise criteria for a researcher to decide if a child is 'Gillick'[1] competent are not clear, but probably include the understanding of key facts, being of sufficient maturity to understand the consequences of making a particular decision and coming to a reasoned decision. Seeking parental permission can reduce agency, the capacity for the child to make choices and to impose those choices on the world, but when considering consent, it is important that giving the child the decision to participate or not should be in the best interest of the child rather than the research.

The gatekeeper role is usually to control access to children of the school who are not legally capable of granting informed consent (Homan, 2002: 23). However, teachers researching their own practice are insider researchers and as such have an advantage over outsiders: they know the children and are in a good position to judge each child's maturity and reasoning ability when deciding whether they need to seek parental consent or allow the child to decide. Yet as Dewey (1963) argues, with the best interests of the student in mind, formal education is responsible for creating authority-dependent subordinates deprived of citizen status by teachers and academics. Nevertheless, as Masson makes clear, if a child has the capacity to make the decision then it is the child's to make:

> Where children have the capacity to make a decision, parents' power over that area of their child's life is ended unless preserved by statute law. Consequently, a parent cannot consent to research on behalf of a competent child.
>
> (Masson, 2000: 39)

Coyne (1997) found that most children aged seven to 15 in her research were keen to give their own consent, rather than rely on the consent of their parents and cites an example where not only consent but also confidentiality was tested:

> On one occasion a father asked about the content of the child's interview when it was completed. The request was made casually in front of the child (boy aged 13 years). His request was politely refused with the explanation that all interview data was confidential. It was suggested that he could ask his child directly for information. The child seemed pleased with the researcher's response and immediately said that he did not want to share the data with anyone.
>
> (Coyne, 1997: 414)

The difficulty here, as outlined above, is that there is a fine line of judgement as to whether a young person is competent and therefore capable of granting informed consent or not. It is a difficult decision to make for a gatekeeper, whether a parent, teacher or head teacher, to make, and care must be taken to avoid denying a young person the right to consent as outlined above in the Gillick case and supported by Articles 3 and 12 of the United Nations Convention on the Rights of the Child (1989).[2] One person's opinion may not be the same as the next person's. Clearly there are very different perspectives of discourse depending on whether you are a researcher, a teacher, or both. As Usher (1996: 27) claims, 'knowledge, being relative to discourses, is always partial and perspectival'. The decision to give permission for research should be made on the behalf of the children in the school but as Heath *et al.*'s (2004) report into researchers' views and experiences shows this is not always the case with regard to consent.

> However, most [respondents] could provide examples of what they considered to be bad ethical practice in relation to research ... in particular in relation to a denial of young people's rights to exercise consent in school based settings.
>
> (Heath *et al.*, 2004: 25)

There is the added difficulty in that the head teacher has responsibility for the professional development of the staff in their school. Head teachers across England will have to make some difficult decisions with 31,000 teachers engaging in postgraduate professional development with a research element in partnership with HEIs.

Withdrawal

A colleague worked with an arts group on a week-long cross-phase (primary) project to 'trial' an approach to arts in school. Two of the children working with the group were from the special needs unit attached to the school, with moderate learning difficulties. Parental permission was sought and received. One of these children produced stunning work during the course of the week and absolutely thrived working in the way that the group was approaching the tasks. Although she and the teacher had discussed the various aspects of the week very carefully and clearly at the start of the project and she was more than happy to be involved, by the end of the week she had forgotten everything about the discussion, arrived from home in a very bad mood and said she didn't want to be involved at all. The research group had to decide whether this invalidated everything relating to her from the week as a whole. Two days later, she forgot the bad mood and remembered the original conversation and wished the group was still working with her. This example was a matter for much discussion in the group. Since consent had clearly been withdrawn, whatever her understanding of it might have been, the teacher felt it was inappropriate to do anything other than respect that. During the project the child had produced some stunning artwork, and the group all felt that was something they wanted to use in presentations about the project – the girl was asked for her permission to use that, which she was more than happy to give.

Permission was sought from the girl and her parents to participate in the research but, by withdrawing, the agency of the girl was exercised and accepted. Benefits for the girl were evident in that she thrived from the new approach, yet she decided to withdraw. She may have enjoyed the work up to a point, then not. The girl may have wished to withdraw but could not or did not want to articulate why. Perhaps she did not fully understand all the aspects of the week so was not as informed as the researchers had believed. Whatever the case, she withdrew her consent as BERA's ethical guidelines suggest she is fully entitled to do without duress, prejudice or future repercussions. The research group acted ethically in recognising there was distress and discomfort and respecting her decision to withdraw without pressure to re-engage and then by considering her understanding of any consent given. Would using just the parental consent be an ethical decision or a way to get around using her work and completing the research? The research group could have decided that the girl was not Gillick competent and relied on the consent of the parents to justify not invalidating her contribution, although BERA guidelines are clear in that researchers must make known any detriment to the girl to her parents who should be given the opportunity to reconsider their consent. The research group acted ethically in respecting the agency of the girl in what Dewey calls an 'educative relationship' where there is recognition of the girl as a human being capable of making her own decisions and speaking for herself (McNiff, 2001).

The dilemma appears to be that the researchers, by invalidating everything related to the girl, lost a lot of data. It is a research problem that may have been brought about by following ethical principles but not an ethical problem or indeed dilemma BERA guidelines suggest researchers examine their actions to assess whether they contributed to the decision to withdraw. In a case such as this, where the participant forgets the original discussion and consent, the researchers might also use implied consent before each data collecting activity, as well as the discussion at the beginning.

Confidentiality

Maintaining confidentiality is considered the norm for educational research (BERA, 2004). It means not having identifying characteristics such as a name or description of physical appearance disclosed so that the participants remain unidentifiable to anyone outside the permitted people promised at the time of informed consent. Anonymity is only one aspect of ensuring confidentiality. It involves using a fictional or no name rather than a participant's real name. Anonymity is usually easier during quantitative research involving the analysis of numerical data when unnamed and unmarked questionnaires or surveys can be distributed and collected in such a way that even the researcher cannot associate an answer with a person. Quantitative research methods quite often involve analysis of data such as words from interviews or interpretations of observations.

This next scenario involves a teacher who had never undertaken educational research but agreed to assist a leading educational sociologist, as did all those working in the school. On reflection, the teacher feels he was too naive to ask the researcher about how he would be represented in the study. At the time a man teaching in Key Stage 1 was most unusual. Everyone at the school was flattered that this researcher had chosen their school for a major piece of research. It was only after a book had been published that the teacher saw 'himself' in print. All the female teachers were attributed a colour, e.g. Mrs Green or Mrs White. This teacher was Mr Black. Everyone throughout the area knew who Mr Black was, while his female colleagues remained anonymous.

Were anonymity and confidentiality considered? While the man was not identified by his name, the fact that he was the only man involved in the research, and the term 'Mr' was used, meant he was easy to identify by people familiar with the context. Single-setting research such as this makes it even more difficult to conceal the identity of participants. Measures to keep data confidential are needed and consideration of how a participant's identity will not be disclosed in any publication should be decided before publication; unless of course it is the participant's wish to be identified with, or credited for, aspects of their input in the research or with a product of the research. Of course, it may have been the intention of the sociologist to make it known there was a man in Key Stage 1 to give the reader a sense of the research population. In the absence of a promise or an agreement for confidentiality was he being unethical? Alternatively, because he is an experienced researcher of education, should he not have a personal definition of ethics or an ethical code that includes the ideas of fairness and respect for the privacy of his participants? Should the experienced researcher have done more? Should the school have done more?

The NTRP is concerned about schools' reluctance to take part in research carried out by outsiders, and in particular the problems that arise when schools feel it necessary to pull out of research projects once they have started. It believes that whilst knowledgeable and discerning hosting by schools may pose initial challenges to research teams, it will also provide the most fruitful context for improving the quality and accessibility of research outputs. In 2003 the NTRP produced a document after consultation with schools aimed at securing benefits for schools, teachers and researchers while hosting research in schools. The panel, rather than lay down a set of guidelines, developed a series of questions to help schools through the issues involved and to help them negotiate confidently with research teams to inform dialogue between teachers, schools and research teams about how to make the processes of large-scale research activities, as well the eventual outcomes, mutually beneficial. One part of the NTRP document addresses the questions schools need to ask about the conduct of the research:

> Is there a code of practice for the ethical conduct of the research? Are there assurances about the following?
>
> - Will the school and/or teachers remain anonymous?
> - Will the contribution of the school and the teachers be acknowledged and how?
> - How is the data to be collected about teachers, teaching and learning or other aspects of school organisation and how checked with those involved in generating them? For example, will teachers who are interviewed have access to records of the interview? Will the teachers or the school have a chance to comment on profiles, draft questionnaires, proformas, interview schedules?
> - Will the sample target a range of teacher effectiveness and how is this to be defined? If so, what will teachers need and want to know about how their work is being evaluated?
> - Will the teachers and/or the school have the chance to comment on written outputs?
> - How will disagreements about data or reports be negotiated and reconciled?
> - Are there are proper arrangements in place for observing pupils and for parental permission?

Reliability

In the final scenario, the teacher, for her MEd dissertation, wanted to report a sensitive situation that involved a head teacher that she had worked for. In her view it was a vital piece of evidence. It would not have taken much detective work to discover who this person was and that discovery would have caused embarrassment on all sides. In the end, she did use the information about her head teacher but she had to think long and hard about the implications. She decided it unlikely that he would ask to read her dissertation and that she would dream up some excuse for his not seeing it if he did. No one else at school asked to read the dissertation either so she escaped any embarrassing situations. She still feels uneasy about it though.

In this scenario the researcher was not a professional researcher but a teacher researching and the work was not for publication (beyond the postgraduate supervisor) but for a postgraduate qualification. As an inexperienced researcher conducting research for a postgraduate degree, she must have been guided by a supervisor about including the vital information that would cause embarrassment, yet, from the little detail given, the decision to include the 'vital bit of evidence' is difficult to justify. It clearly cannot be justified by the public's right to know because the public would not be allowed see it. Research, particularly at postgraduate level, is about adding to knowledge. It could be argued that this research was a vehicle for a master's in education and what this research was about is almost irrelevant because the vital piece of evidence that was used resulted in the work's being buried rather than shared with colleagues. However, that argument does not take into consideration the nature of practitioners as researchers. Teachers as researchers quite often conduct action research: researching their own learning, reviewing their current practice with a view to understanding it and taking action, or changing it while conducting the research rather than as an afterthought at the end. It could be that the purpose of this research was not to represent the world but to represent the case (Stake, 1998). As in the PPD programme, research is a part of the teacher's professional development, therefore the findings of the enquiry may not be as important as the personal enquiry itself. The outcome of research can result in action from dialogue rather than a dialogue of results typical of traditional, scientific research.

It may be that the head teacher was unaware of his appearance in the research and that a person other than the head teacher or researcher, possibly someone with a grudge, may have contributed the evidence used in the dissertation. In which case, how reliable is the data? Because people construe the world in similar, but not the same ways, there are different understandings of what is real and it is therefore unsurprising that people have different views of the world (Bassey, 1999). As a result, the data recorded can be no more than the researcher's understanding or interpretation of the construction of others' interpretations. It may have been the researcher's observations that were recorded. Therefore, in either case, it is no more than the researcher's construction. It would be important for the teacher above to show how those interpretations are arrived at during the research. Clandinin and Connelly (1998) describe the process of writing research text as being on a knife edge – struggling to capture the participants' experiences and representing their voices, while attempting to create a research text that will reflect upon those voices. Non-participants should not expect to find themselves identified in the text of another's research without the informed consent, anonymity, confidentiality and care from the researcher they would be entitled to if they were a willing participant in the research. Further, the head teacher should have been made aware of any expected detriment arising from the research, or informed immediately if unexpected detriment arose (BERA, 2004). If he were a willing participant then how credible would the data appear if the head teacher, or another participant, were to challenge it once completed, and possibly published without having had the opportunity to check, correct or validate their responses? If the data was collected by interview, then it is good research practice to give transcripts of interviews back to the respondents to validate. This may appear at first to be another job to do that prolongs the research write-up process, or could mean longer contact with the participant, but researchers must not falsify, sensationalise or distort findings (BERA, 2004). Stake (1998) goes further and suggests allowing the participant to review the material for palatability as well as accuracy. Respondent validation is a helpful way of triangulating the researcher's observations and interpretations. Koch (1998) emphasises a reflexivity that acknowledges interpretations exist in a 'complex matrix of alternative representations', and that the constructions represented are 'faithful descriptions' so that the head teacher in this case can recognise the description when confronted with it.

Researching *with* rather than *on*

The term 'participant' has been used throughout this chapter rather than the other often used term 'subject'. Participant suggests an active, willing engaging role rather than a passive and possibly oblivious character in the text. The dilemmas from just about all of the scenarios offered for inclusion in this chapter involved the participant somehow losing out, but the only problems identified for the researchers were dilemmas in acquiring data and the danger that the research could not be completed. A lot of time, effort and commitment are needed for practising teachers to successfully complete a postgraduate certificate, diploma, master's or doctorate, so the threat to that success cannot be underestimated given the rigours faced in completing. There is something to be gained for the researcher in that success. New qualifications can open doors to a promotion or a change of employer. In addition, because research is a process and not simply a product, such as a report or a text that forms a dissertation, the research process can, and probably should, give the researchers the opportunity to reflect on their practice and improve it as well as present the opportunity to generate and share new knowledge – ends that are worth working towards. Yet we cannot get away from those that have contributed by way of data, time and effort for the research to be conducted. Detriment may have resulted, or oppression, from those in more powerful positions when an ethical stance based on care, duty, fairness and empathy has not been considered and adopted. Ethics cannot be ignored in research, nor should actions that ensure an ethical position, such as seeking informed consent and ensuring confidentiality, be ignored or worked around like tax avoidance. In the world of educational research, ethics avoidance is ethics evasion.

Guidelines such as those of BERA (2004) are just that, a guide or foundation to build an ethical stance upon. Teachers conducting research need to fuse the best of each of the disciplines of teaching and researching to develop a new perspective that considers not only the teaching or researching aspects but also the participants. It is perhaps appropriate to finish here with the final sentence of the visionary book by Stenhouse (1975), *An Introduction to Curriculum Research and Development*, to highlight the benefit of researching *with* rather than researching *on* people – whether adult or child: 'Communication is less effective than community in the utilization of knowledge'.

Notes

1 In 1986, the House of Lords decided in the case Gillick v West Norfolk and Wisbech Area Health Authority that parental rights are not absolute rights. They are rights exercised by parents on behalf of children too young to exercise them for themselves. The case concerned a teenage child's right to consent to medical treatment without the parents' knowledge. Lord Fraser said that the degree of parental control varied according to the child's understanding and intelligence.
2 Article 3 requires that in all actions concerning children, the best interests of the child must be the primary consideration. Article 12 requires that children who are capable of forming their own views should be granted the right to express their views freely in all matters affecting them, commensurate with their age and maturity. Children should therefore be facilitated to give fully informed consent (BERA, 2004: 7).

References

Bassey, M. (1999) *Case Study Research in Educational Settings*, Milton Keynes: Open University Press.
BERA (2004) *Ethical Guidelines*, British Educational Research Association, www.bera.ac.uk
Berg, B. (1989) *Qualitative Research Methods for Social Sciences* (3rd edn), Boston: Allyn and Bacon.
Campbell, A. (2002) Paper presented at the Annual Conference of the British Educational Research Association, University of Exeter, England, 12–14 September 2002. The text is in the Education-line Internet document collection at www.leeds.ac.uk/educol/documents/00002296.htm
Clandinin, D. and Connelly, F. (1998) 'Personal experience methods', in N. Denzin and Y. Lincoln (eds) *Collecting and Interpreting Qualitative Materials*, London: Sage.
Coyne, I. (1997) 'Researching children: some methodological and ethical considerations', in *Journal of Clinical Oncology*, 7(5): 409–416.
Dewey, J. (1963) *Experience and Education*, New York: Collier.
Foucault, M. (1978) *The Archaeology of Knowledge*, London: Tavistock.
Heath, S., Charles, V., Crow, G. and Wiles, R. (2004) 'Informed consent, gatekeepers and go-betweens', paper presented to stream on 'The Ethics and Social Relations of Research', Sixth International Conference on Social Science Methodology, Amsterdam, August 2004.
Homan, R. (2002) 'The principle of assumed consent: the ethics of gatekeeping', in M. McNamee and D. Bridges (eds) *The Ethics of Educational Research*, Oxford, UK: Blackwell Publishing.

Koch, T. (1998) 'Story telling: is it really research?', in *Journal of Advanced Nursing*, 28(6): 1182-1190.

Masson, J. (2000) 'Researching children's perspectives: legal issues', in A. Lewis, and G. Lindsay, (eds) *Researching Children's Perspectives*, Buckingham: Open University Press.

McNiff, J. (2001) Keynote address presented at the Register of Primary Research Seminar Conference, Action Research in the Classroom, Royal Geographical Society, 8 March 2001. The text is in the Education-line Internet document collection at: www.leeds.ac.uk/educol/documents/ 00002397.htm

NTRP (2003) www.standards.dfes.gov.uk/ntrp/ourwork/hosting research/

Shor, I. (1993) 'Education is politics: Paulo Freire's critical pedagogy', in P. McLaren and P. Leonard (eds) *Paulo Freire, A Critical Encounter*, London: Routledge.

Shor, I. (1996) *When Students Have Power: Negotiating Authority in a Critical Pedagogy*, London: University of Chicago Press.

Shor, I. and Freire, P. (1987) *A Pedagogy for Liberation*, New York: Bergin and Garvey.

Stake, R. (1998) 'Case Studies', in N. Denzin and Y. Lincoln, (eds) Strategies of Qualitative Inquiry, London: Sage.

Stenhouse, L. (1975) *An Introduction to Curriculum Research and Development*, London: Heinemann.

Usher, R. (1996) 'A critique of the neglected epistemological assumptions of educational research' in D. Scott and R. Usher (eds) *Understanding Educational Research*, London: Routledge.

Chapter 7

Ethics in practitioner research

Dilemmas from the field

Nicole Mockler

Introduction

The 'emancipatory' or 'democratic' project of which the teacher-as-researcher is a key component has long been assumed as 'given' in scholarly work on practitioner research. This path to teacher emancipation, however, comes not without considerable ethical challenges and dilemmas relating to the processes, products and contexts of the work being undertaken. This paper will examine ethical dilemmas for school-based practitioner–researchers through the eyes of one who engages with and supports practitioner research teams in a variety of capacities and contexts. Taking as its starting point a number of illuminating 'critical incidents' (Tripp, 1993, 1997), it will address some key ethical challenges and issues for teacher–researchers, contextualised within an understanding of practitioner inquiry as a vehicle for ethical and transformational teacher professionalism.

> 'I'm telling you stories. Trust me.'
>
> (Jeanette Winterson, 1987: 5, 13, 69, 160)

This is the refrain of *The Passion*, Jeanette Winterson's novel about truth, story and perception set during the French Revolution. Far from the way it was originally imagined, this chapter has turned out to be its own reflection on story, truth and perception, for it is the story of a number of ethical dilemmas framed within an ethical 'meta-dilemma' which emerged only at the point at which I set about committing my thinking to the writing of an account. The meta-dilemma cuts to the heart not only of issues relating to ethics, but also to those relating to the telling of stories, the nature of evidence, and the ontological and epistemological perspectives which frame thinking, research and practice.

In this chapter I argue that the ethical enactment of practitioner research relies on an alignment of a number of different ethical 'frames' – those of consent, confidentiality and transparency. It uses the narrative form to demonstrate and describe the ways in which both data and researcher become compromised when alignment of these frames is absent, and the ways in which such alignment creates conditions and circumstances within which a story such as this might itself be regarded as trustworthy.

This chapter began life as what was intended to be a simple example of 'second order action research' (Elliot, 1991), utilising a research method which I have assisted and supported many teachers in using over the past years, as a way of reflecting on or evaluating aspects of their practice, as well as developing a capacity for professional judgement. Based on David Tripp's (1993, 1997) notion of the 'critical incident', the methodology I had initially intended to use to explore the dilemmas, but rather have used to explore the meta-dilemma itself, involves three distinct phases: initially, the description of an incident from which an ethical dilemma issued; secondly, the explanation of the incident in the light of the ethical dilemma, and finally, the broadening of the implications of the incident to draw a more general meaning and interpret the events in the light of the broader context of the school, society, and in this case, the field of practitioner research. My original intention had been to use this methodology as a framework within which to discuss three ethical dilemmas, variously related to the context, the processes and the outcomes of practitioner inquiry. The ethical meta-dilemma emerged from consideration of the dilemmas themselves, and as I grappled with questions such as 'Where do I start?', 'What do I tell?', 'What do I include and what do I leave out?' and 'How do I tell these stories in ways which are both sensitive to the players but true to their essence?'. The ensuing discussion is the result of the meta-dilemma which emerged.

Describing ethical dilemmas in practitioner research: a simple task?

Having decided to use a number of dilemmas as the starting point, I set about writing the story of the 'incident' which had been the catalyst for each of the dilemmas, from my own perspective. Because of my commitment to write these stories of research and practice in ways that were sensitive to the players and the context within which they took place, it soon became apparent that the task was not as easy as it seemed. Plagued by questions about the evidence I was drawing on, the origin and validity of the perspective I held and the ethics of using this very methodology, I came to the realisation that the task of discussing the ethics of practitioner research was more complex than I had initially taken into account, and that perhaps this task needed to be approached in a different way.

Explaining ethical dilemmas: more complex than they look?

The decision to use a number of ethical dilemmas 'from the field' as the basis for this chapter was an easy one. For the past ten years I have been engaged in practitioner inquiry, as a practitioner–researcher, facilitator and leader of practitioner research, and advocate for practitioner research within both schools and academic circles. During that time, I have worked with teachers within and across diverse backgrounds, and encountered and engaged with a myriad of ethical dilemmas, relating variously to the ethics of consent, the ethics of anonymity and confidentiality, the ethics of purpose and outcome and so on. The process of choosing three discrete dilemmas to use as a starting point was slightly more difficult – I felt that the dilemmas themselves had to be significant enough to justify constituting a 'dilemma' rather than a 'question' in the first place and be such that they were substantially different from each other so as to highlight a range of ethical dilemmas within practitioner research. Eventually, I settled on the framework of context–process–product as a useful one and chose one substantial dilemma for each.

In all three cases, the dilemma came about as the result of a complex chain of actions performed by a group of people which in some way produced a situation where the team, the facilitator or both were led to grapple with a range of ethical issues. One dilemma related to the ethics of confidentiality, where a group of teachers felt that they were unable to 'opt out' of being participants in a research project for which they were to be interviewed for fear of reprisal, as it would be possible to identify from the data collected who had chosen to participate and who had not. The second related to the ethics of transparency, where a group of practitioner–researchers who had been given, and in turn had themselves given, assurances that the results of a research endeavour would be made available to the entire community had presented their report to the school executive to find it censored prior to being released to the community. The final dilemma related to the ethics of consent, where a group of teachers had given their informed consent for participation in a focus group interview. A senior member of staff, however, wanting access to the data for reasons other than those for which it had been collected, put significant pressure on the staff member who had facilitated the focus group to release the recording of the interview.

These descriptions, brief as they are, are offered as a concise overview of the dilemmas themselves, rather than a detailed account. The writing of the detailed account, however, posed a number of problems, and it was at this point that the ethical meta-dilemma emerged. For while, as I have indicated above, the stories were mine insofar as in each case I and others had been pushed to take a particular ethical stance, which reached resolution with various degrees of personal satisfaction, in another sense, it felt as though these stories were not entirely mine to tell. Implicit in the telling of the detail of each one in the context of an 'ethical transgression' was a passing of judgement on the actions of others. Torn between an unwillingness to claim my own truth as 'the truth' and an equally strong unwillingness to condone what, as a leader in each of these situations, I regarded as questionable behaviour by my silence, to take 'the option of least risk' (Calland and Dehn, 2004: 4), I struggled with what to do.

As a student of feminist history in years past, I have long been aware of the impact of my background as a historian on my life as an educationalist and researcher, and in this particular case I found myself grappling with questions which were as much historical as overtly 'ethical'. For while the earlier ethical dilemmas were about the mechanics of research ethics, this second-order dilemma, the meta-dilemma, is about the ethics of story. Winston Churchill offered a very particular insight into the ethics of story when he wrote, 'History will be kind to me, for I intend to write it', and for me, this dilemma cuts to the centre of age-old questions about the nature of story and the nature of history, such as those below.

- Whose story gets told?
- Who has the right to tell it?
- Whose story is privileged above others and why?
- Whose story makes 'history'?

On a very practical level, considering the dilemma through the lens of the ethics of story raised some interesting ethical questions, around, for example, anonymity and nuance, consent on the part of the players, and reflexivity and negotiation. In writing the stories in such a way as to make the contexts and the players anonymous, a variety of nuances and particularities were necessarily omitted. While, on the one hand, this was essential for the protection of those individuals and communities involved, on the other hand, the omission of some salient details seemed to me almost to be 'tampering with the evidence'. Further, relating to the issue of anonymity, it became apparent to me that regardless of how I tweaked or omitted finer details of the stories to preserve anonymity, it might be possible for people to recognise themselves or their colleagues within the stories. In addition, while these stories are the stories of my own experience, consent had not been sought from other key players, and had it been sought, given the purpose of the request, would probably not have been given by all involved. Whether that meant that in fact the reporting of my own experience would be unethical, I was unsure, but as a researcher committed to the notion of reflexivity and negotiation with research participants, my sense of unease grew. While I knew from experience that my perspective on the incidents which would form the basis of the stories was shared by some others, I was unsure that that was enough to justify the documenting of such judgements in a forum such as this.

Almost in direct opposition to these concerns, however, a range of others grew. For while the earlier concerns related to the ethical consequences of telling the stories, a similar range of concerns emerged at this stage in relation to the consequences of not telling the stories. Does my silence in relation to these events and unwillingness to subject them to the tides of debate and discourse in fact condone ethically questionable practices? Does an unwillingness to tell these stories represent a 'moral muteness' (Bird and Waters, 1989) and in fact compromise my professional integrity, contributing to a greater culture of individualism which sees injustice perpetuated within organisations and society at large?

Theorising ethical dilemmas: what can we glean?

The notion of 'moral muteness' itself raises some interesting issues in relation to this dilemma. First developed by Bird and Waters in their study of organisational ethics and managerial collaboration (1989), it refers to what they observed as a lack of willingness on the part of organisational leaders to discuss ethical problems and dilemmas. They identified three key causes of 'moral muteness', concisely summarised by Simon Longstaff (2001: 1) as:

- A perceived threat to harmony caused by the possibility of conflict when underlying values are made explicit and used to assess actual behaviour in the organisation

- A perceived threat to efficiency caused by 'moral talk''s being a waste of time or even a 'barrier' to getting the job done

- A perceived threat to a preferred image of power and effectiveness by seeming too idealistic or utopian or even being exposed as inadequate when it comes to the task of talking about ethics.

While it is apparent to me that each of these 'perceived threats' played a part in this context, the parameters of Bird and Waters' study are such that their discussion is confined to the enactment of moral muteness within the organisation in question, not necessarily beyond it. The discussion of ethical dilemmas in forums and arenas broader than the organisation, such as this, raises an additional range of ethical considerations. Of teacher research itself, Lawrence Stenhouse wrote:

> What seems to me most important is that research becomes part of a community of critical discourse. But perhaps too much research is published to the world, too little to the village.
>
> (1981: 17)

In terms of ethical dilemmas such as those which formed the basis for this paper, perhaps they too, are best published to the village rather than to the world, becoming part of the village-based community of critical discourse within the school. What then, of the village-based community of critical discourse within the practitioner research community more broadly? If ethical dilemmas relating to practitioner research are situated at least partly within the school context, and should therefore be confined to the school context for discussion and debate, then how does the broader practitioner research community engage in generative debate and discussion across schools, universities and other institutions? At what point does 'moral muteness' in terms of the outside world stop being generative for the 'inside community' and become, instead, oppressive?

In an attempt to begin theorising this dilemma, I turned initially to the grow-ing literature on practices and cultures of 'whistleblowing'. While the act of whistleblowing itself is construed in the literature as one riddled with ethical dilemmas (Calland and Dehn, 2004; Lovell, 2003; Campbell, 1996), prevailing thinking on whistleblowing is focused specifically on criminal, rather than unethical, activity, and as such seems infinitely more clear-cut than my meta-dilemma. In addition, in terms of my own professional identity, having forged a role and image of myself as one who is actively engaged in 'working alongside', assisting teachers to build on their professional knowledge and develop their professional judgement as a means for both professional development and what Stenhouse would refer to as 'emancipation': 'The essence of emancipation, as I conceive it, is the intellectual, moral and spiritual autonomy which we recognise when we eschew paternalism and the rule of authority and hold ourselves obliged to appeal to judgement' (1979: 163), the notion of 'blowing the whistle' seems counterproductive. In the first place, where might the adoption of such an approach begin and end: if the only approach to take in this case is to 'blow the ethical whistle' and call 'foul', what of the situation where I observe what might be seen by some as unethical practice in the classroom in the form of, for example, transmission-style learning and children deprived of any sense of power and agency in their learning? To approach this situation with whistle in hand would be to transgress all that I believe and understand about teacher pro-fessional learning and the importance of trust within the learning relationship. In addition, such an approach brings to bear a more adversarial than forensic approach (Groundwater-Smith and Mockler, 2003) to evidence and truth, and while I can appreciate the similarities between the two in this context, as Anthony Weston points out:

> The real point of ethics is to offer some tools for thinking about difficult mat-ters, recognising from the start – as the very rationale for ethics, in fact – that the world is seldom simple or clear cut. Struggle and uncertainty are part of ethics, as they are a part of life.
>
> (Weston, 1997: 4)

No conversation about ethics is simple, for as Weston indicates, the field of ethics itself exists as a response to 'hard questions' and 'hard issues', and as such the ensuing conversation is almost always about shades of grey. An additional level of complexity is brought to this particular conversation when one considers that the ethics of practitioner research lies at the crossroads of the ethics of research and the ethics of practice, so the conversation is confined neither to the usual consid-erations of research ethics and the intent therein that one should 'do no harm' nor to the applied, or 'implied' (Todd, 2001) ethics of professional practice, but must instead straddle both. Just as practitioner research itself blurs the line between research and practice, so too does due consideration of the ethics of practitioner research take both into account.

I offer this observation not because I believe that one operates out of a dual or conflicting ethical framework as a practitioner–researcher, indeed I agree with Elizabeth Campbell's (2003) argument that 'professional ethics is simply an extension of everyday ethics into the nuances of the professional's practice' (p.12), in the same way as I would claim that the research ethics is a similar extension of everyday ethics into the researcher's sphere of work. Yet this would be simply because we cannot talk about research ethics in relation to practitioner inquiry without discussing professional practice and therefore professional ethics and the ethical dimensions of teaching.

Furthermore, if we are to embrace teacher research and practitioner inquiry in a way that pushes beyond a 'project' approach and embeds an inquiry approach within teaching practice itself, reaching toward what Marilyn Cochran-Smith and Susan Lytle have termed 'inquiry as stance' (2001, 2007), then we are further confronted with the research/practice nexus. Because, for teacher inquiry and teaching practice to be seamlessly integrated, ethical concerns which might previously have been thought to be the province of research suddenly become salient for practice and vice versa. To borrow from the title of Cochran-Smith and Lytle's chapter in this current volume, under such circumstances, 'everything's ethics'. Clearly a holistic approach to teacher research and professional practice is required in order to think robustly about ethics within this context.

Ethics and ethical approaches to teaching are very much a part of the emerging discourse of 'new professionalism' (Sachs, 2003) and related thinking about the potential of practitioner research for professional renewal. Mike Bottery (1996) nominates five ethical aspects of new teacher professionalism which he argues are essential in the formation of authentic professional practice. They are as follows:

- An ethic of truth disclosure which must override personal advantages.
- An ethic of subjectivity, for each individual must recognise the limits of his or her perceptions, the individuality of his or her values.
- An ethic of reflective integrity, as each professional recognises the limits of personal perception, of the need to incorporate many understandings of a situation.
- An ethic of humility as each professional recognises that such subjectivity means that personal fallibility is not a failing but a condition of being human.
- An ethic of humanistic education of the duty to help [others] help themselves.

(p.193)

Elsewhere (Groundwater-Smith and Mockler, 2007), Susan Groundwater-Smith and I have posited a series of ethical guidelines for practitioner research, some of which are linked to a traditional conceptualisation of research ethics, while others flow from the discourse of the 'ethical professional':

- That it should observe ethical protocols and processes. Practitioner research is subject to the same ethical protocols as other social research. Informed consent should be sought from participants, whether students, teachers, parents or others, and an earnest attempt should be made to 'do no harm'.
- That it should be transparent in its processes. One of the broader aims of practitioner research lies in the building of community and the sharing of knowledge and ideas. To this end, practitioner research should be 'transparent' in its enactment, and practitioner–researchers accountable to their community for the processes and products of their research. Publication whether to the 'village' or to the 'world' (Stenhouse, 1981: 17) is part of this transparency.
- That it should be collaborative in its nature. Practitioner research should aim to provide opportunities for colleagues to share, discuss and debate aspects of their practice in the name of improvement and development. The responsible 'making sense' of data collected from within the field of one's own practice (through triangulation of evidence and other means) relies heavily on these opportunities.
- That it should be transformative in its intent and action. Practitioner–researchers engage in an enterprise which is, in essence, about contributing to both transformation of practice and transformation of society. For as Marion Dadds (1998: 5) writes:

> At the heart of every practitioner research project there is a significant job of work to be done that will make a small contribution to the improvement of the human condition in that context. Good practitioner research, I believe, helps to develop life for others in caring, equitable, humanising ways.

While these aspects and guidelines go some way toward developing and enacting a practical, ethical teacher professionalism and research protocol, on their own they are not enough to ensure that the conditions and circumstances for the alignment of the ethics of consent, confidentiality and transparency are created. For while guidelines and protocols and charters are useful for the formation and development of individual teachers and groups of teachers, work which a truly mature profession undertakes as a self-regulatory duty, the prior question relates to context and culture. The alignment of the ethics of consent, confidentiality and transparency grow out of, and in turn feed into, the development of organisational cultures which are themselves ethical in nature and framed by trust and 'generative politics' (Giddens, 1994). Such organisational cultures do not develop by happenstance, and neither are they, contrary to much writing and thinking on the notion of 'organisational ethics' (see, for example McDaniel, 2004), created through the behaviour modification the so-ethical-employer performs on the less-than-ethical employees who through having ethics 'instilled' in them, come to behave in ethical and appropriate ways.

In making a case for the development of what might otherwise be seen as ethical classroom practices, in the form of 'critical pedagogy', Michael Apple

(2001: 154) cites the following elements as the central tenets of a community within which such an ethical approach might flourish:

- caring and connectedness
- a sense of mutuality, trust and respect
- a freedom to challenge others
- a commitment to challenge the politics of 'official knowledge' whenever and wherever it is repressive.

It is through the building of such school cultures and contexts, where active trust and truly generative professional discourse flourish, that not only are the ethics of consent, confidentiality and outcome more likely to be aligned, but the threats identified by Bird and Waters as conditions for 'moral muteness' are more likely to be minimised. Furthermore, the very act of discussing and critiquing ethical dilemmas such as these thus becomes a much less risky affair, both within and without the immediate context, as the process of discussion and debate itself becomes part of the collegial professional learning process, and dissonance and dissent become opportunities for growth and development rather than threats to the world order.

Conclusion

In the final analysis, these ethical dilemmas hold implications which are much broader than the context within which they emerge, and also broader than the context of practitioner inquiry itself. Given that much of the work of teaching is in its very nature 'ethical work', and that judgements taken by teachers about students, learning, welfare, leadership and a range of other salient issues are inescapably related to ethics, unless the door is open to conversation and critique around ethical issues, we risk losing the scope for professional discourse around the core issues of education and schooling. Furthermore, the residual effects of such misalignment hold the potential to give rise to ongoing mistrust of people and processes, and diminish the very process, not only of practitioner research but also the professional learning of which it is a part, for, in the words of Margaret Somerville:

> Many people believe that the beginning and end of doing ethics is to act in good personal conscience. They are right that this is the beginning, but wrong that it is the end. We all need to do ethics and, therefore, to learn how to do it. But doing ethics is not always a simple task: it is a process, not an event, and in many ways, a life long learning experience.
>
> (Somerville 2000: 284)

This chapter began with the recurring plea from the narrator of *The Passion*: 'I'm telling you stories. Trust me'. The plea itself recognises the importance of trust within the relationship between the teller and the recipient of the story, a contract entered into by both parties. At the end of the day, that trust is sometimes contingent upon stories not being told out of turn or out of context, and being told only by those whose stories they truly are to tell.

References

Apple, M.W. (2001) *Educating the 'Right' Way: Markets, Standards, God and Inequality*, New York: RoutledgeFalmer.

Bird, F. and Waters, J. (1989) 'The moral muteness of managers', *Californian Management Review*, 32: 73–88.

Bottery, M. (1996) 'The challenge to professionals from the new public management: implications for the teaching profession', *Oxford Review of Education*, 22(2): 179–197.

Calland, R. and Dehn, G. (2004) *Whistleblowing around the World: Law, Culture and Practice*, Cape Town: ODAC.

Campbell, E. (1996) 'Ethical implications of collegial loyalty as one view of teacher professionalism', *Teachers and Teaching: Theory and Practice*, 2(2) Oct: 191–208.

Campbell, E. (2003) *The Ethical Teacher*, Buckingham: Open University Press.

Cochran-Smith, M. and Lytle, S.L. (2001) 'Beyond certainty: taking an inquiry stance', in A. Lieberman and L. Miller (eds) *Teachers Caught in the Action*, NY: Teachers College Press.

Cochran-Smith, M. and Lytle, S.L. (2007) 'Everything's ethics: practitioner inquiry and university culture' [current volume].

Dadds, M. (1998) 'Supporting practitioner research: a challenge', *Educational Action Research*, 6(1): 39.

Elliott, J. (1991) *Action Research for Educational Change,* Bristol, PA: Open University Press.

Giddens, A. (1994) *Beyond Left and Right: The Future of Radical Politics*, Oxford: Polity Press.

Groundwater-Smith, S. and Mockler, N. (2003) *Learning to Listen: Listening to Learn*, Sydney: The University of Sydney/MLC School.

Groundwater-Smith, S. and Mockler, N. (2007) 'Ethics in practitioner research: an issue of quality', *Research Papers in Education*, special issue on Research Quality.

Longstaff, S. (2001) 'The problem of moral muteness', *Living Ethics*, 43. Available online at: www.ethics.org.au/things_to_do/ethics_workout/ article_0201.shtm (accessed 14 November 2006).

Lovell, A. (2003) 'The enduring phenomenon of moral muteness: suppressed whistleblowing', *Public Integrity*, 5(3): 187–204.

McDaniel, C. (2004) *Organisational Ethics*, Hampshire: Ashgate.

Sachs, J. (2003) *The Activist Teaching Profession*, Buckingham: Open University Press.

Somerville, M. (2000) *The Ethical Canary: Science, Society and the Human Spirit*, Toronto: Viking.

Stenhouse, L. (1979) 'Research as a basis for teaching', in L. Stenhouse (ed.) *Authority, Education and Emancipation*, London: Heinemann Press.

Stenhouse, L. (1981) 'What counts as research?', *British Journal of Educational Studies*, 29(2) 103–114.

Todd, S. (2001) 'Bringing more than I contain: ethics, curriculum and the pedagogical demand for altered egos', *Journal of Curriculum Studies*, 33(4): 431–450.

Tripp, D. (1993) *Critical Incidents in Teaching: The Development of Professional Judgement*, London and New York: Routledge.

Tripp, D. (1997) 'Critical incidents', Booklet 6 of *SCOPE: Supporting Workplace Learning*, Perth: Education Department of Western Australia.

Weston, A. (1997) *A Practical Companion to Ethics*, New York: Oxford University Press.

Winterson, J. (1987) *The Passion*, London: Bloomsbury.

Chapter 8

Ways of telling

The use of practitioners' stories

Anne Campbell and Olwen McNamara

Introduction

A great deal of human learning occurs through storytelling; it is a time-honoured way of informing others about what has happened in life and work. Elliott (2005: 15) in her work on using narrative in social research stresses three key features of narrative that link it to human learning and communication: firstly, it has a temporal or chronological dimension providing a series of events or experiences rather than describing a state of affairs; secondly, it communicates the meaning of events or experiences through temporal and evaluative statements; and thirdly, there is an important social dimension to narrative which is a popular form of communication. This chapter will draw upon approaches promoting storytelling, narratives and fictions in practitioner research. In particular, it will address how ethical issues can be investigated and developed through presenting ideas and data in the 'real' and 'fictive' voices of practitioners and others in stories, pen portraits and vignettes. It will discuss how, through fictions and telling stories about professional practice, ethical issues and dilemmas can be raised, illustrated and discussed; and how the storytelling process can help develop practitioners' professional learning, values and ethical practice. It will also raise questions about the ethics of storytelling itself. The chapter will introduce and problematise a range of story types such as 'real' and 'true' stories, 'fictional' and 'hypothetical' stories, 'cover' stories and 'positive' and 'negative' stories. It will then discuss the pen portrait methodology as developed in Campbell *et al.* (2004) to illustrate how teachers in their professional development can be encouraged to identify and be supported in reflecting upon ethical issues in their professional lives.

What types of stories can be used to raise ethical and professional issues?

Moral imagination is almost inevitably partial and influenced by the lives we lead. Our moral understanding may thus be limited, and if we want to be ethical in our behaviour, and specifically in our professional practice, we need to rehearse scenarios, decisions, reasons and justifications. Engaging with events or experiences through stories before we encounter such situations in the world, can be a good way of 'limbering' up for the real thing. Doing so can help us to clarify and sharpen our ethical thinking (See Fairbairn *et al.*, 1995)

Real stories and true-to-life stories

Real stories may be described as authentic accounts of actual living, or once living, people who are experiencing, or have experienced, the events that are described. Piper and Simons (2005), for example, use a real story of a research project commissioned by the Royal Society for the Protection of Animals (RSPCA) to raise and discuss issues of 'situated ethics and ethical reflexivity'. The research was exploring the causes of violence towards animals and one hypothesis being tested was that the animal abusers had themselves experienced abuse elsewhere (Ressler *et al.*, 1988). A dilemma arose when the researchers were considering how to respond if children, being interviewed about cruelty to animals, disclosed that they had been, or were being, abused. Were the researchers to report the abuse to the child protection agencies? Or was the information gathered from interviews to be confidential? UK legislation and the ethical concerns of the researchers themselves meant that a position of maintaining confidentiality was no longer tenable. After much discussion the team prepared a statement which was communicated to respondents at the beginning of the interview which indicated that information given would be treated as confidential unless it led to concern for the respondent's or another's safety.

Real stories can be very powerful in illustrating aspects of professional practice, or in raising issues; however, it is clear that they can cause ethical problems, because of the need to protect the characters whose real lives they portray. This is one reason that other genres of storying are useful. True-to-life stories describe events in the lives of the practitioners, clients and pupils, whose experiences, values, worries and fears they narrate. Such stories are not 'real' in the sense that they are constructed about actual people, who have lived or are living the life that they recount, but they are (re)constructed in the sense that there are real people with lived experiences and identities that replicate and authenticate the narrative accounts of the characters who inhabit the apocryphal tales. The reconstruction of stories of real people, pupils, teachers, classroom assistants, dinner ladies, allows us to protect their privacy whilst using them to engage our professional and personal knowledge, skill and experience and challenge our ethical thinking.

A well-conceived, 'true-to-life' story will be experienced as authentic by those who encounter it. Ironically, real stories are sometimes so unbelievable that students and colleagues form the view that they must have been invented. The ability to write true-to-life stories about areas of professional practice is, at least arguably, a sign of expertise, because convincingly true-to-life stories can best be written by those who know and understand situations well enough to allow them to create stories that hang together in a credible way.

Fictional and hypothetical stories

Other examples of story types to be found in the literature are fictional and hypothetical stories. Fictionalised stories draw on autobiographies and biographies, amalgamating and meshing together selected characteristics and behaviours from a variety of people to illuminate ethical dilemmas and other problems faced by practitioners in their professional lives. They have some similarity to true-to-life stories, but differ from them in that they may be based on empirical data but subject to poetic licence, whereas true stories draw on one's own experience or the shared experience of others. Clough (2002: 8) comments on the usefulness of narrative approaches in educational and social research with reference to social consciousness:

> The fictionalization of educational experience offers researchers the opportunity to import fragments of data from various real events in order to speak to the heart of social consciousness – thus providing the protection of anonymity to the research participant without stripping away the rawness of real happenings.

Fictionalised stories provide a means of presenting research data in readable and accessible formats. This in itself is a valuable aim and may promote audience engagement with the issues the data raises. Campbell and Kane (1998) developed this methodological approach in a fictional primary school. In their book, fictionalised stories were used in reporting the results of empirical research carried out on teachers' and student teachers' experience in the process of mentoring in school-based teacher education initiatives. In doing so a *Canterbury Tales* approach was used in which fictionalised stories depicted the experience of mentoring, by telling the tales and developing portraits of those who were travelling on the 'mentoring journey'. Stories were presented from different viewpoints, including those of mentors, students, children, governors and parents in order to explore professional and ethical dilemmas in school-based teacher education.

In doing so they developed a range of stories that included among others:

- a high-achieving student who got so 'close' to her mentor that there were complaints from colleagues and parents about the propriety of their relationship
- a 'struggling' student who claimed to have been the subject of discrimination which raised ethical issues concerning racial stereotypes
- two undergraduate students whose small-scale research projects seemed to be closer in both form and content than could have occurred by accident. Issues about plagiarism and undue influence of mentors on student work were raised in this story
- a 'failing' student, who possessed many of the 'right' attributes for success but not necessarily in the right order, and failed to relate to children: this story raised ethical issues with regard to his personality and suitability for teaching.

The following excerpt illustrates one of the ethical pitfalls that 'Mike' encountered in a professional context:

> In an attempt to come to terms with the disruption in his class. Mike (a student teacher) thought he would try to motivate and remediate his disruptive pupils by awarding them gold stars when they managed a session without disruptive behaviour. Though his scheme seemed to have some success in achieving his goal of changing the behaviour of those who were causing the disruption it clearly raised ethical issues, which were highlighted when the parent of another child in his class asked why her very well-behaved daughter's name was not on the displayed 'chart of honour'. It was difficult to explain that he only awarded gold stars to disruptive pupils. He seemed to be operating a system that rewarded only those who exhibited bad behaviour, and ignoring those who were well behaved.
>
> (Adapted from Campbell and Kane, 1998)

What are the ethical principles here? Is it OK to reward naughty children when they are good but not reward good children when they are good? Whilst many teachers may feel it justifiable to have a system which rewards only naughty children's good behaviour, many parents of well-behaved children may well, quite justifiably, feel it ethically incorrect not to reward the good behaviour of their own children.

Like true-to-life stories, fictionalised stories can be useful in both raising and illustrating ethical and professional issues in educational and professional development contexts, and in encouraging readers and workshop participants to view storytelling as a way of learning and of exploring issues. Of course, fictionalised stories for these purposes could also draw both on previously identified issues from other research studies and on others' reported experiences. Thus, it is possible to play with data collected by developing scenarios, creating tales, telling stories, and developing metaphors, whilst at the same time attempting to formulate and construct arguments for and against theories arising from research into school-based teacher education.

Hypothetical stories are the kinds of stories that philosophers use to provoke thought; they have a kind of 'what if' character and are constructed to fit occasions when the intention is to push the boundaries of thinking. The use that philosophers make of such stories has some similarities to the classic scientific enterprise in which scientists test hypotheses through experiments in which the number of variables is controlled. For her part, the philosopher wants to keep under control the number of factors that might influence the way in which moral decisions are reached. Having outlined a situation in which an individual or group faces a moral decision, she can then alter the story line in various ways, in order to clarify the factors that are important for people in coming to decisions. Hypothetical stories are particularly useful in creating 'moral gymnasia' (Fairbairn and Campbell, 2003) for discussing and exploring ethical issues. They are often complex and rather far-fetched, and not infrequently they have a science fiction flavour, especially in areas such as medicine and in particular in genetics. Here, however, is a short and extremely simple example:

> John, a bright nine-year-old can make a lot of progress in a short time using the one computer available to his class in a rural primary school. David, who is in the same class, can make the same amount of progress, but it takes him much longer to do so – perhaps ten times as long. What must the teacher in the story do, if she wants to treat David and John equally? Should she allow each the same amount of time on the computer, or give David more time? Will it make a difference to how she acts if she knows that one of the boys has easy access to a computer at home?

Secret, sacred and cover stories

Clandinin and Connolly (1996: 25) discuss the ways in which teachers address the dilemmas that they face via the stories that they tell, and these, the authors claim, take a variety of forms: secret, sacred and cover stories. Secret stories they define as 'lived' stories of classroom practice told to other teachers. Sacred stories they define as being theory-driven views of practice shared by practitioners, policy-makers and theoreticians. Sacred stories can help practitioners to develop their ethical thinking, by drawing their attention to the ways in which reconstructing events can cast them in a more positive light, even when they involve serious professional mistakes or even misconduct.

Cover stories can be characterised as stories in which practitioners agree or collude with a version of events and portray themselves as 'experts', sometimes to 'protect' their professional behaviour or the participants in the story. Sometimes stories that are told in professional settings undergo changes of a more subtle kind in a sort of Chinese whispers phenomenon, until gradually they become 'liveable with'.

Through these stories we can deepen our understanding of the 'professional landscapes' characterised by Clandinin and Connolly (1996: 30) as 'complex places with multiple layers of meaning that depend on individuals' stories ... as well as the landscape's own narrative history of shifting values, beliefs and stories'. Clandinin and Connolly's (1996) cover stories may be told to interpret situations, shift meanings and disguise what really happened while hiding real feelings. Examining the cover stories that may be told to make more palatable events that happen in practice, can be useful in helping practitioners to develop their ethical thinking.

There are complex ethical issues and decisions involved in collecting cover stories. Consider for example a situation in which

> a social worker told a colleague the story of a child's court case in great detail, but gave scant comment on her own role, focusing on the actions of the other players. In this case, as the discussion between the social worker

and her colleague proceeded, it emerged that her role was crucial both to the resolution of the case and to the child's being taken into care.

This social worker's unhappiness with her role led her to be economical with the truth in the story that she told her colleague.

Sometimes stories result from collusion on the part of colleagues. Consider, for example,

> an experienced teacher who knew that a newly qualified colleague in the class next door was having some discipline problems and had resorted to threatening to use Sellotape to cover the mouths of persistent offenders. Knowing about this threat left her with a number of ethical dilemmas – for example, about whether she should intervene or not; and if she did how she could do so without making the new teacher feel inadequate. The situation became more difficult when she realised that on at least one occasion her colleague had actually carried out his threat. In the end she made sure that her newly qualified colleague was in no doubt about how unacceptable his behaviour was, but colluded with him in creating an acceptable story to explain his behaviour, because she believed that in behaving in the way that he had, he was unwise rather than unethical.

Positive and negative stories

Practitioners in the caring professions face moral decisions every day. That is why it is important that they are enabled to grow as reflective and ethical individuals able to think through the kinds of situations in which they find themselves or may find themselves in the future. We have suggested that stories can be useful in providing them with opportunities for such reflection and ethical development. We have discussed some examples from the wide range of types of story that can be useful.

We want to move to a focus on skill in telling positive rather than negative stories about the lives of clients and pupils and service users. This dichotomy is introduced by O'Brien and O'Brien (2000). Many practitioners may need support in developing the ability to tell positive rather than negative stories which could arguably form part of a programme of moral development for caring professionals. To illustrate how the ability to tell positive stories can avoid negative stereotyping we use the two following stories:

Story I

Mr Davis has a mental age of 3 years, 2 months. IQ = 18. Severe impairment of adaptive behaviour, severe range of mental retardation. Becomes agitated and out of control. Takes [medicines] for psychosis. Severely limited verbal ability: inability to comprehend abstract concepts. Learns through imitation. Has learned to unlock the coke machine and restock it, and to crank a power mower and operate it. His family is uncooperative. They break appointments and do not follow through on behaviour management plans.

Story 2

Ed lives with his mother and sister in a housing project. Ten of his relatives live nearby and they visit back and forth frequently. Ed is at home in his neighbour-hood. He goes to local stores with his sisters and helps with shopping. He goes to church. Ed dresses neatly, is usually friendly, and shakes hands with people when he meets them. He is a very big man, with limited ability to speak. When he gets frustrated and upset he cusses and 'talks' to himself in a loud voice. These char-acteristics often frighten other people who do not know him well. He has been excluded from the work activity centre because he acts 'out of control' there. He has broken some furniture and punched holes in the walls there and scares some of the staff people very much.

Ed likes people and enjoys visiting in the neighbourhood. He loves music, dancing, and sweeping. He likes loading vending machines and operating mechanical equipment. He likes to go shopping. He likes to cook for himself and for other people and can fix several meals on the stove at home. He likes to hang clothes and bring them in off the line. He likes to stack wood and help people move furniture. He prefers tasks that require strength and a lot of large muscle movement.

(O'Brien and Mount, 2000)

The first profile, in the genre of a medical report, is pithy, focused on measure-ment of performance and, as such, is judgemental and evaluative. The sketch presents a rather negative picture of Mr Davis's accomplishments and behaviour. The story about Ed, however, is descriptive rather than evaluative and analytic without being overtly judgemental; it gives a more comprehensive account of his life and relationships. Many of the harsh realities of Ed's life are presented but they are tempered by more detail in Story 2. Stories we tell can change the ways in which the characters are viewed and so while the story about Mr Davis is likely to leave us with the idea that he can't do very much and that he can be rather a dif-ficult person, the story about Ed makes him sound much more human and connected. Readers may be surprised to learn that both stories are about the same individual and arguably demonstrate how a positive approach to reporting and style of writing can generate different pictures of the same person. Whilst we would not advocate always taking a positive approach to storytelling, it does have a powerful influence on views of people with learning or other disabilities.

Fictionalised pen portraits

Fictional pen portraits were used in a recent research project, Teachers' Perceptions of Continuing Professional Development (Hustler *et al.*, 2003), which we as part of a team conducted on behalf of the English government's Department for Education and Skills (DfES). In the project we undertook case studies and used these to develop fictional pen portraits of teachers; the pen portraits were vignettes used creatively to illustrate the teachers' professional lives and their attitudes towards, and perceptions and experiences of, professional learning and development. The methodology adopted was far more structured than the approaches outlined above and was used effectively to raise dilemmas posed in the data in relation to the professional identities, lives and contexts of the case study schools and the staff that inhabited them.

The pen portraits were constructed from data gathered on visits made by the team of researchers to 22 case study schools. The schools were selected to be representative of the overall sample for the baseline survey including variables such as: government region; rural, suburban, urban contexts; phase; diversity in size and type of school. In each case study school a minimum of four teachers was interviewed; they were selected to represent a mix in terms of experience, curriculum specialisms and attitudes to continuing professional development (CPD). The semi-structured interview lasted approximately 45 minutes and covered the following areas:

- career history and progression/career stage and individual needs
- definition and perceptions of CPD
- anecdotal evidence and memorable experience of CPD
- CPD in subject knowledge, classroom practice, teaching style
- ideas about professionalism/management of CPD
- constraints and facilitators of CPD
- impact of CPD on practice and career
- identification of needs and description of good quality CPD.

The interviews with teachers were transcribed and a framework devised for analysing key features, and drawing on previous research in the field, notably that of Day (1999), Harland and Kinder (1997), Ovens (1999), and Smith and Coldron (1999).

The framework included:

- the effectiveness and value and impact of types of CPD activities, e.g. courses, conferences, team teaching, coaching, school inset days, personal research and online learning
- the tensions between individual needs, school needs and government priorities
- the degree to which ownership and autonomy and participation in agenda setting for CPD was experienced
- differing learning styles of teachers
- teachers' assessment of the content of curriculum focused CPD
- experiences of CPD providers that produced some 'types': for example, guru, national expert, likeable amateur, local whiz, knowledgeable colleague, out-of-date has-been, 'too-long-away-from-the-chalk-face' consultant.

In this way, the pen portraits were based on empirical data collected through semi-structured interviews. Recurrent and common issues were identified and logged. The team then fashioned a number of fictional characters based on its reading of the transcripts and relating to the sample of teachers interviewed. An amalgam of major characteristics, personal histories and common experiences was then produced as a typology and used to formulate the first draft pen portraits.

Team discussion and analyses of the data fleshed out the characters and the 'fictionalising' and writing of pen portraits was undertaken. Creating fictional characters from 'real' teachers' stories is a task requiring imagination, knowledge of storytelling and creativity (see Campbell, 2000). The intention was to create characters that reflected the careers and professional development stories that illustrated and illuminated the ethical, professional and personal issues encountered by teachers in schools. One of these pen portraits, Julia, is presented below to illustrate how professional and ethical issues about teacher learning can arise in narrative interviewing:

> Julia, aged 30, taught for four years in a small, rural, secondary school.
> I've been here for four years ever since I qualified. I'm in the history department. I started off in Public Relations, got made redundant, then worked with adults with learning difficulties, that's what got me interested in teaching really. Professional development to me is about advancing my skills, keeping up to date, finding new ways of teaching, using resources. I've had one absolutely brilliant experience through the Bursary Scheme – I used the bursary money to go over to Auschwitz, it was fabulous, inspired my teaching of the Holocaust and I've got so many new resources and photographs. Normally I don't go on many courses. I did go on one Information, Communications and Technology [ICT] course that was great. Peter Jackson was a classroom teacher and you could use his ideas with the pupils, you felt as if you had learned something new, it wasn't just 'sharing ideas' like one appalling session I attended where Sheila Sharp gave us no ideas, no material. This government's New Opportunities Fund [NOF] training stuff has annoyed me too, a complete and utter waste of time. The best training days are the ones when you have time to prepare or go on the Internet – there's so much good stuff there. To be honest about teaching, I'm not prepared to lose out on having a life … in fact I'm not really sure I will stay with the job, I keep thinking I might go back into PR again, or get a job with Marks and Spencers.

Julia was in the history department – indeed she *was* the history department in her small rural secondary school. Her situation and that of many like her means that in any real account of 'a Julia' she would be identifiable; her confidentiality would be impossible to protect.

Julia was made redundant and found her way into teaching through her passion for history and interest in teaching adults with learning difficulties, but already her commitment is waning and she is thinking of leaving the profession. A number of recent government recruitment drives have been aimed at persuading potential entrants to make mid-life career changes: is this useful? Does Julia seem the kind of person we want to attract into teaching?

A considerable amount of money has already been invested into Julia's training and induction. Was it right that Julia should be thinking of leaving teaching now? In particular, would Julia be right to leave simply because she is not prepared to 'lose out on having a life'? The European Union Working Time Directive and the UK government's pledge on work–life balance have recently become other 'plates' for schools' senior management teams to spin. Characteristically, workforce statistics tell us that teachers three/four years into their careers are most at risk of leaving. What is it about this watershed that makes retention such an issue? A number of government initiatives have been targeted at teachers at this stage of career development in order to increase retention. Is it ethical to induce teachers at this stage in their careers to stay in teaching, whilst not rewarding those that have remained loyal to teaching for many years?

The teacher bursary scheme was one such covert 'retention' initiative that was targeted at teachers with three to four years' experience. Julia applied for and received a teacher bursary and used the money to visit Auschwitz – the funding amounted to hundreds of pounds – should such money be available to one individual for professional renewal? Julia's experience reinvigorated her history teaching. The Holocaust was on the syllabus; would it have been OK if it hadn't been? Many teachers used bursary monies without direct benefit for teaching or curriculum. Should the money have been available for personal renewal? Would a course in basket weaving have been a 'bona fide' use of public funds? How much responsibility should Julia accept for her own professional learning? Should it be her responsibility to manage her own CPD?

Discussion of issues raised in the chapter

The particular power of narrative, biography and telling stories about professional development is in our view an important way of researching the ethical dimensions of teachers' lives and careers. Connolly and Clandinin (1990), Goodson and Sykes (2001) and Clough (2002) acknowledged the growth of narrative and storytelling in research about teachers and recognised that as a result of these, informal, person-centred genres such as narrative and biography, autobiography, life history and anecdote have become quite widely accepted within educational research and professional development. Birkeland (2002) explored how stories could impact on teachers' ideas of their educational world and asserted that stories had particular relevance when developing reflective practice. Apple reminds us of the centrality of ethical and aesthetic sensitivities in inclusive practice and the importance of personal, moral stories to the development of practice:

Much of the impetus behind personal stories is moral. Education is seen correctly as a way to reawaken ethical and aesthetic sensitivities that, increasingly, have been purged from the scientific discourse of too many educators. Or it is seen as a way of giving a voice to the subjectivities of people who have been silenced.

Apple (1996: xiii)

Research into professional development, through biography and autobiography, can be a powerful way of discovering concerns about the ethical dimensions in research. Critical reflection and evaluation can aid a developing understanding of moral problem-solving in professional settings. There are also strong links across the professions, as attested by the work of Bolton (2001) on reflective writing in the health and care professions, Fairbairn (2002) on ethics and storytelling in professional development, and Clements (1999) and Neisser and Fivush (1994) on autobiography.

Ethical guidelines are available for educational researchers to consult. The British Educational Research Association (BERA, 2004) and British Psychological Society (BPS) discuss how research should not disadvantage participants. There is, not surprisingly, little specific detail on ethical concerns regarding the use of particular methodologies such as narrative or storytelling methods. Elliott (2005) highlights personal and moral relationships in the data collection and analysis phases of narrative methodologies and the issues around 'informed consent' as especially important. Graham (1984) suggested that storytelling approaches provided a more authentic 'voice' for participants who were interviewed.

Issues of power are at the centre of Goodson and Sykes (2001: 92) when they discuss ethics in life history research which relate closely to narrative and storytelling methods of research. They discuss doing research in a covert or overt manner and argue that 'studies of powerful groups or individuals or investigations into socially unacceptable or even illegal attitudes, behaviours or practices' may be difficult to research overtly due to lack of cooperation of informants. They do, however, stress the need for active participation and collaboration with participants but raise questions about the degree to which 'informed consent' is a reality. For example Measor and Sykes (1992) in their life history research with teachers failed to tell participants about the 'real' focus on racist attitudes. Honesty and truth are problematic issues in narrative and fictionalised accounts. Arguably, what researchers need to do is to be careful in their justifications of purposes and methodology. They should consider ethics in the design and conduct of their research and in the topics they wish to study.

Issues of anonymity and confidentiality are problematic in action research and practitioner research. Somekh *et al.* (2005: 3) raise the issue of power in their discussion of ethical issues in social research:

Knowledge confers power, so in collecting data researchers need to be guided by principles of respect for persons and obtaining informed consent. The publication of outcomes confronts social scientists with the need to consider the possible impact of their reports on the people who have been part of it. Standard procedures such as 'anonymizing' particular participants and organisations raise further ethical questions since people's ideas can be seen as their intellectual property and in some cases it would certainly be unethical to quote them without accrediting the source.

Piper and Simons (2005: 57) highlight the need for separate consideration of confidentiality and anonymity stating that confidentiality allows 'people to talk in confidence but also to refuse to allow publication' whereas anonymisation 'is a procedure to offer some protection of privacy and confidentiality' and state that anonymisation may not be appropriate for action and participatory research where participants are researching their own contexts. Eisner (1997: 6), in a discussion of alternative data representation, stresses the use of critical reflection and the need for context when 'exploring the edges' of new and alternative methodolgies. We need to be careful in our search for empathy with practitioners' lives.

In this chapter we have tried to share some of the thinking that we have done about the kinds of stories that can be useful in the ethical and professional development of practitioners. In doing so, we have discussed some of the ways in which we might use them. However, we have stopped short of a detailed discussion of the sort of approaches to storytelling that we have used for work in professional and ethical development. Imagination is one powerful way of getting people to examine their immediate responses to stories in which ethical dilemmas are posed; whether the stories are true, real, fictionalised or hypothetical, particular emphasis needs to be placed on the use of imagination to develop empathy. The process of imagining is claimed by Hardy (1986) as the link between 'storying' and theorising cited in Campbell and Kane (1998: 136). Winter (1988: 235) acknowledges the contribution of imagination to the introduction of 'play' to the process of research. He identifies 'play' as 'the mode of innovative understanding' allowing the researcher to play with 'the actual and potential discontinuities within experience, using metaphorical processes of language to manipulate elements in a state of affairs'. In a way, collecting practitioners' stories is akin to what Kemmis (1980: 133) describes as case study research:

> By demonstrating the rigour of the process of the imagination of the case and the invention of study, the case worker provides an internal justification for the study: s/he demonstrates its reasonableness ... If case study is to create platforms of understanding and action it must be an educative process.

Alternative ways of representing data collected about professional identity, development and experience such as narratives, biographies, storytelling and fictional accounts have much potential for bringing theory and practice together in a powerful emancipatory fusion, which can enthuse and enthral readers and incite them to rediscover the joy and passion in teaching and learning. Campbell and Kane (1998) in their tales of a fictional primary school hoped that exploring the edge of new methodologies to research school-based teacher education through fictional–critical writing and tale telling would stimulate teachers' interest in research and provide platforms of understanding.

We would also hope that using practitioners' stories would open up the personal, ethical, moral and human side of being a practitioner. We hope that readers and listeners might identify and relate to the characters, perhaps even recognise in them traits of a well-known practitioner, client or colleague. Or themselves.

References

Apple, M. (1996) 'Education, identity and cheap french fries', in M. Apple *Cultural Politics and Education*, Milton Keynes: Open University Press.

BERA (2004) *Ethical Guidelines,* British Educational Research Association, www.bera.ac.uk.

Birkeland, L. (2002) 'Storytelling and staff training: a narrative approach to reflective practice', in N. Hall (ed.) *Occasional Papers*, 2002, University of Greenwich and European Teacher Education Network (ETEN).

Bolton, G. (2001) *Reflective Practice: Writing and Professional Development*, London: Paul Chapman.

Campbell, A. (2000) 'Fictionalising research data as a way of increasing teachers' access to school-focussed research', *Research in Education*, 63, May: 81–88.

Campbell, A and Kane, I. (1998) *School-based Teacher Education: Telling Tales from a Fictional Primary School*, London: David Fulton.

Campbell, A., McNamara O. and Hustler, D. (2004) 'Researching continuing professional development: the use of fictional pen portraits to illustrate and analyse teachers' perceptions and experiences', *Professional Development Today*, Spring.

Clandinin, D.J. and Connolly, F.M. (1996) 'Teachers' professional knowledge landscapes: teacher stories/stories of school/school stories/stories of school', *Educational Researcher*, 25(3): 24–30.

Clements, P. (1999) 'Autobiographical research and the emergence of the fictive voice', *Cambridge Journal of Education*, 29(1): 197–205.

Clough, P. (2002) *Narratives and Fictions in Educational Research*, Buckingham: Open University Press.

Connolly, F.M. and Clandinin, D.J. (1990) 'Narrative, experience and the study of curriculum', *Cambridge Journal of Education*, 20(3): 241–253.

Day, C. (1999) *Developing Teachers: The Challenges of Lifelong Learning*, London: Falmer Press.

Eisner, E.W. (1997) 'The promise and the perils of alternative forms of data representation', *Educational Researcher*, 26(6) 4–10.

Elliott, J. (2005) *Using Narrative in Social Research: Qualitative and Quantitative Approaches*, London: Sage.

Fairbairn, G. J. (2002) 'Ethics, empathy and storytelling in professional development', *Health and Social Care*, 1(1): 23–32.

Fairbairn, G. and Campbell, A. (2003) 'What kinds of stories should we be using in professional ethics teaching?', paper given at the Association for Moral Education Annual conference, Krakow, Poland, July 2003.

Fairbairn, G.J., Rowley, D. and Bowen, M. (1995) *Sexuality, Learning Difficulties and Doing What's Right*, London: David Fulton Ltd.

Goodson, I. and Sykes, P. (2001) *Life History Research in Educational Settings*, Buckingham: Open University Press.

Graham, H. (1984) 'Surveying through stories', in C. Bell and H. Roberts (eds) *Social Researching*, London: Routledge and Kegan Paul.

Hardy, B. (1986) 'Towards a poetics of fiction: an approach through narrative', in M. Meek, A. Warlow, and G. Barton (eds) *The Cool Web: The Patterns of Children's Reading*, London: Bodley Head.

Harland, J. and Kinder, K. (1997) 'Teachers' continuing professional development: framing a model of outcomes', *British Journal of In-Service Education*, 23(1): 71–84.

Hustler D., McNamara O., Howson J., Campbell, A. (2003) 'Teachers' perceptions of CPD: a baseline survey', DfES research report no. 429, London: DfES.

Kemmis, S. (1980) 'The imagination of the case and the Invention of the study', in H. Simons (ed.) *Towards a Science of the Singular*, Norwich: University of East Anglia.

Measor, L. and Sykes, P. (1992) 'Visiting lives: ethics and methodology in life history research', in I. Goodson (ed) *Studying Teachers' Lives*, London: Routledge.

Neisser, U. and Fivush, R. (eds) (1994) *The Remembering Self*, New York: Cambridge University Press.

O'Brien, J. and Mount, B. (2000) 'Telling new stories: the search for capacity', in J. O'Brien and C.L. O'Brien *A Little Book about Person Centred Planning*, Toronto: Inclusion Press.

O'Brien, J. and O'Brien, C.L. (2000) *A Little Book about Person Centred Planning*, Toronto: Inclusion Press.

Ovens, P. (1999) 'Can Teachers be Developed?', *Journal of In-Service Education*, 25(2): 275–306.

Piper, H. and Simons, H. (2005) 'Ethical responsibility in social research', in B. Somekh and C. Lewin *Research Methods in the Social Sciences*, London: Sage.

Ressler, R.K., Burgess, A.W. and Douglas, J.E. (1988) *Sexual Homicide: Patterns and Motives*, Lanham, MD: Lexington Books.

Smith, R. and Coldron, J. (1999) 'Conditions for learning as a teacher', *Journal of In-Service Education*, 25(2): 245–260.

Somekh, B., Burman, E., Delamont, S., Meyer, J., Payne, M. and Thorpe, R. (2005) 'Research communities in the social sciences', in B. Somekh and C. Lewin *Research Methods in the Social Sciences*, London: Sage.

Winter, R. (1988) 'Fictional critical writing: an approach to case study research by practitioners and for in-service and pre-service teachers work with teachers', in J. Nias and S. Groundwater-Smith (eds) *The Enquiring Teacher*, London: Falmer Press.

Chapter 9

Student voice

Essential testimony for intelligent schools

Susan Groundwater-Smith

Introduction

Increasingly, there is an awareness that we cannot continue to debate the nature of schooling without consulting the consequential stakeholders, the students themselves. During the 1960s the *Observer* newspaper in the UK ran a competition asking children of secondary-school age to design the school of their dreams. Edward Blishen used the 1000 entries to put together a book that clearly indicated the difficulties that students were experiencing with their schools (Blishen, 1967). Some 40 years later the *Guardian* newspaper ran a similar competition, K-12. This time they received 15,000 entries, many of them being multimedia. Again a book resulted from the competition which indicated that not much has changed. In their introduction to the book Burke and Grosvenor (2003) wrote: 'There is a history of not attending to the expressed experience of children within schools; everyday neglect in this sense has become institutional'. While, in the main, it is true that schools rarely consult their students and take them seriously, it is the case that there are schools both in the UK and in Australia where there have been systematic policies and practices that have enabled students' voices to be heard and have even given students agency in designing, investigating, analysing and interpreting studies of learning (Needham and Groundwater-Smith, 2003; Groundwater-Smith and Mockler, 2003; Arnot *et al.*, 2004). That being so, there are serious ethical issues to be considered when schools engage in practitioner inquiry where students become integral to the research. These ethical issues revolve around vulnerability and the extent to which young people may be manipulated or coerced. As well, there are matters of various and competing accountabilities and the ways that these are played out in the many and diffuse practices of the school.

Consultation with students: considering the case

It is a truism to suggest that schools could not exist without their students, but it is also curious that as the key stakeholders in the education enterprise they are rarely consulted about the conditions under which they learn. In effect they live in a kind of 'borderland'. Gloria Anzaldua has written most evocatively of borderlands in her meditation upon the existence of those living on the frontiers between cultures and languages, that is Chicanos in an Anglo culture (Anzaldua, 1987: 11). Culturally determined roles are imposed from the outside and dictate who is acceptable and who is not; what is acceptable and what is not:

> Borders are set up to define the places that are safe and unsafe, to distinguish us from them. A border is a dividing line, a narrow strip along a steep edge. A borderland is a vague and undetermined place created by the emotional residue of an unnatural boundary.

Anzaldua's 'borderlands' are a metaphor for the political and psychological positioning of those denied power. In a similar, if not as heartbreaking a fashion, young people in our schools also occupy a borderland where an unnatural boundary is created between them and those who determine what their experiences will be. Others speak *on* their behalf: they speak *for* them, they speak *about* them, but they rarely speak *with* them. And yet, as Antoine de Saint-Exupery wrote in *The Little Prince*, grown-ups cannot on their own understand the world from the young person's point of view and therefore they need children to explain it to them.

One of the significant dilemmas facing those advocating the need to consult with young people is that, in many cases, it is the young people themselves who are the 'border guards'. As Johnson (2004: 10) has noted in her investigation for the National College of School Leadership, 'school leaders most often refer to elected school councils as examples of pupil participation in their schools'. It is a rare school council that chooses to be transgressive and challenge what is taking place. Rather they work at the behest of those who hold the power. Holdsworth (2005: 7) alerts us to some of the dangers inherent in investing in student leaders at the expense of broader participation:

> I have been concerned that the dominant language has shifted over the years from 'participation' to 'representation' to 'leadership' and that each shift has marked a narrowing of concepts and of increasingly elite ideas.

And yet there are voices who advocate the right of students to be heard, for they are the witnesses to what takes place in schools, both within and outside their classrooms:

> What pupils say about teaching, learning and schooling is not only worth listening to, but provides an important – perhaps the most important – foundation for thinking about ways of improving schools.
>
> (Rudduck *et al*. 1996: 1)

Jean Rudduck, Professor Emeritus at Cambridge University, has long been an advocate of the rights of students to be heard. In naming but of few of her many publications on student voice spanning well over a decade (Rudduck and Flutter, 2000, 2004; Flutter and Rudduck, 2004; MacBeath *et al.*, 2003; Rudduck, 2001, 2002), it is clear that she has an enduring concern for students to be more participative in the decisions that govern the place in which they spend so much of their young lives.

Ruddock actually employs the term 'pupils' to describe young people in schools. In the Australian context the preferred term is 'students', that is intended to invest them with greater agency than the former designation would suggest.

Of course it should not be taken that, if and when they are consulted, young people will necessarily wish for more radical or innovative schooling. Howard and Johnson (2000) found, in the Australian context, that young people who were consulted about the possibility of changing the ways in which the early years of secondary school might be operated in order to assist them in making the transition more effectively generally opted for the status quo. It was argued that because the current conditions were the only ones that they knew and experienced, it was unreasonable to ask them to 'imagine how things might be managed differently, because it is asking them to put their present success at risk' (p. 8). Partly the research results could be attributed to the researchers only seeking the views of 'resilient students'. However, the caution is worth observing in that it raises an interesting ethical point, 'What we are to do if students themselves are the conservative forces?'. This is an issue to which I shall return later in this discussion.

Of course, not all young people wish for things to remain the same. This has been illustrated when they have been more broadly consulted, via the mass media, in an investigation of 'the school I'd like'.

The school I'd like

A concern for listening to students is not a discovery of the twenty-first century. During the 1960s, as noted above, the *Observer* newspaper in the UK ran a competition asking children of secondary-school age to design the school of their dreams. Not only did these young people indicate something of the school they'd like, they also told of the features of their schooling that they were unhappy about, even actively disliked. At that time, one 15-year-old girl wrote that 'the institutions of today are run on the principles of yesterday'. So what has changed?

In the *Guardian* follow-up (see above), the editor of the day, Dea Birkett, summed them up in this way: 'I have never read so much that was so full of complaints and criticisms, of schemes for imaginative innovation, and yet that was, as a whole so very sober' (*Education Guardian*, Tuesday, 5 June, 2001). As observed in the Introduction – but it is worth repeating – Burke and Gosvenor commented: 'There is a history of not attending to the expressed experience of children within schools, everyday neglect in this sense has become institutional'.

Introducing a similar competition, in 2005, the *Sydney Morning Herald*'s then education editor, Linda Doherty, reflected that today's students are very different from those who sat in classrooms decades ago. They are sophisticated users of information and communication technologies, engaged in forms of communication unimaginable in their parents' or teachers' own schooldays. It is certainly the generation that has had the greatest engagement with digital technologies. Today's students have never known life without mobile phones, computers, and voice mail (Chester, 2002); they are globally aware and locally savvy. There is very little that they have not seen or heard through the electronic media that is saturated with explicit messages and vision. Young people may be place bound, but they can operate freely in cyberspace.

Of course such competitions have not been the only ways in which young people have been consulted. In a somewhat different context, two Glasgow school leavers, Craig and Kevin (Jones and Smith, 2004: 17) reported on a two-day event that offered students the opportunity to use multimedia, including making a documentary on schooling. They made a number of telling observations upon both their own and their peers' experiences of learning. They suggested that schooling had changed little from the 1920s classroom that they had been researching. They posed the question:

> Why not ask the pupils what they think would help them most to learn, because they're the ones that are going to learn? Not many pupils of our age have this option; most are conditioned to believe that all the rules laid down are correct. They have been battered with this stuff over the centuries; all these artificial pressures have been put on teenagers. Their views aren't encouraged; instead they are dictated to by teachers who take all the responsibility that shapes their character. Even today, school is not really different from the 1920s. They don't have permission to batter us, but we're still in an institutional straightjacket.

While, in the main, it is true that schools rarely consult their students and take them seriously, it is the case that there are schools in the UK, the USA and in Australia where there have been systematic policies and practices that have enabled students' voices to be heard and have even given students agency in designing, investigating, analysing and interpreting studies of learning (Cook-Sather, 2002; Needham and Groundwater-Smith, 2003; Groundwater-Smith and Mockler, 2003; Arnot *et al.*, 2004; Danby and Farrell, 2004; Johnson, 2004). In Sydney, Australia, a network of schools has been working upon the development of authentic inquiry-based processes that involve students at every point in the research.

The Coalition of Knowledge Building Schools as learning network

The Coalition of Knowledge Building Schools (Groundwater-Smith and Mockler, 2003) has as its purpose:

- developing and enhancing the notion of evidence-based practice
- developing an interactive community of practice using appropriate technologies
- making a contribution to a broader professional knowledge base with respect to educational practice
- building research capability within their own and each other's schools by engaging both teachers and students in the research processes
- sharing methodologies which are appropriate to practitioner enquiry as a means of transforming teacher professional learning.

The processes that it has adopted are:

- developing new practitioner research methods; sharing methodologies which are appropriate to practitioner inquiry
- engaging in cross-researching in member schools
- considering forms of documentation
- reporting and critiquing research
- engaging in collaborative writing and reflection.

Altogether, 13 schools (seven government secondary schools, two government primary schools and four independent schools) meet with and visit each other to fulfil these purposes. They see themselves as 'intelligent schools' as understood by MacGilchrist *et al.* (2004) and believe that a significant component of working intelligently is to attend to the testimony of their students.

To demonstrate the Coalition's commitment to taking account of student voice, two studies will be examined: one in which students were central to the investigation of bullying with a need to develop more proactive academic care policies; the other where students considered their own teachers' learning and how it impacted upon classroom practices.

Countering bullying at Independent Girls' School

Independent Girls' School (IGS) has been a foundation member of the Coalition of Knowledge Building Schools. As such, it has become confident not only in consulting its students regarding various practices within the school but also engaging them in the inquiry processes themselves. While the school has given thought in the past to such matters as bullying and intimidation, it perceived that before moving towards more enduring solutions it was important that further evidence be gathered regarding the ways in which the phenomena are understood, in particular by students, in order to inform the development of resources that can be used by them and by their teachers in addressing the various associated issues.

It was strongly believed that in order to gather this intelligence the principal source of information should be the students themselves. Consequently, a student research programme was formed as one that would assist in the organisation and collection of data, the interpretation of results, the formulation of strategies and the development of resources. In effect, the students would act to validate the operational definition of bullying and its consequences and support teacher professional learning to assist them in addressing some of the associated challenges. Importantly the processes that have been adopted have been embedded into the normal practices of the school through curriculum development resource evaluation and student leadership. In this context 'student leadership' is not a term applying to an elected student body, but a role that students may take – the view is that on different occasions and for varying purposes students will be identified, or identify themselves as leaders. While the undertaking of the project has been multidimensional and far-reaching it can be seen that a study of this kind can be a part of the curriculum and not apart from it.

Strategies adopted by the study were:

1   A website on the school intranet, for use by students, has been instituted and used extensively by students – this site has yielded insight into student perceptions of bullying, its nature and incidence within the school. The website has clear protocols for its use. Students refer to behaviours rather than the names of those perceived to be bullying or being bullied. They are aware that staff responsible for academic care do know their identities, but they are able to use pseudonyms on the website.
2   Student focus groups have been conducted, using information from the Senior School Climate Survey data, in order to provide an enriched and informed perspective from the student point of view. These focus groups have been conducted by trained Year 11 students who have engaged with a significant number of Year 8 and Year 10 students.
3   Students have developed posters for display in various areas of the school in order to raise awareness and understanding of the need for the school community to be one where cooperation is applauded and difference celebrated. These posters have fallen into two categories: the first of these has been at the initiative of the middle school and enjoin cooperation, friendship and the celebration of difference. The second set of posters was developed by the junior school with coaching and support from the older students and featured a similar set of concepts. Another publishing strategy which was enacted was related to gathering designs to support the school's 'Respecting Difference Policy' to be published as a revamped brochure. Students were requested to document and encourage proactive policies. This has been conducted as a 'Speak Out' competition within the middle and senior schools.
4   A number of teaching/learning resources and strategies have been adopted, developed and/or evaluated to be used in relation to affective concerns (relationship building, human skills development). For example an integrated curriculum initiative in personal development, health and physical education (PDHPE), 'The Power in Me', has been designed and enacted. The use of Rigby's maxim 'speaking out makes a difference' as an explicit pedagogical device has been adopted during such occasions as assemblies. The Learning to

Learn programme has been adapted to meet identified needs. The 'Snakes and Ladders of Life Game' has been evaluated by Year 5 in 2004 and Year 6 in 2005 and there has been a multimedia approach to developing further insights about bullying as a behaviour through picture book and film analysis.

5   Student leadership groups have met to discuss the results arising from the various strategies and to recommend ongoing action. A particularly noteworthy issue has been the redesign and refurbishment of the senior student common room in order for interaction to be more open and public.

6   Dance, drama and speech programmes are currently under way. These challenge students to question the 'you can't do anything about it' stance. Students in the junior school and Year 8 Empowerment Programme are involved.

Following an analysis of results that also involved teachers, as practitioner–researchers, and the writer of this chapter who has long been the school's 'researcher-in-residence', a group of Year 11 student leaders convened to discuss their impact on school policies and to develop a PowerPoint presentation that would be used for teacher professional development.

Reflecting on teacher professional learning: Outer Western Comprehensive High School

Outer Western Comprehensive High School (OWCHS) is a government school and is established on Sydney's western fringe. It is a more recent member of the Coalition and joined as a result of its involvement in the Australian Government Quality Teaching Program. Having participated in a number of projects, it could see the merit in terms of consulting students with respect to the ways in which learning could be assisted. Thus it was with some enthusiasm that it agreed to take part in a small pilot study to which students might contribute by considering their teachers' professional learning and the ways in which such learning might be improved.

Altogether 13 students participated, seven girls and six boys from Year 12. The group was observed by an officer from the New South Wales Department of Education and Training Professional Learning Unit and a deputy principal.

When asked to comment on their perception of their teachers as learners and how they learn their skills, the group responded with a list of desirable skills: have rapport with students; be able to listen; be able to handle and control difficult students; have good communication skills; speak clearly; be skilled in presenting concepts in a manner that will facilitate learning; be insightful about identifying students experiencing problems in order to prevent those students being demeaned in front of their peers; be friendly; and finally, have a passion for their work.

They believed their teachers learned by making mistakes and from experience in life and in the classroom. When the information that teachers learned from making mistakes was reported back to the School Principal she smiled, as she had only that day talked at the school assembly of the learning that can arise from making mistakes and the importance of taking risks in learning. Students perceived that extended experience in the classroom enabled the teacher to be less nervous. In response to a question asking them to tell a story about a time when they detected that one of their teachers had learned something new and how it impacted on them, several students recounted in detail occasions when they believed that this had happened and the way that the teacher had applied this new learning in the classroom. They discussed the issue of learning through experience and gave the example of a beginning teacher who, they believed, needed to learn and grow and to accept that negative behaviours are not necessarily a personal attack on her but may require the teacher to work out objectively why students react as they do.

When questioned about whether they were aware when their teachers were attending professional learning events, the students affirmed that their teachers would advise them when they would be away attending courses and often described the course they were attending. They shared several examples of occasions when their teachers returned with lessons enriched from these experiences. They assumed that staff development days were occasions when teachers talked about their students and teaching. In response to 'What kinds of things would you like to see your teachers learn?', students stated that they would like their teachers to be more skilled in behaviour management. They understood the balance that a teacher had to maintain between being friendly and maintaining a professional relationship underpinned by a sense of authority. Students valued teachers who did not 'just put a book in front of you'; they needed interaction. They appreciated teachers who explained the work rather than saying 'just do it'. They wanted their teachers to recognise 'personal learning methods'. However, it was seen that it could be difficult for teachers to reach 'every student when they need to get through the syllabus'.

In this instance, the feedback from the students was intended not only to inform professional learning plans within the school, but also to assist in advising policy more broadly across the system. To this end a number of other schools also participated in this project (for more information see McLelland, 2005). What was revealing was the extent to which the schools themselves responded to the students' perceptions. In the case of OWCHS the information was well received. Consulting students was not new to this school and it was believed that their testimony was dependable and useful. However, as is suggested by the title to McLelland's paper, 'Why should we tell them what we learn?', referring as it does to the teachers whose learning was being discussed, in other areas the desirability of consulting students was questioned.

Consulting students cannot be seen as unproblematic. The process generates a number of challenges and dilemmas which in turn surface some serious ethical concerns.

The challenges and dilemmas of consulting students

Just as Jean Rudduck has given over a considerable part of her academic life to reflecting upon issues surrounding consulting with students, so too has Michael

Fielding devoted much of his time to these concerns (Fielding, 2004). His recent analysis of the very real difficulties in working in this manner reminds us of the range of practical concerns that we must address if we are to move forward:

> [We need to] resist the constant pull for either 'fadism' or 'manipulative incorporation' ... Fadism leads to unrealistic expectations, subsequent marginalisation and the unwitting corrosion of integrity; manipulative incorporation leads to betrayal of hope, resigned exhaustion and the bolstering of an increasingly powerful status quo.
>
> (Fielding, 2004: 296)

He asks a series of penetrating questions, among them:

- How confident are we that our research does not redescribe and reconfigure students in ways that bind them more securely into the fabric of the status quo?
- How clear are we about the use to which the depth and detail of data is likely to be put? Is our more detailed knowledge of what students think and feel largely used to help us control them more effectively?
- Are we sure that our positions of relative power and our own personal and professional interests are not blurring our judgements or shaping our advocacy?

> (Fielding, 2004: 302–304)

In effect we might ask ourselves 'Are we capturing student voice in order to tame the unruly?'. As Cook-Sather (2002: 8) asks in the context of current United States educational reform, are we 'authorising' student perspectives only to later ignore them: 'Most power relationships have no place for listening and actively do not tolerate it because it is very inconvenient: to really listen means to have to respond.'

The more cynical among us might see shades of just this kind of appropriation of student voice in the current work directed towards 'personalised learning' (Hargreaves, 2004: 7). Student voice is seen here as mainly being about

> How students come to play a more active role in their education and schooling as a direct result of teachers becoming more attentive, in sustained and routine ways to what students say about their experience of learning and of school life.

There seems little room here for the possibilities of debate and dissent so strongly advocated by Fielding. Indeed, when addressing dissent in the publication Hargreaves notes:

> Dissent on issues that are of evident importance to students is natural and should always be expected and accepted; it does not have to be ignored or

suppressed. As John MacBeath has suggested, there are in a school so many voices (some of which may not be verbal) that there are harmonies and discords; strident shrieks, soft whispers and silences, both natural and enforced. Replacing cacophony with just the right acoustic balance is the task of leadership.

(Hargreaves, 2004: 9–10)

There is a shadowy elision here. The dialogic encounter may occur, but it will be resolved by those in power, the school leaders; any hint of genuine reciprocity has gone. Is student voice being employed to promote teacher professional development, or to discipline, manage and control both teachers and their students? As Noyes observes (2005: 536) 'Voices are nothing without hearers', the question is, 'Who is doing the listening and to what purpose?'. This brings us, then, to the very significant ethical concerns that require attention in this field of practice.

Ethical concerns

It must first be observed that the ethical concerns of which I write are themselves dilemmas. There are costs and benefits whichever way we turn. If we consult students, we may put them in positions of vulnerability. If we do not consult them, we risk overlooking the important contribution that they can make. If we treat them as vulnerable, we may be patronising them and imagining them to be powerless and irresponsible (Morrow, 2004). If we regard them as invulnerable, we may underestimate their fragility. As Simons (2000) notes, it is a matter of 'damned if you do and damned if you don't'. The fundamental ethical principle is to prevent harm or doing wrong to others; it is a concern to promote the good and to be respectful and fair.

In order to address the ethical concerns in attending to student voice in the intelligent school I pose six questions:

- To what extent are students given the right to exercise informed consent?
- What provision is made to ensure confidentiality and anonymity?
- Who is consulted?
- What are the opportunity costs?
- How is student voice sustained and nurtured?
- How is the information yielded through student voice disseminated and acted upon?

The right to say 'no'

Schools are typically places where students are not asked their permission to participate in whatever is taking place. Indeed they have regulatory influences on children's experiences even when they are home (Danby and Farrell, 2004: 38). They are expected to come to school every day, to write when they are told to write, to calculate when they are told to calculate; to work cooperatively in small groups when they are required to and so on. Informed consent is a fundamental ethical precept, but more often observed in its absence than otherwise. Although parental consent may and should be sought, it is also important that the student is provided with an explanation of the project to make his or her own decision regarding involvement. As Danby and Farrell (2004: 39) documented:

Researcher: How did you feel about actually being asked if you wanted to do it or if you didn't want to do it? [provide consent]
Jacob: I was in heaven.
Researcher: Yeah (laughter) how come?
Jacob: Usually I don't get, uhmm, decisions about those particular things like in school.

Generally, we find that young people are willing participants in school-based inquiry projects, yet they may be easily persuaded and at times naive. It is important that they understand that their participation is voluntary and that they can withdraw.

It is interesting to reflect upon issues related to informed consent when data is being gathered unobtrusively such as was the case in IGS where the postings on the bullying website on the school intranet were made available for the research. Tavani and Moor (2001: 6) in their discussion regarding privacy protection in the context of web-based technologies suggest that the concept of privacy is 'best defined in terms of restricted access, not control … it is fundamentally about protection from intrusion and information gathering by others'. Students were posting their responses anonymously in a password-protected environment. The site's webmaster was able to monitor responses through his knowledge of student passwords and intervened only when some example of the school's etiquette code was transgressed, such as naming a student rather than the behaviour that caused alarm. None of this information was available to the school-based practitioner–researchers or the researcher-in-residence. All the same, this is an area where we have to exercise caution. As Tavani and Moor (2001: 7) observe, the individual flow of information cannot be controlled, but individual protection can. The web is something of a blurred area in this respect: 'In general, diverse private and public situations can be imbedded and overlap each other in complex ways'.

Confidentiality and anonymity

Working with young people as authentic witnesses to their own experiences in school requires that they engage with the researcher(s) in a space that will guarantee their privacy. Even where the research may be being conducted by their peers, it is important that every care is taken to ensure that they are not overheard and their responses commented upon by third parties. Young people need to feel safe and comfortable when their opinions upon what might be quite contentious issues are being sought. This raises some real issues for practitioner–researchers when they know and are familiar with the students with whom they are working. In the focus group discussion conducted at OWCHS it was noted that the Deputy Principal was present. The purpose of this was to continue to build capacity in the school to undertake this kind of inquiry. The students themselves had already taken part in a number of such discussions and appeared at ease. However, when sensitive issues are being discussed protocols need to be in place to ensure that students may respond freely and without fear of subsequent consequences. The litmus test is to ask 'Whose interests are being served?'. Will the study contribute important knowledge 'without appropriating participants' experiences, understandings and even their miseries to serve our ends' (Keddie, 2000: 80–81)? As Christensen (2004: 166) reminds us in the context of children's participation in research 'viewing power as inherent to research emphasises that research is a practice that is part of social life, rather than an external contemplation of it'.

Who is consulted?

Reflecting back on the earlier cited Howard and Johnson study (2000), it was argued that the very fact that they consulted 'resilient' students led to some unintended consequences for their research in that these were students who opted for the status quo because it had served them well. In considering who is consulted in inquiries involving young people, it is important to take account of issues related to equity and social justice. Are only those students who are likely to put a good face on things the ones who meet the researcher? Have some been excluded because they may have difficulties in formulating their ideas? Perhaps they have speech or learning difficulties, or are just being seen as 'difficult'.

Atweh and Bland (2004: 13) remind us that students' voices are not singular. Perspectives will be mediated by factors such as ethnicity, gender, degrees of cultural and social capital, all working and interacting in complex ways. 'Working with students in collaborative research, adults should be conscious of the differential experiences and expertise that each participant brings to the process of collaboration.' Some of these variations can be dealt with through the employment of mixed methods which not only lend authenticity through triangulation but also allow for voices to be expressed through a variety of media such as in the case of IGS where surveys, focus groups, product analysis and a web-based discussion were all part of the data set.

Opportunity costs

Some studies will take a considerable amount of student time. Good relationships need to be built in order for trust to be established. This is time away from other opportunities. Students need to feel that their contribution has been worthwhile. In the IGS study it was possible to embed a number of data collection strategies into the curriculum itself. Consequently, when students were engaged in developing their information literacy skills they conducted their searches around some of the key questions that the study was investigating. Similarly, they evaluated various visual and written texts as a normal part of classroom practice.

Sustaining student voice

Practitioner–researchers who work with students to provide the conditions that allow them to be heard and respected know well that the process is not one with which to be lightly engaged. It is not a tap to be turned off and on, but rather a continuous and developmental process. There are serious ethical questions to be asked with respect to raising expectations that consultation with students will be ongoing and embedded in the culture of the school. If this is to occur, then schools also need to have ongoing plans for ways in which they can sustain student voice inquiry. Fielding and Bragg (2003: 41) advocate developing students' roles, developing the identity of the work, and involving different staff and developing staff roles. As one Year 10 researcher in their Students as Researchers Project put it:

> We'd like to see the present Year 9 training up new students like we did, so we're continually developing students throughout the year groups on research and presentations … We shouldn't be the main people in this because we're eventually going to go. If we take control, they won't know where to start, we need to make sure they have the skills.
>
> (Year 10 researcher)

Similarly, continuity is dependent upon staff commitment. Kaye Johnson, Principal of Woodville Primary School in South Australia, has been working with young students in her current school for three years, having done so previously for a number of years in prior appointments. She argues that it has taken three years of strategic action to introduce a culture that enables authentic student participation. However, she notes that 'Although an evenly paced, sequential approach to student participation has been in practice for three years, a significant proportion of staff has not participated in all of it' (Johnson, 2005: 47).

Nurturing an inquiring school culture and the capabilities of those within it to fully participate is clearly a significant but warranted challenge.

Dissemination and action

Finally, in reflecting upon the ethical dimensions of listening to student voice in the intelligent school, it is vital that the matter of how studies are to be disseminated and then acted upon is deeply considered. According to Dewey (1916: 87), education in a democratic society is neither for the individual alone or for the society alone. It is for both. It is 'a mode of conjoint communicated experiences' and rests upon principles of communication whereby the responsibility for learning is a whole-hearted endeavour in which all participate in the interests of decency and democracy. It would be an abrogation of the very tenets upon which student voice is developed, if the inquiries to which they had contributed were distorted or withheld. Dissemination of results must be based upon the kind of dialogic encounter so passionately argued for by Fielding (2004). Similarly, unsettling as it might be, actions arising from the inquiries must be clear and transparent. If students indicate that they have consistently experienced negative conditions for learning, then those conditions must change. If students have been enabled to argue that they have a greater need to participate in decision-making, then some kind of provision for them to be so treated must be put into place. Otherwise the kind of cynicism that Alderson (2000) writes of will be bound to flourish.

Conclusion

Early in this chapter I turned to Gloria Anzaldua who has written so evocatively of borderlands. I found it a powerful metaphor for reflecting upon our need to be more inclusive of student voice when considering the educational landscape. In turning back to an interview with Anzaldua I noted:

> What surprised me most was that the metaphor of the borderlands speaks to its time much more than I thought it would. So that it's being taken up by different people who are in different disciplines, who are in different countries. … What it does is thrill me and validate me as a writer that people can take my images or ideas and work them out in their own way and write their own theories and their own books.
>
> (Anzaldua in Reuman, 2000)

Student engagement in practitioner inquiry in educational research may seem a far cry from the new mestiza, but the social geography of the school is one where many borders, both visible and obscured apply. Moving in relationships from power *over* students, to power *with* students is no easy matter; but if the consequence is that the borders are more permeable and the interests more mutual, then the effort will have been worth the game.

References

Alderson, P. (2000) 'School pupils' views on school councils and daily life at school', *Children and Society*, 14(2) 121–134.

Anzaldua, G. (1987) *Borderlands/La Frontera: The New Mestiza*, San Francisco, CA: Aunt Lute Books.

Arnot, M., McIntyre, D., Pedder, D. and Reay, D. (2004) *Consultation in the Classroom: Developing Dialogue about Teaching and Learning*, Cambridge: Pearson Publishing.

Atweh, B. and Bland, D. (2004) 'Problematics in young people as researchers: visions and voices', paper presented to the social Change in the 21st Century Conference, Centre for Social Change Research, QUT, 29th October.

Blishen, E. (ed.) (1967) *The School that I'd Like*, England: Penguin Education Special.

Burke, C. and Grosvenor, I. (2003) *The School I'd Like: Children and Young People's Reflections on an Education in the 21st Century*, London: Routledge Falmer.

Chester, E. (2002) *Employing Generation Why?*, Colorado: Tucker House Books.

Christensen, P. (2004) 'Children's participation in ethnographic research: issues of power and representation', *Children and Society*, 18(2) 165–176.

Cook-Sather, A. (2002) 'Authorizing students' perspectives: toward trust, dialogue and change in education', *Educational Researcher*, 31(4) 3–14.

Danby, S. and Farrell, A. (2004) 'Accounting for young children's competence in educational research: new perspectives on research ethics', *The Australian Educational Researcher*, 31(3) 35–48.

Dewey, J. (1916) *Democracy and Education*, New York: Macmillan.

Fielding, M. (2004) 'Transformative approaches to student voice: theoretical underpinnings, recalcitrant realities', *British Educational Research Journal*, 30(2) 295–311.

Fielding, M. and Bragg, S. (2003) *Students as Researchers: Making a Difference*, London: Pearson Publishing.

Flutter, J. and Rudduck, J. (2004) *Consulting Pupils: What's in it for Schools?* London: RoutledgeFalmer.

Groundwater-Smith, S. and Mockler, N. (2003) *Learning to Listen: Listening to Learn*, Sydney: University of Sydney and MLC School.

Hargreaves, D. (2004) *Personalised Learning – 2: Student Voice and Assessment for Learning*, London: Specialist Schools Trust.

Holdsworth, R. (2005) (ed.) *Student Councils and Beyond*, Northcote, Victoria: Connect.

Howard, S. and Johnson, B. (2000) 'Transitions from primary to secondary school: possibilities and paradoxes', paper presented to the Australian Association for Research in Education Annual Conference, Sydney, December.

Johnson, K. (2004) 'Children's voices: pupil leadership in primary schools', *International Research Associate Perspectives*, Nottingham: National College for School Leadership, Summer edition.

Johnson, K. (2005) 'Students' voices: strategies for promoting student participation in primary schools', in R. Holdsworth (ed.) *Student Councils and Beyond*, Northcote, Victoria: Connect, pp. 44–47.

Jones, C. and Smith, K. (2004) 'Listening to the learner', in M. Selinger (ed.) *Connected Schools*, London: Premium Publishing, pp. 16–25.

Keddie, A. (2000) 'Research with young children: some ethical considerations', *Journal of Educational Enquiry*, 1(2): 72–81.

MacBeath, J., Demetriou, H., Rudduck, J. and Myers, K. (2003) *Consulting Pupils: A Toolkit for Teachers*, London: Pearson Publishing.

MacGilchrist, B., Myers, K., and Reed, J. (2004) *The Intelligent School* (2nd edn), London: Sage Publications.

McLelland, M. (2005) 'Why should we tell them what we learn?', paper presented at the International Practitioner Research/CARN Conference, Utrecht, 4–6 November.

Morrow, V. (2004) 'The ethics of social research with children and young people – an overview'. Available online at www.ciimu.org/wellchi/reports/wsh1/pdfs/pdf%20 securitzats/morrows.pdf (accessed 30 September 2005).

Needham, K. and Groundwater-Smith, S. (2003) 'Using student voice to inform', School Improvement Paper presented to International Congress for School Effectiveness and Improvement Sydney, January.

Noyes, A. (2005) 'Pupil voice: purpose, power and the possibilities for democratic schooling: a thematic review', in *British Educational Research Journal*, 31(4) 533–540.

Reuman, A. (2000) 'Coming into play: an interview with Gloria Anzaldua'. Available on line at www.findarticles.c om/p/articles/mi_m 2278/is_2_25/ ai_ 67532171/#continue (accessed 5 October 2005).

Rudduck, J. (2001) 'Students and school improvement: "transcending the cramped conditions of the time",' *Improving Schools*, 4(2): 7–16.

Rudduck, J. (2002) 'The transformative potential of consulting young people about teaching learning and schooling', *Scottish Educational Review*, 34(2): 123–137.

Rudduck, J. and Flutter, J. (2000) 'Pupil participation and pupil perspective: "carving a new order of experience",' *Cambridge Journal of Education*, 30(1): 75–89.

Rudduck, J. and Flutter, J. (2004) *How to Improve your School: Giving Pupils a Voice*, London: Continuum Press.

Rudduck, J., Chaplain, R. and Wallace, G. (eds) (1996) *School Improvement: What can pupils tell us?*, London: David Fulton.

Simons, H. (2000) 'Damned if you do; damned if you don't: ethical dilemmas in evaluation research', in H. Simons and R. Usher (eds) *Situated Ethics in Educational Research*, London: Routledge.

Tavani, H. and Moor, J. (2001) 'Privacy protection, control of information, and privacy-enhancing technologies', *Computers and Society*, 31(1): 6–11.

Chapter 10

Going round in circles

Key issues in the development of an effective ethical protocol for research involving young children

Caroline Leeson

Introduction

Research with children is generally perceived, rightly or wrongly, as requiring great sensitivity and robust ethical consideration. Proposing to do research with children who reside in the state care system, who are usually viewed as extremely vulnerable, demands protocols that demonstrate higher levels of sensitivity and formidable ethical constraints.

This chapter traces a personal journey towards an effective ethical protocol for research looking at the levels of participation of children and young people in the decision-making processes of the care system. It highlights the many dilemmas and key moments encountered, many of which, frequently, felt like going round in circles. The research project was designed as a co-construction of what it feels like to be a child in care and thus demands a child-centred approach from the researcher, encouraging the children to take a lead in what they wish to talk about and how they wish to be represented. Child-centredness in this piece of research is further supported by involving the children as co-collaborators, by continuously reflecting on whether questions asked and materials used are appropriate and by maintaining an awareness of the researcher as an adult in the child's world.

This approach is not without ethical controversy. How is the researcher able to maintain objectivity, be sensitive to any distress and satisfy the anxieties of the adult gatekeepers?

This chapter seeks to explore the dilemmas, obstacles and difficulties when developing an ethical protocol for research with young children. It also seeks to contribute to the current debate concerned with developing real opportunities for the voices of young children, aged four to six years of age, to be heard. The research, from which this chapter has arisen, focuses on the issue of involvement in decision-making processes when children are in the care of the local authority, during court proceedings, subsequent reviews and permanency planning meetings. These are forums where traditionally young children, aged four to six years, have been excluded or marginalised with the voices of caring adults being heard in preference to their own. This is a key area of interest as this is an arena, like no other, where agents of the state, rather than parents or children themselves are deciding children's lives.

There have been several research projects looking at children's ability to take part in such decision-making processes (Blueprint 2004; Thomas, 2000). The results seem to suggest that whilst older children should be empowered to have their views heard, children younger than five are unable to participate in the decision-making process. However, much of this work has looked at the abilities of children over the age of six (Shemmings, 2000; Thomas, 2000), and not engaged children who are younger. Thus, I developed an interest in investigating the following questions.

- Can young children participate fully in these decision-making processes or is this idealistic rhetoric engaged in by the well-meaning?
- Is failing to engage the young child a paternalistic adult concept or misguided altruism, or is it based on sound knowledge and understanding of the cognitive processes of young children?
- What are the implications of failing to promote decision-making skills in the young, for other areas of a child's life?

The research project designed to address these questions was constructed in the following way:

1   Accessing the views of older children, aged eight to 13, establishing the issues relevant to children who have already experienced divorce or care proceedings. This would inform the later stages of research with younger children
2   Interviewing parents and practitioners in this field
3   Working with young children aged four to six using a variety of techniques (Clark and Moss, 2001; Thomas and O'Kane, 1998; Lancaster, 2002)
4   Taking this work back to the first group of children and working with them to analyse and understand how it feels to be a young child in care, faced with these processes. With this group of children, discussing how this work might be disseminated to a wider audience.

In order to understand more fully how it feels to be a child in this position, I felt it important to work to a child-centred agenda, co-constructing the project and, as far as possible, working in collaboration within the cooperative paradigm (Heron, 1998). Acknowledging the child's right for personal autonomy, to make decisions about the research process and the direction it should take, are important facets of the child-centred nature of the research and imperative to be recognised within the ethical protocol for the work. The first stage, working with slightly older children would help to develop a clearer idea of the areas that are relevant to children and which need answers. This group of children would then be actively engaged as co-collaborators in the research process, helping to construct and conduct some of the interviews and activities with the younger children, analysing responses and suggesting ways forward.

This final research plan was quite different from the original intention which had involved interviews with older care-leavers, teenagers and young adults, with opportunities to observe younger children engaged in care planning. Reflecting on this initial plan, I became uncomfortable. Where was the genuine voice of the child? How was I getting *alongside* children (Rogers and Stevens, 1967; Dahlberg and Moss, 2005), listening to their stories and understanding the experience through their eyes, as opposed to the eyes of the adults around them, myself included? I began to question the concept of childhood I was using when planning the research. I came to realise that I was, in fact, seeing the child as an object (Christensen and Prout, 2002), which contradicted my intention. I had to find another way. But a research methodology that meaningfully engaged young children aged four to six years old would be complicated to construct, involving considerable negotiation with several adults in order to gain consent to a process that might be difficult and would require their participation. It would be complex, requiring significant debate and discussion with sensitive attention to detail to satisfy anxieties and demonstrate a structure that takes care of all participants.

In attempting to construct this protocol, I encountered a number of difficult issues that caused me to pause, question my stance and debate the ethical rights and wrongs of possible courses of action. I came to describe these as moments of going round in circles, internal debates about the research project and the ethical dilemmas posed at these key times. These were serious moments, potentially sticking points that created temporary halts, whilst I thought carefully about what I was attempting. This chapter seeks to explore those circular moments, shedding light on the various issues and looking at the resolutions that finally stopped me spinning.

How can the research conform to accepted ethical protocols advocated by various key academic and professional stakeholders?

The first circular voyage was encountered at the beginning of the research. This research was grounded in feminist values of care: a refusal to deceive participants and a desire to redress power imbalances by seeking to empower all involved in the research process (Christians, 2000; Punch, 1998; Edwards and Mauthner, 2002). How could an ethics protocol be developed that reflected the above values? This was a serious issue, as I increasingly felt uncomfortable attempting to fit my purpose into a tailored protocol developed by the University. In order to understand what lay behind this unease, I needed to explore the arguments for and against the existence of ethical codes and protocols, and come to a decision about the implications for my research.

Understanding the ethical imperatives demanded by research communities and establishing a working protocol are essential components of any research project (Aubrey *et al.*, 2000; Miller and Bell, 2002). Researchers are required by their institution or funding bodies to submit detailed ethical protocols that show a systematic and sensitive awareness of a variety of issues that may arise during the research, such as consent, confidentiality and identification of risks (Silverman, 2005). Bronfenbrenner (1952) talks about the need to think through all ethical issues carefully prior to commencing data collection, arguing that trying to do this whilst doing the research has the potential to raise such severe anxieties that the project is unlikely to succeed. Protocols and codes are intended to help individual researchers to ask questions of themselves and their research design to ensure that key ethical issues are addressed. According to Alderson (2004), such issues include:

- respect and justice – doing good research because it is right to do so
- upholding the rights of the participants – effective listening to all who are taking part, especially children
- best outcome – balancing the costs and benefits for all who will experience the impact of the research.

Thus, the intention is that ethical codes should offer guidance on how to plan, instigate and develop research projects, focusing attention on the philosophical stance taken and on any individual issues considered.

However, Punch (1998: 157) argues that slavish adherence to ethical codes can limit rather than enhance research. He feels researchers should 'just get on with it', pausing for thought before commencing and maintaining that thoughtfulness throughout the process, rather than trying to fit their work into a particular mode to meet the demands of funding bodies and educational institutions:

'I would warn against leaning too far toward a highly restrictive model for research that serves to prevent academics from exploring complex social realities that are not always amenable to more formal methods.'

Thus, it could be argued that ethical codes may prevent rather than permit action, stifling research creativity by setting a rigid agenda before fieldwork commences. Dahlberg and Moss (2005) suggest that ethics cannot deal with certainties. Ethical questions are ambivalent and uncertain, often having to be addressed in the field, so they are contextual, emergent and situational, dependent upon the relationship between the researcher and the participants and what is mutually discovered through the process. Thus, researchers need to be flexible in their approaches, prepared to work reflexively in the field (Etherington, 2004) and to acknowledge that additional skills, such as effective listening and caring for the people before them are essential parts of the ethical researcher's tool bag (Dahlberg and Moss, 2005).

But protocols and codes exist for very good reasons. They have been developed over many years, most notably since the Second World War and the revelations about Nazi atrocities (Aubrey *et al.*, 2000). Such protocols and codes are 'universalist' in nature (Dahlberg and Moss, 2005), with clear distinctions between right and wrong and an acknowledgement of obligations and rights as two sides of the same coin. Dahlberg and Moss (2005) would much rather reject the use of such protocols, described as calculative and based on rational thinking, to concentrate instead on personal codes that take responsibility for the 'other' and have respect for otherness. Small (2001: 391) agrees, arguing that protocols 'take over the moral responsibility that each researcher should have for his or her behaviour'.

This should lead to a more intuitive approach to ethics ensuring that each individual piece of work is thought through carefully in terms of its own needs, rather than being fitted into a prescriptive pattern of requirements. According to these arguments, prescriptive, 'pro forma' protocols may be viewed as failing to meet the expressed aim of protecting participants from experiencing harm whilst engaged in research by taking too rigid a stance from the start and not encouraging the degree of reflexivity required to take care of all participants.

An additional difficulty with 'pro forma' protocols is they rarely address the issue of doing research with children as active participants in the process. The Nuremberg Code of 1947, agreed after the war, focused on research with adults, assuming that children were too immature to be involved (Alderson, 2004). The increasing interest in collaborative research with young children, inevitably includes a discourse on ethics (Alderson, 2004; Dahlberg and Moss, 2005; Christensen and Prout, 2002), raising a fundamental question: should there be different ethical protocols or codes for children and for adults? Key writers appear to argue this should be the case (Allmark, 2002; Alderson and Morrow, 2004). Aubrey *et al.* (2000) argue that research with young children should involve increased sensitivity as their age and level of cognitive ability require that additional thought must be given to how to inform them about the aims of research in ways they can understand:

> It may be impossible to inform young children fully about the research, so their consent may seem more like exploitation. Further, because most children are very trusting and wish to please adults, it is often difficult to know if they feel comfortable both with what is being asked of them and with the person who is asking, who may be relatively unfamiliar.
>
> Aubrey *et al.* (2000: 164)

This raises the question as to whether young children can differentiate between their own interests and those of others. I am not sure children are so different from adults that they require special ethical considerations. Christensen and Prout (2002) suggest that it is the researcher's own attitudes towards children and their competence or ability to be engaged in research that affects the way projects are designed and ethical protocols are drawn up:

> ... the perspective on children that a researcher works with has important implications for his or her research practice. It influences the choice of methods (including the researcher's role), the analysis and interpretation of data as well as ethical practice.
>
> (Christensen and Prout, 2002: 481)

They advise a practice of 'ethical symmetry', where ethics is regarded as a continuum where all features of the research project and the needs of the participants, children, adults, children or adults with any special needs are acknowledged. Any differences between participants, their ages or levels of competency, should be allowed to emerge rather than their being assumed. Each research proposal is thus considered on its merits rather than following differentiated 'pro forma' protocols, one for adults and one for children. The protocol for this piece of work needed to reflect a view of young children as competent, to encompass an organic ability to adapt to changes in circumstance and consider each individual participant's needs and requirements. Therefore, considerable personal exploration and thought had to be invested to ensure there was no loss or compromise of those values as I established the research programme. I was determined to take an ethical stance throughout the research (Birch and Miller, 2002), to actively listen to my participants at all times (Dahlberg and Moss, 2005) and to ensure that the research was collaborative (Heron, 1998) and empowering (Edwards and Mauthner, 2002).

Structuring the research to facilitate the authentic voice of the younger child

As discussed above, the original idea was to engage with older care-leavers where questions could be asked about their memories, whether they had participated in decision-making and the impact this level of involvement had made on their lives and their ability to make decisions as they grew up. Younger children would not be asked these questions, but might be observed participating in decision-making meetings.

On closer investigation, this plan showed an underlying assumption that younger children would be less competent than older children and adults in relaying their experiences (Hutchby and Moran-Ellis, 1998) – that age mattered. I began to realise I had created a research project with an adult perspective, regarding young children as vulnerable (Hendrick, 2003), incapable of telling their own stories and understanding what was happening around them. Given the topic area, this was ironic – exhorting others to regard children as competent social actors and doing so through research that treated them as objects (Christensen and Prout, 2002). This was also an issue for the University and other gatekeepers with whom I was in contact. There was also evidence of reluctance, from the University ethics committee and Social Services, to agree to the research on the grounds that young children would not understand what I was doing and therefore would be unable to give their informed consent. With such a focus (assessing children's competency on the basis of their age rather than recognising different maturities and abilities), there would be an inherent danger of excluding younger children on the assumption that they would not yet be sufficiently competent:

> ... our concept of such qualities should not influence ways of approaching children in social science research. It should be open to empirical investigation to

explore the significance of age and status within different contexts and situations, to explore 'doing' rather than 'being'.

(Solberg, 1996: 63–64)

Alderson and Montgomery (1996: 7) suggest that the quality of experience of research participants should be considered as a guide to involvement: 'Experience is far more salient than age in determining children's understanding'. They elaborate, arguing from research with children making health care choices, that the child receiving treatment is in a better position to describe what is happening to them, how it feels and what they would prefer, than the healthcare professionals, or even their parents. This is an intense experience for them, not an abstract concept and therefore it is important for them to discuss and engage with it. This argument would appear to be pertinent to the experience of inclusion or exclusion in decision-making processes for the young child. Children may have deep feelings about what is happening to them and the researcher needs to find a way of helping them to explore those emotions in ways that are helpful, collaborative and meaningful. It could be argued that young children may not have the 'stock of experience' that adults have, but they probably have significant experience of the area under investigation and it is up to the researcher to help them to find the vocabulary using appropriate methods to facilitate communication and develop an understanding of the child's concepts of the world. This might be viewed as a research design issue – how does one identify the appropriate population for the research question? But it is also an ethical issue as one tries to determine whether this is an appropriate topic for young children to be engaged in thinking about. The difficulty is that there are few ethical guidelines established for researching with young children (Hill, 2005).

Allmark (2002) uses the Royal College of Paediatrics and Child Health (RCPCH) Guidelines, which advocate that research should only be undertaken with children if it cannot be done with adults. Following these guidelines, this piece of research could be done with adults, but would seem to lose some of its power by not engaging with the very group whose views it seeks to explore. Allmark also argues that the impact of participating in research may remain with participants for many years to come. This may have particular significance for young children, especially when examining the quality of relationships with people they are close to, such as parents and social workers. The child may begin to call into question how helpful and supportive a significant adult was when important decisions were being made and this may raise doubts in the child's mind about the relationship. If Allmark is right, then this is likely to have more serious consequences for the younger child who is in a more powerless, dependent role than for an older child or adult who may be able to do something about those feelings and doubts. My ethical protocol, needed, therefore, to show that this issue had been considered and that appropriate safeguards were in place. Finally, I decided to work with two age groups of children, aged four to six and eight to 14, putting more responsibility for collaborative work on the older group, but nevertheless, adopting the same principles when working with the younger children.

Activities would be created to facilitate engagement with the topic. These activities would need to be child-led rather than researcher-led, enabling co-construction and authentic articulation of what they want to say rather than what I want to hear.

How could I avoid causing distress when looking at an experience that was painful and probably traumatic for the child and his/her family? Surely it is unethical to work in this area with such young people?

This was an extremely serious debate that could have spelt the end of the whole process, had it not been resolved. Obviously, any research should attempt to avoid or minimise any upset caused when people are invited to recount or remember experiences. But what if you are talking about something that is distressing in its own right? Experiences of being removed from families, placed in foster care or a children's home, attending court, for example, are all potentially distressing events. With a particular lens of wanting to protect children who are seen as innocents or victims (Hendrick, 2003), it seems difficult to countenance planning a research project looking into areas that may provoke strong emotions that are hard to deal with. Hill (2005) argues that care needs to be taken when looking at such situations with children, as they will already have undergone several interviews looking at their experiences with the professionals working with them. He asks that researchers think very carefully before asking children to relive these events once again and to be very clear on the benefits there may be for them in that circumstance. Attempts to select children who seem able to cope with the demands of working in a group without getting too distressed may lead to bias in the research and deny children the right to self-select and work on something that they feel strongly about. Again, Hill (2005) debates this issue, feeling it is inevitable that the children selected for such research may not be typical of their population. King (1996: 179) addressed the inherent difficulty in deciding to proceed when people become distressed after she found herself intervening in an interview when the respondent became upset:

> Because of the highly personal and interpersonal nature of in-depth interviewing, such enquiry is likely to be more intrusive than most other research methods, and may well open up issues that are highly sensitive for the interviewee. This risk needs to be clearly expressed, and an 'opt-out' clause given in order that the interviewees are made aware that they are not obliged to answer all the questions should they prefer not to, and that they can stop the interview should they so wish.

This raises significant issues when thinking about research with young children. How will they feel about telling an adult they do not wish to answer some questions? The perceived power imbalance between adults and children

(Robinson and Kellett, 2004) and the lens regarding young children as in need of protection (Hendrick, 2003) require that we avoid causing distress at all costs, which could render this piece of research unjustifiable. On the other hand, perpetuating this stance means children are denied any access to knowledge and power, which could also be viewed as abusive. Robinson and Kellett (2004: 93) argue that researchers can explore difficult areas by careful ethical research design: 'Researchers can take seriously power differentials between themselves and children and seek to address these in the design, implementation and dissemination of their work'.

Issues of consent: who is able to give consent and who should give consent?

To maintain a child-centred approach, it would appear axiomatic that the child is the principal consent-giver, but this is an ethical, legal and moral minefield. On the ethical side, there are issues of competency and understanding – how does the researcher know that the child understands the project sufficiently to be able to give informed consent (Cocks, 2006)? On the legal side, there is the issue of whether the courts regard children as competent to give consent. The Gillick ruling (Gillick v. W. Norfolk, 1985) makes legal demands on all practitioners to make decisions about a child or young person's competency to consent. The assumption with this ruling was that very young children would be unlikely to be seen as Gillick competent (Masson, 2004) and therefore would require the consent of a parent or adult with parental responsibility (DoH, 1989, s3 (1)). Masson (2004: 48) points out that adults making decisions about competency will be operating from their own concepts of childhood and may favour a judgement of incompetence with regard to very young children as they seek to protect them:

> Where information about research in general and the particular study can be given clearly and simply, quite young children are able to consent to take part. In order to give a valid consent, a child needs to understand the nature of his or her engagement with the researcher and how that differs from that of other adults who may seek information in order to take decisions about or for that child.

Legally, parents are responsible for their children (DoH, 1989, s3 (1)) and therefore have a right to be informed about, and give consent to, research being done with their children. This is seen as diminishing with age, older children being able to give their consent as they move towards adulthood and establish a right to self-determination. It could be argued that this rule perpetuates the belief underpinning the Gillick ruling that younger children are incompetent. This renders them potentially defenceless, as they are not able to offer their opinion or thoughts without another's permission. Schenk and Williamson (2005: 4), in their ethical guidelines for research with children, consider that researchers working with children under the age of consent (16 in the UK) should obtain parental consent prior to asking the children if they wish to take part. They group all children under 16 in a category of people with diminished capacity and therefore in need of special protection.

There is a serious issue of power here – the power of adults over children means we have to have safeguards to ensure that the power is not used irresponsibly or dangerously (Alderson and Morrow, 2004; Homan, 2001; Williamson *et al.*, 2005). But this power might also be used to deny children the right to be heard (Robinson and Kellet, 2004). Nieuwenhuys (2004: 212) highlights the dependency of children on adults and the importance of acknowledging this at the beginning of any research project: 'Children's dependency on adults for the fulfilment of even simple needs is so great that one can hardly expect them to co-operate in a research programme that does not from the outset address these needs seriously'.

Having worked hard to ensure that the children can understand what they are consenting to, and that all relevant adults agree that this is right and proper, has a researcher created a situation where a child cannot refuse an adult request? How can the situation be created where children feel safe to say 'no' to take part, or to refuse to continue their involvement when it becomes difficult? Williamson *et al.* (2005) demonstrate that it can often be difficult to ascertain full comprehension, that children understand different things by words such as 'harm', 'confidentiality' and 'child protection' that are used in research. This means that it could be difficult to ensure that consent is informed and freely given when working with young children.

In the case of children in care, the persons with parental responsibility may include the child's social worker as well as either or both parents. This makes gaining their consent potentially complicated and time-consuming. It also keeps the child at arms length, further removed from giving consent on their own behalf. Maintaining a stance of being child-centred and working in a cooperative paradigm (Heron, 1998), I emphasised the importance of the child's active consent to take part, whilst acknowledging that gatekeepers would expect their consent and that of the parents to be gained first. All stakeholders were encouraged to think positively about the children in their care, to think widely rather than narrowly when identifying possible participants in order that a situation would occur whereby the children could choose to be involved for themselves. Recruitment would therefore be 'opt in' rather than 'opt out' (Alderson and Morrow, 2004), and children would be encouraged to think for themselves whether they wished to join in.

Can all discussions and activities be kept confidential and anonymous?

The area under investigation is one fraught with potential difficulties in terms of child protection, potential evidence for court hearings (Masson, 2004) and the issue of responsibility towards gatekeeping adults. Whilst it may be possible to guarantee anonymity in documentation and in the final report, neither anonymity nor confidentiality could be guaranteed in the interview situation as disclosures may be made that need further action, i.e. abuse allegations. However, this could be problematic when trying to be clear with young children about the parameters of the research prior to gaining their consent. As previously stated, research by Williamson *et al.* (2005) found that children interpreted the words differently and, therefore, might not understand researchers' attempts to explain instances of when they may have to deny confidentiality because of concerns for the child's safety. Also, neither anonymity nor confidentiality could be guaranteed in any group work situation. Group rules might be established involving not talking about each other's comments and experiences outside the group, but there is obviously no control other than self-control to ensure that this happens. It is difficult to predict how children, or any research participant, might act in the future, after being involved in a research process. All a researcher can do is remain ethical in the choice of participants and maintain an ethical stance throughout, picking up any cues that raise concern, and responding responsibly and effectively.

What sort of relationship will I have with the children I am working with?

The piece of research I am referring to requires considerable close contact with adults and children who have been through painful experiences that have significantly shaped their lives. Therefore, contact needs to be carefully and sensitively planned and executed to minimise pain and help to make sense of what has happened. This involves the creation and development of meaningful relationships that allow people to feel safe to discuss such sensitive matters; relationships that are founded on guiding principles of genuineness, trust and empathy (Rogers and Stevens, 1967). The relationship would be based on the children's perceptions of me, not only as a researcher, but also as a person, a tangible individual with whom they can identify and work (Rogers and Stevens, 1967).

This begins to move away from the traditional idea of researchers being on the outside of their research, with little or no impact on the matter under discussion and reportage that is not written in the first person (Richardson, 1996). The role of researcher is, nevertheless, fundamentally different from that of a social worker, a previous role held by me. As a researcher, I am involved in the children's lives for a very short time, looking at a specific issue I have generated an interest in (Milner and O'Bryne, 2002), rather than being there to help them with their lives (Aubrey *et al.*, 2000). My aim, therefore, must be to make a different type of relationship from one normally seen between a social worker and a child where it is most commonly related to the agenda of the child and his/her family (Milner and O'Bryne, 2002). The research relationship is thus formed for a specific, time-limited, purpose and should not enter into the areas of therapy or advocacy, as this may blur the relationship and become unethical (Aubrey *et al.*, 2000; King, 1996). By working with the children as collaborators, seeking to follow their agendas and facilitate their exploration of their own experiences, the research thus moves towards the paradigm of cooperative inquiry (Heron, 1998) where researchers and researched work together to develop the research project and attempts are made to create a relationship that is equal and active. This raises an important question about the boundaries between researchers and researched. King (1996) explores this, suggesting researchers ask themselves questions such as whether they are going to self-disclose, whether this is appropriate to the research being undertaken and whether to encourage the development of long-term relationships. This self-disclosure is especially difficult to maintain, particularly when looking at powerful life events that evoke strong emotions. King acknowledges this, suggesting the development of a stance of self-aware-ness and acceptance in order to promote empowerment of participants in the research process. Duncombe and Jessop (2002) raise similar questions demon-strating, through their own work, a sense of discomfort at having created a close relationship that they cannot sustain. Taking all of this into account, clarity of purpose appeared most appropriate. I had a need to ensure that participants are aware that the relationship would be time limited and that there would be no con-tact following its termination. This position requires significant support as looking at such an intimate topic is bound to create close relationships. Therefore the role of research supervisors as consultants to discuss potential over-identification and over-involvement, is crucial. I was also resolved to con-tinue to clarify the limits of the relationship throughout the research and not assume the message was still loud and clear, several weeks down the line.

Conclusion

The design of the ethics underpinning this research required close examination of important issues and personal values and led me to seek to develop a better under-standing of my perceptions of childhood and of doing collaborative research with young children. It had been thought through thoroughly with key issues identified and debated in full. It was with some reluctance that I had embarked on fitting my purpose within the established format required by the University. By exploring the reasons for my reluctance as well as other issues that confused or concerned me, I have begun to develop a clearer perspective on the role of ethics both in gen-eral and particular and begun to understand my own ethical stance. An ethical protocol has been designed that enables gatekeepers to feel secure in allowing me access to the children they are responsible for. It allows for constant review of the appropriateness and advisability of some of the decisions made at the outset, per-mitting changes to be made in consultation with the research co-constructors, namely the children, any gatekeepers and the supervisory team. I would recom-mend to fellow researchers that they do not allow themselves to be put off by the anxieties of others, but challenge the basis of those fears, to investigate the model of children that lies at the heart. I would also recommend researchers to be ethi-cally authentic, to maintain an internal dialogue that keeps questions of ethics and good practice at the forefront of the decision-making process. This will assist in developing a real sense of 'the other' with questions about responsibility, power sharing, co-construction and voice.

I would argue that young children should be involved in such research into difficult areas, and that to deny them their voice, with misguided attempts to protect them from distress or concerns over their ability to understand the concept of informed consent, renders them powerless and more vulnerable (Williamson *et al.*, 2005). Researchers such as Alderson (2000), Lancaster (2002), Moss and Petrie (2002), and Thomas and O'Kane (1998) have all shown young children meaningfully interacting with their environment, making sense of what is happening around them and having clear judgements, values and attitudes to voice. They are not passive recipients, people in waiting or citizens in potentia (James and James, 2004: 35), but active participants in their world. Ignoring their voices, or preventing them from being heard through over-zealous notions of protection, is both dangerous and manifestly unfair (Hendrick, 2003; John, 2003).

Thus, it is up to adults to create the optimum conditions for effective listening, not for children to find the way to say what they want to say, or what researchers want them to say.

References

Alderson, P. (2000) *Young Children's Rights: Exploring Beliefs, Principles and Practice*, London: Jessica Kingsley Publishers.

Alderson P. (2004) 'Ethics', in S. Fraser, V. Lewis, S. Ding, M. Keller and C. Robinson (eds) *Doing Research with Children and Young People*, London: Sage.

Alderson, P. and Montgomery, J. (1996) *Health Care Choices: Making Decisions with Children*, London: IPPR.

Alderson, P. and Morrow, V. (2004) *Ethics, Social Research and Consulting with Children and Young People*, Essex: Barnardo's.

Allmark, P. (2002) 'The ethics of research with children', *Nurse Researcher* 10(2): 7–20.

Aubrey, C. David, T. Godfrey, R. and Thompson, L. (2000) *Early Childhood Educational Research*, London: Routledge.

Birch, M. and Miller, T. (2002) 'Encouraging participation: ethics and responsibilities', in M. Mauthner, M. Birch, J. Jessop and T. Miller (eds) *Ethics in Qualitative Research*, London: Sage.

Blueprint (2004) *Start with the Child, Stay with the Child*, London: VCC.

Bronfenbrenner, U. (1952) 'Principles of professional ethics', *American Psychologist*, 7(2): 452–455.

Christensen, P. and Prout, A. (2002) 'Working with ethical symmetry in social research with children', *Childhood*, 9(4): 477–497.

Christians, C.G. (2000) 'Ethics and politics in qualitative research', in N.K. Denzin and Y.S. Lincoln (eds) *Handbook of Qualitative Research* (2nd edn), California: Sage.

Clark, A. and Moss, P. (2001) *Listening to Young Children: The Mosaic Approach*, Norwich: National Children's Bureau.

Cocks, A. (2006) 'The ethical maze: finding an inclusive path towards gaining children's agreement to research participation', *Childhood*, 13(2): 247–266.

Dahlberg, G. and Moss, P. (2005) *Ethics and Politics in Early Childhood Education*, Abingdon: RoutledgeFalmer.

DoH (Department of Health) (1989) *The Children Act*. London: HMSO.

Duncombe, J. and Jessop, J. (2002) '"Doing rapport" and the ethics of "faking friendship"', in M. Mauthner, M. Birch, J. Jessop, and T. Miller (eds) *Ethics in Qualitative Research*. London: Sage.

Edwards, R. and Mauthner, M. (2002) 'Ethics and Feminist Research', in M. Mauthner, M. Birch, J. Jessop, and T. Miller (eds) *Ethics in Qualitative Research*, London: Sage.

Etherington, K. (2004) B*ecoming a Reflexive Researcher: Using Ourselves in Research*, London: Jessica Kingsley Publishers.

Gillick v. W. Norfolk and Wisbech AHA (1985) AC115.

Hendrick, H. (2003) *Child Welfare: Historical Dimensions, Contemporary Debate*, Southampton: Policy Press.

Heron, J. (1998) *Co-operative Inquiry: Research into the Human Condition*, London: Sage.

Hill, M. (2005) 'Ethical considerations in researching children's experiences', in S. Greene and D. Hogan (Eds) *Researching Children's Experience: Approaches and Methods*, London: Sage.

Homan, R. (2001) 'The principle of assumed consent: the ethics of gatekeeping', *Journal of Philosophy of Education*, 35(3): 329–343.

Hutchby, I. and Moran-Ellis, J. (1998) *Children and Social Competence: Arenas of Action*, Guildford: Falmer Press.

James, A. and James, A. L. (2004) *Constructing Childhood: Theory, Policy and Social Practice*, China: Palgrave Macmillan.

John, M. (2003) *Children's Rights and Power: Gearing Up for a New Century*, London: Jessica Kingsley Publishers.

King, E. (1996) 'The use of the self in qualitative research', in J.T.E. Richardson (ed.) *Handbook of Qualitative Research Methods for Psychology and the Social Sciences*, Leicester: BPS Books.

Lancaster, P. (2002) *Listening to Young Children*, London: National Children's Bureau.

Masson, J. (2004). 'The legal context', in S. Fraser, V. Lewis, S. Ding, M. Keller, and C. Robinson *Doing Research with Children and Young People*, Trowbridge: Open University Press.

Miller, T. and Bell, L. (2002) 'Consenting to what? Issues of access, gate-keeping and "informed" consent', in M. Mauthner, M. Birch, J. Jessop, and T. Miller (eds) *Ethics in Qualitative Research*, London: Sage.

Milner, J. and O'Bryne, P. (2002) *Assessment in Social Work* (2nd edn), Basingstoke: Palgrave Macmillan.

Moss, P. and Petrie, P. (2002) *From Children's Services to Children's Spaces*, Bury St Edmunds: RoutledgeFalmer.

Nieuwenhuys, O. (2004) 'Participatory action research in the majority world', in S. Fraser *et al.* (eds) *Doing Research with Children and Young People*, London: Open University Press.

Punch, M. (1998) 'Politics and ethics in qualitative Research', in N.K. Denzin and Y.S. Lincoln (eds) *The Landscape of Qualitative Research*, California: Sage.

Richardson, J.T.E. (ed.) (1996) *Handbook of Qualitative Research Methods for Psychology and the Social Sciences*, Leicester: BPS Books.

Robinson, C. and Kellett, M. (2004) 'Power' in S. Fraser *et al.* (eds) *Doing Research with Children and Young People*. London: Open University Press.

Rogers, C. and Stevens, B. (1967) *Person to Person, the Problem of Being Human*, USA: Real Person Press.

Schenk, K. and Williamson, J. (2005) 'Ethical approaches to gathering information from children and adolescents', in *International Settings: Guidelines and Resources*, Washington DC: Population Council.

Shemmings, D. (2000) 'Professional attitudes to children's participation', in Decision-making: Dichotomous Accounts and Doctrinal Contests, *Child and Family Social Work*, 5(3): 235–243.

Silverman, D. (2005) *Doing Qualitative Research* (2nd edn), London: Sage.

Small, R. (2001) 'Codes are not enough: What philosophy can contribute to the ethics of educational research', *Journal of Philosophy of Education*, 35(3): 387–406.

Solberg, A. (1996) 'The challenge of child research: from "Being" to "Doing"', in J. Brannen and M. O'Brien (eds) *Children in Families*, Falmer Press: London.

Thomas, N. (2000) *Children, Family and the State: Decision making and Child Participation*, Chippenham: MacMillan Press.

Thomas, N. and O'Kane, C. (1998) *Children and Decision Making*, Wales: University of Wales.

Williamson, E, Goodenough, T., Kent, J. and Ashcroft, R. (2005) 'Conducting research with children: the limits of confidentiality and child protection protocols', *Children and Society*, 19 November, pp. 337–409.

Chapter 11

Behind the vision

Action research, pedagogy and human development

Petra Ponte

Introduction

Action research as a strategy for teachers' knowledge development is often described in terms of 'praxis': development of knowledge through independent and purposeful action. This means that teachers should continually link three areas of knowledge: the ideological, the technological and the empirical areas of knowledge. I will argue in the paper that action research merely serves instrumental aims when theories about pedagogy are reduced to methods or to the technological area of knowledge and theories about ethics are reduced to the ideological area. This reductionism can even cause inadequate practices to persist: an ethical basis for action research needs an explicit theory about the link between the ideological and the technological, in theory and practice. This link has not been made that well in the pragmatic vision of 'pedagogy as method', which has been dominant in the Anglo-Saxon tradition. In the tradition of 'pedagogy as human science', however, which has been more dominant in the European tradition, it has been more common to study the relation between action and underlying assumptions about human development. This ethic of pedagogy could enrich the ethics of justice and critique (based on social theories) which are dominant in the debate about action research. In this chapter I will elaborate my assumption by arguing that teachers' views on human development will have a strong influence on their action research. The confession to a particular view, or at least the consciousness that these outlooks play a role, should not be a matter of personal intuitive preference but a result of a collaborative and rational process of knowledge construction by teachers.

When Carr (1994) asked 'Whatever happened to action research?' and Cochran-Smith and Lytle (1999) warned about the dangers of popularising action research in the field of education, they were both expressing sentiments that many will recognise: concern about the quality of action research and especially about the motives for this type of research. Is action research used for what it should be used and is it used appropriately? Do those engaging in action research ask relevant questions, leading to relevant knowledge and relevant actions? Moreover, what is relevant? Relevant for whom or what and who decides this? These are essentially ethical questions and such questions are not easy to answer, certainly not when action research is being used as a strategy for the professional development of teachers or student teachers, as in in-service and pre-service education. Action research in this context soon degenerates – according to its critics – into a handy, instrumental method for solving immediate problems or for learning from practice, or – the opposite – a handy way to apply academic knowledge in practice; a method that leaves existing inadequate practices as they are. This will certainly be the case when action research is not aligned to the ethical questions as mentioned above. Instead action research should be critical, according to many authors, based on social–philosophical theories such as those of Gadamar (1976) and Habermas (1981). These are prominent theories in the literature discussing the legitimacy of action research, in which the ultimate aim is to establish a democratic, just society. Among the leading scholars in this area are Carr and Kemmis (1997: 224), who concluded their book, *Becoming Critical* by saying,

> If the central aim of education is the critical transmission, interpretation and development of the cultural traditions of our society, then the need for a form of research which focuses its energies and resources on the policies, processes and practices by which this aim is pursued is obvious as well. Emancipatory action research, as a form of critical educational science, provides a means by which the teaching profession and educational research can be reformulated so as to meet these ends.

This chapter contends that action research in education based on social theories could be enriched by pedagogical theories. I am not referring here to 'pedagogy as method', which has been dominant in the Anglo-Saxon tradition. I am referring to 'pedagogy as human science' which was dominant in the continental European tradition until the 1980s. Pedagogy as human science seeks to understand the development of children towards adulthood as well as to contribute to the practice of those who are responsible for helping the children in this process, like parents and teachers.

The bases for pedagogy as human science were in fact laid down as long ago as the seventeenth and eighteenth centuries by Locke (1632–1704) and Rousseau (1712–1778). Locke saw the newborn human child as a sheet of blank paper (*tabula rasa*) on which things learned through the child's upbringing and education would be written. Rousseau pleaded for the child, who was good by nature, to be given a natural upbringing. His view was that the child's development should be protected from harmful and stunting influences in the culture. Educationalists in the Locke tradition reduced the experience of being a child to 'that which not yet is', but through discipline and education must become, as soon as possible, in accordance with the standards of the established ideology of the church or state. Educationalists in the Rousseau tradition felt that the child should develop as soon as possible into a human being who does not allow himself to be guided by any authority other than his own judgment; only in this way could education contribute to a better society. In both cases, being a child is understood from a perspective about what the child is not yet, but should become as quickly as possible (Miedema, 1997: 31). In the humanist pedagogy of the twentieth century, however, being a child was seen as a development process that is always driven from two sides: the environment, especially the parents and teachers, and the drive coming from the child him- or herself to become someone. In this outlook, being a child is seen as a distinct form of human existence with specific qualities and characteristics which clearly distinguish this stage from other stages of life (Langeveld, 1967). The idea that children have a right to a protected youth was described by Dasberg (1975) as '*Grootbrengen door klein-houden*' (raising children by keeping them young). She argued, however, that while the shielding from the adult world had indeed resulted in separate juvenile law, children's literature and child-centred education, it had also isolated children from the adult world; by that children are not prepared for the adult world.

In addition to the humanist movement, the other most influential movements in pedagogy have been: critical pedagogy based on the sociological work of the Frankfurter Schule (Jay, 1973); cultural historical pedagogy and constructivism based on the work of Vygotsky (1971); and empirical pedagogy based on the work of Popper (1972) and Brezinka (1971). It is worthy of note that pragmatism based on the work of the American, Dewey (1984), is also seen as one of the movements within European pedagogy as human science.

There in a nutshell we have a number of important developments in pedagogy as human science. I will return to this later, but it will be clear that, although there is general consensus about the need to raise children towards adulthood, to help them in the process of growing up and gradually growing into society, there is no consensus about what 'raising children' should be or lead to. There is no consensus because definitions of 'raising into adulthood' are based on anthropological, normative assumptions. Conditions, methods and objectives all vary depending on the prevailing views about what it is to be a civilised human being and, moreover, how children can be helped to become such human beings (Thoomes, 2000). It can be assumed, therefore, that teachers' views on human development will have a strong influence on their action research: the issues that are raised, the knowledge that is constructed and the actions that are taken to transform practice. The confession to a particular view, or at least the consciousness that these outlooks play a role, should not be a matter of personal intuitive preference but a result of a collaborative and rational process of knowledge construction by teachers.

The first part of this chapter focuses on praxis as an ethical framework for action research. It is argued that this framework usually consists of three ethics: the ethic of justice, the ethic of critique and the ethic of professional development. I will add a fourth, namely the ethic of pedagogy based on pedagogy as human science. The background to this pedagogical ethic may then be explored, leading to a model for knowledge construction by teachers who are carrying out their action research.

One final remark needs to be made in this introduction. With the exception of empirical pedagogy, continental European pedagogy as human science has been dominated by an interpretative approach. *Geisteswissenschaftliche* pedagogy, for example, is based on hermeneutics and phenomenology; critical pedagogy is strongly oriented on *Handlungs Forschung* (action research). It seems ironic that the dominance of pedagogy as human science (including action research methodologies) in continental Europe stopped at some point in the 1980s, while at the same time there was a revival of interest in action research in the Anglo-Saxon world. It seems reasonable to assume that globalisation and the consequent inevitable dominance of the English language had a role to play in this (Scholte, 2000). That is not a problem in itself, of course, were it not that the dominance of the English language was accompanied by an almost automatic orientation toward the pragmatic Anglo-Saxon literature of that time, especially toward product approaches in curriculum development (see Westbury, 2000). I think it is therefore worth making the effort to explore whether linking the Anglo-Saxon action research tradition and the continental European pedagogy tradition could help to address current concerns about the quality of action research.

Praxis as an ethical framework for action research

The concept of action research as used in this chapter is mainly based on educational action research as a strategy for teachers' professional development. The essence of this research is the simultaneous development and application of knowledge. This means that the construction and use of professional knowledge are aspects of a cyclical process that teachers are themselves responsible for: they use knowledge to achieve certain goals and when using this knowledge they construct new knowledge, which they then use again, and so on. The construction of professional knowledge through such self-reliant and purposeful action via action research is often linked in the literature with the Aristotelian concept of 'praxis' (see, for instance, Grundy, 1995; Carr and Kemmis, 1997). Grundy argues, for example (1998: 40), that, 'Professional knowledge is knowledge that is intrinsically connected with practice. This is not knowledge that informs practice, or that has practical intent, but knowledge, which is embedded in "praxis": reflective knowledge in and through action'.

Following Gadamar (1976) and Habermas (1981), knowledge based on praxis – *phronesis* – can be distinguished from knowledge based on *theory* (modelled predictions of educational reality) and *techné* (potential skills, techniques and strategies). Riedel (1977) – a proponent of pedagogy as human science – stated that technical or theoretical knowledge is not the insight and understanding of the practising teacher, but knowledge itself, knowledge that the teacher could have mastered before practising at all. That is possible because knowledge based on theory and *techné* involves insights and understanding that are surveyable and therefore able to be imparted and explained to others. In that sense they are transferable to students in teacher education (Ponte *et al.*, 2004). The knowledge of a teacher who is acting with a purpose and taking responsibility for his or her own actions is not. It develops through praxis: that is through a situation – limited in time and space – in which teachers intervene purposefully in the reality of others, in this case the pupils. After all, they want pupils to 'learn something' and 'learning something' includes normative choices about what has to be learned and how. According to Schwandt (2001: 207), therefore, praxis demands an intellectual and moral disposition toward right living and the pursuits of human beings and hence a different form of reasoning than is the case with theory or *techné*. Action research can be seen as a form of reasoning in praxis.

The general argument made for action research is often as follows. The reality of educational praxis is complex, changeable and cannot be accurately predicted in advance by academic knowledge. Besides, there is a diversity of academic theories and paradigms; sometimes there is consensus, but more often there is a variety of notions, concepts and findings. This means that teachers' practice cannot be laid down in advance either. Although teachers are bound to a certain extent by the wishes and visions of stakeholders, such as the government, the school, parents and educational science, as they attempt to realise their educational goals, they constantly have to face the question: what in the given circumstances is the best way to act to achieve what is important at the moment? (Stenhouse, 1975; Elliott, 1991). This argument is mainly bound up with a social–democratic agenda (Noffke, 1995). Although there seems to be a consensus in the Anglo-Saxon literature on this social-democratic agenda of practitioner research, different orientations can be found. Dominant in the debate about the action research agenda are the ethic of justice and the ethic of critique, each in a different way related to the ethic of professional development. These are outlined briefly below.

The ethic of justice

The ethic of justice is part of a liberal democratic tradition with a commitment to human freedom, equality of educational opportunity and freedom of belief. It focuses on procedures for making decisions that respect the equal sovereignty of the people (Poliner Shapiro and Stefkovich, 2001: 11). Tolerance, respect and fair treatment are key virtues, not only to make schools more just, but also to educate, so that free and just people emerge from schools. We find this ethic in literature that is based on the work of Stenhouse (1975) and Elliott (1991).

The ethic of critique

The ethic of critique in action research is often grounded in the critical theory of Habermas (1981: see also Carr and Kemmis, 1997; Grundy, 1995; Kemmis, 2005) and other critical theorists. They are suspicious of claims to truth and knowledge and seek to demystify those claims by engaging in critique of ideologies that distort understanding and communication (Poliner Shapiro and Stefkovich, 2001: 11). Their critique of meanings and practices is undertaken for the purpose of transforming society and emancipating individuals from false consciousness. Finally, they are concerned with concrete empirical, economic, social, organisational and political conditions and practices that 'shape human beings as knower and as social agent' (Schwandt, 2001: 44).

The ethic of professionalism

The ethic of professionalism refers to action research as a strategy for professional development and the need for teachers to reflect on education in a research-oriented way. From the ethic of justice perspective, teachers should become professionals addressing the question of how to achieve consensus in interaction with pupils and other stakeholders about what the aims are in given circumstances and the best way to achieve them (see for instance Darling-Hammond and Brandsford, 2005). Their actions are based on shared conferment of meaning and mutual expectations within the educational relationship. From the ethic of critique perspective, teachers should become professionals addressing the question of how they can contribute to social equality and justice in a democratic society (Sachs, 2002). Their actions are based on a critical understanding – acquired through critical dialogue with others – of how teaching contributes or fails to contribute to the emancipation of disadvantaged groups in our society. In both perspectives, lifelong learning is a common ethos for the profession (Day and Sachs, 2003).

An addition: ethic of pedagogy

Although ethics can be viewed from many perspectives, the agenda of action research nevertheless seems to be mainly inspired by the questions, 'What is a good society?', 'What is a good school?' and – based on that – 'What is a good professional?'. These questions are also asked in pedagogical theories, based on the theories of the Frankfurter Schule, and especially those of Habermas. They are asked in an attempt to make pedagogy into a critical social science. The main idea is that growing children can and must be freed from conditions that limit their voice and autonomy in society. Emancipation is the goal, to be achieved through analysis and criticism (Miedema, 1997: 124). The problem for pedagogs with educational science based on the social theories of Habermas, however, is that she cannot provide an answer to the question of how social emancipation can be realised through the concrete education process (Miedema, 1997).

Questions such as 'What is a good society?', 'What is a good school?' and – based on that – 'What is a good professional?' are certainly inspired by commitment to the people that education is ultimately about, namely the pupils. Elliott (1991: 11), for example, argued that the ultimate criterion for action research is the extent to which those engaging in it experience their teaching as something that 'enables or constrains the development of their own power in relation to things that matter'. This kind of commitment is certainly important, but this still does not provide answers to questions like, 'What is our understanding of the children or youngsters we want to teach?', 'What do we see as better education for the children's growth and why?', 'What do we then expect teachers to do on a day-to-day basis with pupils in the name of social and educational goals?'.

Research has also shown that teachers do not usually legitimise their educational actions in the first place because of notions about a better world, doing the good for the human kind (Kemmis, 2005), but mainly because they 'want to do justice to children in their daily practice'. This does not mean that they have no political or social motives beyond their classrooms, but they express these motives mainly through their work and relations with the pupils in their school (Pratt and Associates, 1998). At secondary level, love of the subject and wanting to inspire pupils are additional motives. Teachers' professional identity, according to van Manen (1994: 140), is therefore to be found in the educative relationship with the students, so they will also explore the questions in their action research from that perspective. For example, they ask questions such as 'How can I get dropout among immigrant pupils on the agenda of our school?', 'How can we support mentors in counselling difficult pupils?', 'How can we guide pupils with learning to learn, learning to choose and learning to live?', 'What are the conditions for cooperative learning?', How can I teach ethics to students in the Department of Social Services in a vocational education college?' (these examples are taken from Ponte, 2002). Action research, in other words, will for them be mainly a systematic and empirically based way to identify practical educational problems and to find well-considered practical educational solutions. Any theory about action research as a strategy for the professional development of teachers requires therefore, in my view, explicit linking of an ethic of justice or critique to what I would like to call an 'ethic of pedagogy'. The ethic of pedagogy should focus on the need to maintain an on-going pedagogic relationship in which educators care for the children in their charge, are aware of their responsibility and are also ethically responsible, critically and consciously relating to the surrounding culture and making every effort to enable children to take an effective and responsible part in society in their own way (Thoomes, 2000).

Background to a pedagogical ethic

Although the description above originates in pedagogy as human science, it should also be easy to reconcile with some ideas in the Anglo-Saxon literature on education as moral endeavour (see for instance Noddings, 2002; Hanson, 2001; Goodlad *et al.*, 1990). The important point here, though, is that these theories are not seen as pedagogy as human science and that in the English-language literature pedagogy is usually conceived in a narrow sense as method, addressing therefore the question of what instrumental resources are available with which to shape the teaching. Pedagogy as method is, according to some scholars in the Anglo-Saxon world itself, also dominated by means-to-an-end thinking and often based on a naive child-centred ethos. This ethos proceeds from the assumption that the teacher can allow him- or herself to be guided by the children's needs dissociated from anthropological views of mankind and educational objectives derived from them (Boyd, 1964). Such pedagogy does not, according to these authors, offer a scientific basis to the theory and practice of education, because it does not challenge our views on how life is to be lived and in what direction we should be guiding children. Simon (1999: 38), for example, claimed that 'for a combination of social, political and ideological reasons pedagogy – a scientific basis to the theory and practice of education – has never taken root and flourished in Britain (…) Each [educational] "system", largely self-contained, developed its own specific educational approach, each within its narrowly defined field, and each "appropriate" to its specific social function. In these circumstances the conditions did not and could not exist for the development of an all embracing, universalised, scientific theory of education relating to this practice of teaching'. Simon pleads for a pedagogy which recognises both the power of education to affect human development and the need for the systematisation and structuring of the child's experiences in the educational process. Simon (1999) concurs with van Manen (1994) and Olson (2003) that instead of a pragmatic 'child-centred' ethos – starting from the standpoint of individual differences – a pedagogy is needed that starts from what children have in common as members of the human race and as members of a human society, to establish the general principles of teaching and, in the light of these, to determine what modifications of practice are necessary to meet specific individual needs. Olson (2003) adds to this criticism that contemporary educational theorists who simply put the child at the centre tend to overlook the fact that the church, the nation, science and the economy all have claims in addition to those of parents or the children themselves. Pedagogy has the job of setting out the dimensions on which such debates play out, dimensions that include the entitlements and obligations of states, school systems, individual schools and teachers as well as students, rather than settling on the best methods for achieving specific goals. Pedagogy, according to Olson (2003: 210), should 'not offer methodology;' rather it should 'offer a scientific basis for timely, informed decisions by professionals about balancing the welfare of the individual with the demands of society'.

A central issue in the critiques of these authors seems to be the fact that pedagogy as method does not connect methods to an overall theory of human development, and the role which the family, the school and other institutions have in this development in different social contexts. Boyd in 1964, for example, claimed that in the English-speaking countries in the nineteenth and twentieth centuries 'theories were more or less consigned to plan two' in favour of 'a concentration on mechanical aspects of teaching'; in contrast with the countries on the European continent where theory has always been the 'mainspring of pedagogic debate' (p. 438). So, following the description of van Manen then (1994: 138), one should not confuse the Dutch *pedagogiek* or German *Pädagogik* with the recent popular usage of the term pedagogy in the Anglo-Saxon discourse. These European variations of pedagogy are often translated as 'education' but the Dutch equivalent of education is *onderwijs*, in German *Unterricht*. The Dutch term *pedagogiek* is partly covered by 'education', except that *pedagogiek* takes in the total emotional, intellectual, physical and moral growth of the child for which both parents and teachers or other professionals are responsible. Pedagogy as a human science covers all aspects of knowledge about children, including philosophical, ideological, moral and cultural notions about what is appropriate or inappropriate, good or bad, right or wrong, suitable or less suitable for children's growth toward mature adulthood. According to Benner (1993: 11,12, translation by the author):

> Pedagogy as human science corresponds to a need that is both practical and theoretical, for it supports, for one thing, the gradual problematisation of educational practice. The problematisation of informal educational experience proceeds each time from a situation where the norms and conventions of human co-existence considered by society to be correct become questionable.

With specific reference to education, Benner is pointing to the problematisation of the relationship between child, school and society as the object of pedagogy as human science.

I will attempt to clarify this relationship with reference to the work of Michailova *et al.* (2002). Box 11.1 contains their description of changes in pedagogic thinking before and after the Perestroika period of the early 1990s in Russia.

It is clear from this extract that before Perestroika there was a totalitarian education

---

Box 11.1 Relationship between child, school and society in Russia before and after Perestroika

During Perestroika, coming from a situation where the state controlled every detail of children's' lives as well as those of their parents, a situation in which raising children was seen as a collective enterprise, where human development was seen as an uncritical adaptation of collective values and beliefs, where individuals had no voice at all, Russian educators were forced to explicitly reconceptualise their thinking about human development and this had consequences for their formal education and their teacher education. Research has shown that most Russian teachers are oriented toward group-centred norms and values, which prescribe modelling the child according to the standards of the society. The humanistic norms and values, which require the child to be approached, not from the perspective of 'what (s)he ought to become', but 'what (s)he is like today, how (s)he lives, what (s)he feels, and how this influences him or her at the moment, as well as what implications this has for his/her future' often remain a mere declaration, therefore, and rarely find their way into practice. Consequently the teacher–educator should strive to help the teacher to recall, record and reflect on all situations, actions, and outcomes that involved treating the child not as a student but as a person. The teacher–educator supports reflection aimed at awareness of the potential contradictions between the adult-imposed 'ought to' and the child's' perspective on the very possibility of achieving that.

(based on Michailova *et al.*, 2002: 423)

model based on the idea that the individual is not only subordinated to the collective, but also needs the collective to come to that subordinated position. If we disregard the specific content of this educational model in the former Soviet Union, it can be argued that this idea is based in fact on a deterministic view of human development in keeping with that of John Locke: the child's development is purely a response to external factors – in this case they are the school, the youth movement and the family – which are all controlled by the state. Personal qualities, insights or motives play no role in this. Education is entirely in the service of an external ideal and so the child is defined as what it not yet is but must become as soon as possible: in this case 'a servant of the collective'. It is possible to make a comparison here with the traditional Christian ideals of education and upbringing, where the child is seen as 'sinful by nature' who must be fashioned into 'a God-fearing and God-serving person', based on the view of 'man who desperately needs society as a body transcending the individual in order to keep his sinful nature under control and make living together in a community possible' (De Jager, 1975: 31).

During Perestroika, Michailova *et al.* (2002) with their colleagues at the Institute of Pedagogical Innovations in Moscow (with Oleg Gazman as the main leader) laid the foundations for humanist education in Russian schools, basing their approach on the anthropological view that people do not need the state in order to toe the collective line, but that society needs independent and rational people in order to become democratic. Their institute introduced a state-wide system with specialised teachers who teach in class for ten or so hours a week, and then spend the rest of the time offering 'pedagogical support' to individuals or groups of pupils, their parents, and the other teachers who teach those pupils. This support is based on a carefully elaborated strategy which is intended to lead to an open and democratic relationship between teachers and students. Three views on human development can be derived from their work. In the first place there is the humanist assumption that being a child is a distinct form of human existence with specific qualities and characteristics which clearly distinguish this stage from other stages of life: 'approaching the child not from the perspective of what (s)he ought to become', but 'what (s)he is like today', as they put it. Secondly, they seem, however, to also see education as an instrument to raise independent citizens for a democratic society. This is why, they write, teachers' reflection 'aimed at the realisation of the potential contradictions between the adult-imposed "ought to" and child's perspective on the very possibility of achieving that' is necessary. With this belief they seem to be opposed to the natural education of Rousseau based on a romantic picture of the human being as essentially good by nature. They are more in line with Vygotsky's view (1971) that human development should be understood as an interaction between the activities of the individual on one side and the activities of the social and cultural environment on the other side.

Based on the discussion so far, we can assume that teachers shape their relationships with pupils from different perspectives, and that these different perspectives are connected with their (sometimes implicit) outlook on the relation between an ethic of pedagogy on the one hand and an ethic of justice or critique on the other. It can also be assumed that it is precisely these different perspectives that will determine what problems they identify in their action research and what solutions they find. These assumptions can be briefly illustrated using the basic positions of pedagogy as human science already mentioned, namely the position stemming from Locke's '*tabula rasa*' theory and the position stemming from Rousseau's natural education.

In line with Locke (Boyd, 1964; Miedema, 1997), discipline has to be used to raise children in the norms and values of the culture they live in. Teachers with this perspective who carry out action research will ask themselves questions such as: 'What rules should I get the pupils to follow in order to make them into intellectual people, religious people, or servants of the state or critical citizens?', 'How can I reward and punish pupils so that they follow the rules and how effective are the rules?'. These teachers can give scope to children's voices by, for instance, asking how pupils interpret the rules. They will use this information to formulate the rules more clearly, in order to write on the 'blank sheet' that children, in their view, are, in order to direct them on the right path more effectively. A school could, for example, use an argument like this: 'It is in the interests of society that pupils develop their intellectual capacities and that justifies our calling one pupil "top of the school" every year. What is the best way to organise this and how can we get the pupils involved?'.

In line with Rousseau's natural education (Boyd, 1964; Miedema, 1997), children should be allowed the freedom to develop into rational, religious or critical people. Teachers with this perspective who carry out action research will ask themselves questions such as: 'How can I organise the school environment so that children become aware of the natural good that they have within them?', 'How can I let them experience that lying leads not to punishment, but to discomfort; that effort leads not to "top of the class", but to intrinsic satisfaction?'. These teachers will see enabling children's voices not only as a way to make their teaching more effective, but also as a way to give pupils more control over their own learning process. A school could, for example, use an argument like this: 'It is in the interests of society that pupils develop into rational and independent people. That justifies our allowing pupils to work together, on tasks they have chosen themselves, at their own tempo. What is the best way to do that?'.

Towards a model for knowledge construction by teachers who are carrying out their practitioner research

It remains for me now to answer the question as to how teachers can use their action research to link theories about the relationship between child, school and society with the design of their teaching. As stated in the introduction, making this link should not be a matter of personal intuitive preference but a result of a collaborative and rational process of knowledge construction by teachers. I will now present a model that could facilitate this process. This model is derived from pedagogy as a theory of teaching, which is a branch of pedagogy as human science (Menck, 1999; Simon, 1999; Westbury, 2000). I will explain this pedagogy first before describing the model.

Pedagogy as a theory of teaching is what the German term *Didaktik* and the Dutch term *didaktiek* refer to. Its roots go back to the seventeenth century, when Comenius treated *Didaktik* as a specific pedagogic problem (Blankertz, 1969; Westbury, 2000); that is, a problem for those who are professionally involved in the learning process of children (teachers) in an institutionalised context (schools). After Comenius, *Didaktik* or *didaktiek* continued to develop until well into the twentieth century into a discipline that studied the relationship between child, school and society and – closely associated with that – the relationship between child, teachers and educational content (what is taught).

The idea that the content of the curriculum should be conceived as 'an authoritative selection from cultural traditions that can only become educative as it is interpreted and given life by teachers, who are seen, in their turn as normatively directed by the concept of *Bildung* or formation' (Westbury, 2000: 24) is typical of *Didaktik*. *Bildung* stems originally from a neo-humanist portrayal of mankind, best translated as 'formation', implying both the forming of the personality into a unity as well as the product of this formation, the particular 'formedness' that is represented by the person. Didactics as a branch of pedagogy as human science aspires to offer a framework for reasoning about teaching appropriate for an autonomous professional teacher; a framework which provides teachers with ways of considering the essential what, how and why questions around their teaching of their students in their schools. Pedagogical reasoning in this sense does not, however, begin by asking how students learn or how they can be led towards a body of knowledge (as in the pragmatic approach of pedagogy as method), but by asking what the formative value of teaching and learning is or should be; the formative value of what is learned in cognitive, social, moral and emotional senses, and the formative value of how pupils are taught and how they learn. Here we see a link with the Anglo-Saxon action research tradition. Both approaches are based on the same notion of curriculum, namely the curriculum as a process that teachers put into practice in the classroom or school. Stenhouse had already pointed this link out anyway in 1983. The process-oriented view of the curriculum as education put into practice is at odds with the dominant product-oriented views of the curriculum in the Anglo-Saxon literature, where the emphasis is on the curriculum as a planning document that schools have to implement (Westbury, 2000). Just as with the theory on action research, modern *Didaktik* also stresses the research-oriented role of the teacher in developing the curriculum, for example: 'It celebrates the individuality of each teacher as an active, reflective curriculum maker and theorist rather than seeing the teacher as an agent of a workplace manual of best practices' (Westbury, 2000: 27).

It is important here to note that the *Bildung* concept is often used without any connection with its historical context. It was first formulated by Humboldt for the gymnasia attended by children of the well-off bourgeoisie of the seventeenth and eighteenth centuries. Besides this elite orientation, it was also a philosophical –ideological concept that did not fit into a practically oriented discipline such as modern pedagogy aspired to be in the twentieth and twenty-first centuries. Modern *Didaktik* arose with the growth of education for the masses in the twentieth century and it criticised both the elite character and the abstract philosophical nature of the traditional concept of *Bildung*. Two schools developed out of this criticism at first. The first was embedded in the positivist pedagogy as empirical discipline that strives for objective knowledge about pedagogical issues and the operation of pedagogic strategies. It treats normative statements about the purpose of upbringing and education as unscientific. The second was embedded *Geisteswissenschaftliche* pedagogy, which takes precisely these kind of normative questions as points of reference.

There is in fact also a third school – namely the *didaktiek* that developed within the critical pedagogy based on the philosophy of Habermas which was mentioned earlier. This school developed firstly in response to humanist pedagogy, where concepts such as independence, freedom and self-determination were conceived as relating solely to the pedagogic relationship between teacher/child-raiser and the child's being taught or raised, with no regard for the social context of that relationship. Secondly, it developed in response to empirical pedagogy, which saw no place for normative concepts like independence, freedom and self-determination in a neutral and objective science; a science which should be geared solely to controlling the physical or social reality through knowledge of general laws in the education process. Critical didactics aspires to connect the normative and the empirical into a practice-oriented *Didaktik*, and in so doing to build a bridge between the social theories of Habermas and others of like mind and theories on human development on one side, and available empirical knowledge about education on the other side. Blankertz (1969: 7, translation by the author) said on this:

> My proposition is that the three basic positions of current didactics only appear to compete with each other, that they survive or, in any case, would have a much better chance of surviving through prolific criticism and continual awareness of the problems. For empiricism and theory do not allow themselves to sign up to a continuum, on the contrary, there is a relationship of tension. Not only is specific potential demanded from theory by the control of empirical proof in this relationship of tension; by the same token, theory also criticises reality investigated by empirical methods, including the methods used in doing so.

Riedel (1977) translated this basic principle into a scientific model for *Allgemeine Didaktik und unterrichtliche Praxis*, and his model allows itself to be easily translated into a model for knowledge construction by teachers carrying out action research. Moreover, this model facilitates the placement of an ethic of pedagogy in action research in my opinion. In line with this, one could say that teachers who are carrying out action research should continually link three areas of knowledge.

- The ideological area of knowledge covers the teachers' understanding of norms and values and the objectives based on those norms and values that they want to realise with their pupils. It is therefore concerned with the 'desired effects' of their teaching.
- The technological area of knowledge covers the teachers' understanding of methods, techniques and strategies that they want to use to realise the objectives they have formulated. This means that it is concerned with the 'desired phenomena' of their teaching.
- The empirical area of knowledge covers the teachers' understanding of educational reality. It is concerned with the relationship between 'real phenomena' and 'real effects' in relation to their teaching.

These areas of knowledge are integrated into the concrete professional activities of teachers as praxis, so a distinction can only be made between the ideological, empirical and technological areas in a formal sense (Riedel, 1977). When acting with a purpose and taking responsibility for their own actions in a situation – limited in time and space – intervening purposefully in the reality of others (students), they need to devote proportionate attention to and continuously link the three different areas of knowledge (Ponte *et al.*, 2004). In this way the ethics of justice, critique and pedagogy can be realised in practice. It is easy to make a link with gap theory here, which plays a major role in the literature on action research. Teachers start reasoning about their practice, according to Whitehead (1989), when they experience a discrepancy between what they want to do and what they are actually doing. This could be seen as discrepancy between 'desired phenomena' and 'real phenomena' in their teaching as described above. Only when teachers experience this discrepancy, will they see the need for change (see also Elliott, 1991; Noffke, 1995). The gap between 'desired effects' and 'real effects' of their actions can be explicitly added. The connection between the three areas of knowledge in relation to real and desired phenomena and effects is presented in Figure 11.1. I have added two more components to this figure, namely tasks and communication, which I will now briefly explain.

According to this model, teachers acquire knowledge in the three areas by actually carrying out various 'tasks'. Here these tasks could be formulated in terms of action research models developed by, for example, Stenhouse (1975), Elliott (1991) or Carr and Kemmis (1997). Teachers, however, not only have to be concerned with the quality of tasks in the sense of rules or procedures to be followed, but also with qualities in the sense of aims to be realised. What is important here is that in following rules or procedures teachers can 'get it wrong' and be corrected, but in realising their aims they can 'do badly' (for the good of human kind) and be called to account by others (their facilitators, critical friends,

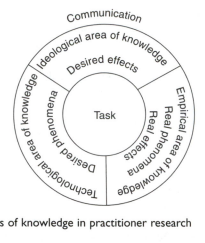

Figure 11.1 Three areas of knowledge in practitioner research

students). Teachers, therefore, do action research by communicating with others about the knowledge that they are constructing in the three areas of knowledge and the tasks that lead to that knowledge construction (Ponte, 2002).

Conclusion

In this article I have only been able to make very general links between the thinking in pedagogy as human science and the ethics of action research. These links are also rather schematic, while teachers will not always be able to act in accordance with these frameworks of ideas in the frequently chaotic practice of their action research. Despite this, the model presented above allows three conclusions to be drawn about the ethics of action research.

Firstly, based on the argument set out above, the ideological area of knowledge can be conceived as ideas that teachers develop through action research about the child–teacher–educational content relationship and – linked to that – knowledge about the child–school–society relationship. In order to do that, teachers have to make an explicit link between an ethic of justice or critique based on social theories and an ethic of pedagogy based on theories about human development, in particular theories about how children develop into adulthood.

Secondly, action research merely serves instrumental aims when theories about ethics are reduced to the ideological area and when theories about pedagogy are reduced to the technological area of knowledge. This reductionism can even cause inadequate practices to persist; an ethical basis for action research needs an explicit theory about the link between the ideological, the technological and the empirical. This link has not been made that well in the pragmatic vision of 'pedagogy as method', which has been dominant in the Anglo-Saxon tradition. In the tradition of 'pedagogy as human science', however, which has been more dominant in the European tradition, it has been more common to study the relation between methods and underlying anthropological assumptions about human development and society.

Third, empirical knowledge cannot be merely knowledge gained from personal experience, that is knowledge immediately available in practice (Laurillard, 1993). On the contrary, it is knowledge about how empirical knowledge gained from experience relates to general pedagogic and social ideas (the ideological area of knowledge) and general knowledge about methods (the technical area of knowledge). Empirical knowledge relates to both systematised knowledge based on the teacher's personal practical experience and knowledge based on academic research, which is the knowledge of others. It is precisely the exploration of this relationship between the two that can help teachers and student teachers to define pedagogic praxis as problematic. This is done by questioning the pedagogic and social norms and values that are taken for granted on which their actual relationships with the pupils are based.

Finally, this kind of analysis of the relationship between child, school and society is not only geared to the personal development of the teacher. The ultimate goal is to develop education that has a place for all pupils, regardless of their social background or personal qualities. As Groundwater-Smith (2004: 12) put it:

> We need to be ready and willing to engage in the notion of informed dissent that is created in authentic conversation where practice speaks to policy and vice-versa. We need to recapture the discourse of virtue where, as good scholars and researchers, we are concerned with truthfulness, respect and authenticity.

References

Benner, D. (1993) *Hauptströmungen der Erziehungswissenshaft. Eine Systematik traditioneller und moderner Theorien*, München: List Verlag.

Blankertz, H. (1969) *Theorien und Modelle der Didaktik*, München: Juventa Verlag.

Boyd, W. (1964) *The History of Western Education*, London: Adam and Charles Black. (Dutch translation: (1969) *Geschiedenis van onderwijs en opvoeding*, Utrecht: Aula-boeken.)

Brezinka, W. (1971) *Von der Pädagogik zur Erziehungswissenschaft*, Basel: Belz Verlag.

Carr, W. (1994) 'Whatever happened to Action Research?', *Educational Action Research Journal*, 2(3): 427–437.

Carr, W. and Kemmis, S. (1997) *Becoming Critical*, London: Falmer Press.

Cochran-Smith, M. and Lytle, S.L. (1999) 'The teacher research movement: a decade later', *Educational Researcher*, 28(7): 15–26.

Darling-Hammond, L. and Brandsford, J. (2005) *Preparing Teachers for a Changing World*, San Francisco: Jossey-Bass.

Dasberg, L. (1975) *Raising Children by Keeping them Young*, (in Dutch: *Grootbrengen door kleinhouden*), Meppel: Boom.

Day, C. and Sachs, J. (2003) *International Handbook on Continuing Professional Development of Teachers*, Maidenhead: Open University Press.

De Jager, H. (1975) *Human Development and Theories about Society*, (in Dutch: *Mensbeelden en maatschappijmodellen*), Leiden: Stenfert Kroese.

Dewey, J. (1984) 'The sources of a science of education', in J.A. Boydston (ed.) *The Later Works: Vol. 5, 192–1930*, Carbondale: Southern Illinios University Press, pp. 3–40.

Elliott, J. (1991) *Action Research for Educational Change*, Buckingham: Open University Press.

Gadamar, H.-G. (1976) *Vernunft im Zeitalter der Wissenshaft: Aussätze*, Frankfurt: Suhrkamp.

Goodlad, J.I., Soder, R. and Sirotnik, K.A. (1990) (eds) *The Moral Dimensions of Teaching*, San Francisco: Jossey-Bass.

Groundwater-Smith, S. (2004) 'Courage: facing the educational agenda', Keynote Address Presented to the Australian Teacher Education Association Annual Conference, Charles Sturt University Bathurst, 9 July, 2004, Australia.

Grundy, S. (1995) *Curriculum: Product or Praxis?*, London: Falmer Press.

Grundy, S. (1998) 'Research Partnerships', in B. Atweh, S. Kemmis and P. Weeks (eds) *Action Research in Practice*, London: Routledge, pp. 37–46.

Habermas, J. (1981) *Theorie des Kommunikativen Handelns*, Frankfurt am Main: Suhrkamp Verlag.

Hansen, D.R. (2001) 'Teaching as a moral activity', in V. Richardson (ed.) *Handbook of Research on Teaching*, Washington DC: American Educational Research Association, pp. 826–857.

Jay, M. (1973) *The Dialectical Imagination*, Boston: Little, Brown and Company. (Dutch translation: (1977) *De dialectische verbeelding*, Baarn: Ambo.)

Kemmis, S. (2005) 'Participatory action research and the public sphere', Keynote Speech at the Joint International Practitioner Research Conference and the Collaborative Action Research Network (CARN) Conference, 4–6 November 2005, Utrecht, the Netherlands.

Langeveld, M.J. (1967) *Concise Theoretical Pedagogy* (in Dutch: *Beknopte theoretische pedagogiek*), Groningen: Wolters-Noordhoff NV.

Laurillard, D. (1993) *Rethinking University Teaching: A Framework for the Effective use of Educational Technology*, London: Routledge.

Menck, P. (1999) 'Didactics as construction of content', in J. Leach and B. Moon, *Learners and Pedagogy*, London: Paul Chapman, pp. 111–124.

Michailova, N., Yusfin, S. and Polyakov, S. (2002) 'Using action research in current conditions of Russian teacher education', *Educational Action Research Journal*, 10(3): 399–423.

Miedema, S. (1997) *Pedagogy in Plural* (in Dutch: *Pedagogiek in meervoud*) (5th edn), Houten/Diegem: Bohn Stafleu Van Loghum.

Noddings, N. (2002). *Educating Moral People: A Caring Alternative to Character Education*, New York: Teachers College Press.

Noffke, S.E. (1995) 'Action research and democratic schooling: problematics', in S.E. Noffke and R.B. Stevenson (eds), *Educational Action Research: Becoming Practically Critical*, New York: Teachers College Press, pp. 1–12.

Olson, R. (2003) *Psychological Theory and Educational Reform: How School Remakes Mind and Society*, Cambridge: Cambridge University Press.

Poliner Shapiro, J. and Stefkovich, J.A. (2001) *Ethical Leadership and Decision Making in Education: Applying Theoretical Perspectives to Complex Dilemmas*. Mahwah, NJ: Lawrence Erlbaum Associates Inc.

Ponte, P. (2002) 'How teachers become action researchers and how teacher–educators become their facilitators', *Journal for Educational Action Research*, 10(3): 399–423.

Ponte, P., Ax, J., Beijaard, D. and Wubbels, T. (2004) 'Teachers' development of professional knowledge through action research and the facilitation of this by teacher–educators', *Teaching and Teacher Education*, 20: 517–588.

Popper, K.R. (1972) *Objective knowledge: An Evolutionary Approach*, Oxford: Clarendon Press.

Pratt, D.D. and Associates (1998) *Five Perspectives on Teaching in Adult and Higher Education*, Melbourne F: Krieger Publishing.

Riedel, H. (1977) *Algemeine Didaktik und Unterrichtliche Praxis: Eine Einführung*, München: Kösel-Verlag.

Sachs, J. (2002) *The Activist Teaching Profession*, Buckingham: Open University.

Scholte, J.A. (2000) *Globalisation: A Critical introduction*, New York: Palgrave.

Schwandt, T.A. (2001) *Dictionary of Qualitative Inquiry* (2nd rev. edn), London: Sage Publications.

Simon, S. (1999) 'Why not Pedagogy in England?', in J. Leach and B. Moon, *Learners and Pedagogy*, London: Paul Chapman, pp. 34–46.

Stenhouse, L. (1975) *An Introduction to Curriculum Research and Development*, London: Heinemann Educational Books.

Thoomes, D. (2000) 'The necessity of education and the importance of maintaining pedagogics as an independent discipline'. Available online at www.socsci.kun.nl/ped/whp/histeduc/thoomes.html (accessed 30 November 2006).

van Manen, M. (1994) 'Pedagogy, virtue and narrative identity in teaching', *Curriculum Inquiry*, 24(2): 135–170.

Vygotsky, L.S. (English translation in 1971, original written in 1921/1923) *Educational Psychology*, Boca Raton, FL: St. Lucie Press.

Westbury, I. (2000) 'Teaching as a reflective practice: what might Didaktik teach curriculum?', in I. Westbury, S. Hopmann and K. Riquarts (eds) *Teaching as a Reflective Practice: The German Didaktik Tradition*, Mahwah. NJ : Lawrence Erlbaum Associates, pp. 15–40.

Whitehead, J. (1989) 'Creating a living educational theory from questions of the kind: "How do I improve my practice?"', *Cambridge Journal of Education*, 19(1): 21–43.

Chapter 12

Pedagogical research in higher education

Ethical issues facing the practitioner–researcher

Lin Norton

Introduction

Researching into the practice of one's own institution raises a number of ethical dilemmas. Having worked in higher education for 18 years as a practitioner–researcher, I convince myself that the research I do on students' learning and on teachers' teaching at university is for the greater good of improving both. But what happens if my research shows the institution where I work in a bad light, or the student, or the teacher, or the subject? How do I know I am not abusing my power as a teacher who is also a researcher? How can I examine the effects of interventions in a controlled experimental way without disadvantaging students in the process?

This chapter is not about the many codes of conduct and the regulatory frameworks that currently exist. These serve a useful purpose but the danger is that they sometimes get treated in a rather superficial and pragmatic way. In my view, carrying out research ethically is not just about procedures; it is about a fundamental moral duty, which is ultimately the personal responsibility of the person who is doing the research. In this chapter, I think through the moral obligations of researching ethically, by considering the implications of balancing the aims of the research and the researcher with those who are researched on, in the context of the institution. I do not claim to have the answers, but I will raise many questions in my chapter.

Overview

Ethics in higher education is an increasingly important subject. Keith-Spiegel and Carr (1996) argue somewhat chillingly that there is a vested interest in universities to engage in a scholarly debate and investigation of the ethical issues of every profession except their own. The situation is changing. Barbara Blake of the Council for Industry and Higher Education is currently involved in producing ethical guidelines for universities and has this to say:

> A university or college may not be quite like any other business but the opportunity for malpractice or simply poor practice is enormous and can

have a devastating effect on the reputation and future of the institution ... There is currently much good practice within institutions. This was evidenced in the responses to our first consultation earlier this year when around 100 institutions provided information on their current procedures. However, it was apparent that much of what was being done was ad hoc and more likely to be a response to legal requirements or to a specific crisis than a considered approach to communicating and embedding the values of the institution. There is no doubt that institutions want to work within an ethical framework that is fair, transparent and based on best practice.

(Blake, 2005: 24)

Some universities already have codes of ethics or ethical principles drawn up and disseminated (see for example the Canadian Society for Teaching and Learning Ethical Principles for University Teaching, 2000), and there are currently some excellent examples of ethical codes such as those produced by the British Psychological Society (BPS), the British Educational Research Association (BERA) and the American Psychological Association (APA) but producing yet another code of ethics is not the only answer. Courses to help students think about ethics are currently being taught such as those described in the joint Ethics project, a one-year initiative funded by the Learning and Teaching Support Network, now the Higher Education Academy. This project covered six disciplines and produced an online guide to ethics teaching (Illingworth, 2004). In this online guide, Beale (2004: 34) makes an important point when she says that when teaching students about ethics it is important to '"think ethically" rather than simply adhere to a set of rules or guidelines. This involves thinking through any intended research and considering what effect it might have on the participants, any organisations involved and other parties'.

In the same vein, I will argue that the onus is on each academic practitioner–researcher who carries out pedagogical research to 'think ethically' about the consequences of carrying out research on students who are vulnerable and dependent on us (we grade their work and ultimately determine the classification of their degree) and on fellow university teachers, who work in the same institution as we do, which in itself may cause potential conflicts of interest. This is the focus of my chapter. Since any text on ethics addresses a complex range of issues, I have been selective and discussed those that have impacted on my own practice and research. These are: the negative effects of research on students' learning; the over-use of psychology students in research, the issue of fairness, and, specific ethical issues in pedagogical action research.

Review of the literature

In order to set the context of this chapter, I define pedagogical action research as research in learning and teaching which aims to modify practice, influence policy and strategy and produce publishable outcomes. As such, it falls half way between the distinction that Gordon *et al.* (2003) make between PedD (pedagogical development) and PedR (pedagogical research).

When reviewing the literature, I found remarkably little on the ethics of carrying out pedagogical research in higher education. An ERIC search revealed only seven sources which mentioned ethics in the context of pedagogical research. A quick random survey of five journals which publish studies in pedagogical research in higher education (PedR) showed that of 39 articles related to PedR, only five mentioned ethical issues at all (see Table 12.1). Bearing in mind this was a convenience sample of journals and so may not be representative of all, nevertheless, this shows that only 13 per cent of articles which directly reported on studies involving human participants made no mention of ethical issues apart from bald statements such as 'participation was voluntary'. This brief survey confirms that this is an area which is under-represented in the literature and in actual research practice.

The potential negative effects of research on student learning

A recent working party paper by Poole and Maclean (2005) was one of the few sources I found that specifically address ethics in pedagogical research. As they point out, there is a real dilemma in pedagogical research which is usually carried

Table 12.1 Analysis of articles for evidence of ethical issues as part of the research design

Journal title	Date	Vol. no.	Part no.	No. of PedR articles	No. citing ethical issues
Educational Action Research	2005	13	2	3	0
Educational Action Research	2003	11	1	2	0
Educational Action Research	2000	8	3	3	1*
British Journal of Educational Psychology	2003	73	4	1	1*
British Journal of Educational Psychology	2002	72	1	1	0
British Journal of Educational Psychology	2001	71	2	1	0
Studies in Higher Education	2005	30	3	6	2*
Studies in Higher Education	2002	27	4	4	0
Studies in Higher Education	2001	26	3	5	0
Active Learning in Higher Education	2005	6	2	5	0
Active Learning in Higher Education	2002	3	1	4	1*
Teacher Development (Special issue on teaching in HE)	2000	4	1	4	0
Totals				39	5

*These articles make some mention of ethical issues and are included later in this chapter:

Clegg (2000); Evans *et al.* (2003); Bell and Taylor (2005); Kirkwood and Price (2005); Howard (2002).

out with the express aim of improving the quality of student learning, but in doing that research, we are inevitably interfering with or affecting the students' learning itself. To tease out some of the difficulties in trying to resolve this tension, I am going to describe a number of case studies drawn from my own research, which I hope will illustrate some of the practical as well as moral difficulties. The first is concerned with the problem of carrying out a study which might unfairly advantage some students in their assessed work.

Case study 1: Improving essay writing through feedback

When I wanted to find out if writing feedback in a certain way would help my students write better essays, I was faced with this particular dilemma. My research design was to look at the effects of three types of feedback on essays that were part of a third-year class assessment: The three types were:

  (i)   using a standardised essay feedback form where the criteria were specified
 (ii)   responding to students' requests for specific feedback
(iii)   building feedback on what I had said before.

To do this, I assigned students in the class on the basis of their previous essay marks to one of the three conditions, so that I would have an equal spread of essay writing ability in each group. I then marked their essays, gave the feedback and asked them to complete a short questionnaire on how helpful they found the feedback in raising their academic self-esteem and in knowing what they needed to do to improve on their next essay.

Some might say that the answer to this dilemma was that I should have not used real essays but the difference between artificial laboratory-type tasks and real-life naturalistic research is one where, ever since my PhD research, I have come down firmly on the side of the naturalistic. Another solution might be to argue that, since I did not know which of these types of feedback would be more helpful, then there was no ethical dilemma for me to worry about. But that inner sense of unease would not let me settle for that. If I let students choose which type of feedback they preferred, not only would the responsibility be transferred to them, which seems unfair, but that would compromise the attempt to be objective in terms of balancing out essay writing ability in the three groups. So what did I actually do? All students were informed about the purpose and design of the study and told that I genuinely didn't know which type of feedback would be the most useful. Students were also told that if they wanted additional feedback, if the condition they had been allocated to didn't help them, then I would give them individualised face-to-face feedback as well after they had completed their questionnaires. In the event, no student asked for this and the results showed no difference between types of feedback – a consequence I think of my bending over backwards to give the fullest feedback possible in all three conditions. So the ethical dilemma was solved, in part, but I feel the study was compromised, and most disappointingly of all, I feel none the wiser from this study about which types of feedback are the best to help students improve their essay writing. There was, however, another potent ethical issue here. When the researcher is the lecturer, students are vulnerable and dependent. However carefully the request is phrased they may feel very uncomfortable in refusing to take part in the research, even when they are told that it will not affect their marks in any way. Human beings are social animals and a multiplicity of unspoken messages are transferred by our behaviours, so who is to say that the researcher/lecturer would not even unconsciously be affected by her perceptions that 'John' is a lazy unmotivated and/or uncooperative student when marking his work? In this particular research, everyone agreed to take part, but perhaps they felt coerced because of this specific concern. This was an area where I felt I did not satisfactorily resolve the issue.

(Norton, 1997; Norton and Norton, 2001)

The 'over-use' of psychology students in research

A subject-specific ethical issue which is of particular concern to me as a pedagogical researcher who comes from a psychology subject background is that psychology students are the most researched students in the world and this does not just apply to pedagogical research – take just about any social science journal and you will find masses of studies carried out on psychology students. Why? The argument goes that by the very nature of the discipline they should be willing and indeed will learn by taking part in research – to the extent that in many universities, psychology students form subject pools whereby they are given academic credit for taking part in a certain number of research studies. On the surface, this would appear to be a win–win situation where both students and researchers gain, but in ethical terms, I am not sure that this is morally defensible. For example Evans, *et al.*'s (2003) study on approaches to learning, cognition and flexibility on 226 Canadian military college students is an example of a typical procedure entry:

> Questionnaires were administered to students during class time in their introductory psychology classes ... Students were made aware that their participation was voluntary and carried no academic implications ... Data were collected from seven classes ... In all cases, the overwhelming majority of students *chose to participate* (greater than 93%).
>
> (Evans *et al.*, 2003: 517, my emphasis added)

My suspicion is that psychology students are used in research because it is easy to do so, but bearing in mind the unequal power dimensions, it is not easy to affirm that students do not feel pressured to take part in research studies such as these.

The issue of fairness

Poole and Maclean (2005) say that 'It is paramount that we be fair to our students with every decision we make regarding their educational experiences'. Nobody could possibly disagree with this statement but who determines fairness and how is it defined? Is it fair, for example, to take up lecture time giving out a questionnaire that might take 15–20 minutes to complete? Is it fair to offer inducements to students to take part in focus groups or interviews which might involve a time commitment of 30–60 minutes or even more? In the desperate quest to obtain data (and it can be quite desperate as my PhD students will bear witness), we are asking students to give up precious learning time – often crucial to today's students who have to fit in study with work commitments and domestic responsibilities. And so often, when they do give of their time graciously, they never get to hear the results of the research that they took part in – is that fair? Case study 2 illustrates this particular dilemma.

Case study 2: Identifying students who might be 'at risk' of academic failure

For a number of years, we have been working at Liverpool Hope University on exploring ways of encouraging students to become more aware of themselves as learners. This has involved a number of methods including asking students to complete a longish learning inventory called the Reflections on Learning Inventory (RoLI) devised by Meyer (2004). Huge efforts have been made to make sure that this exercise is of benefit to the first-year students who are asked to do this task as part of their personal development planning module (which was at the time of the research, a generic 20-credit module but has now been subsumed into the first-year subject modules). Students were given interpretations of their scores in downloadable guides; they were asked to attend a lecture where their 'learning profiles' were explained to them and they were required to discuss what they had learned in the context of their discipline with their Personal Development Portfolio tutors. Part of the research was aimed at seeing if it was possible to identify students who might be at risk of academic failure on the basis of their inventory scores.

The ethical issues here are that the nature of such research requires that we be very careful when determining that certain profiles might dispose students to be at risk or that particular scores might be a danger signal of poor academic performance, so the work is continuing until we are satisfied that we have an indicator which is reliable. Kirkwood and Price (2005) mention in their research how the instruments they used were scrutinised by their University Student Research Projects Panel, but this does not address the problem we are facing of being sure that our results are sound enough to be able to base recommendations to teachers upon them. This is important work but in terms of the students who have taken part, they will derive no direct benefit. In a way, they are being asked to help for altruistic reasons in the hope that the findings may benefit future generations of students. Is this then a justifiable use of their learning time? In this instance because the actual exercise itself was built into the PDP module and was designed to raise awareness of themselves as learners, then the answer is probably 'yes'. However, a related issue is that even though we cannot be certain that certain profiles or scores might suggest potential problems, nevertheless, what should we do about it when we do find these suggested patterns?

(Norton and Norton, 2005; Norton *et al.*, 2004)

Pedagogical action research: specific ethical issues

Action research carries specific problems or ethical issues where the researcher is looking to analyse the effectiveness of her/his own practice. In the university context this means teaching and consequent effects on their students' learning. In this situation it is practically impossible to disentangle the role of the researcher from that of the teacher. Poole and MacLean (2005) highlight two considerations: the extent to which participation is truly voluntary; and the maintenance of anonymity and/or confidentiality. Codes of practice can stipulate that researchers must make sure that students will not be penalised for not taking part and that any findings will be disseminated in ways that make it impossible to identify specific participants. Anonymity is fairly easy to ensure but confidentiality is less so, particularly if the researcher wants to quote students in their findings. Howard (2002) is one of the few authors who has discussed this in any detail in his research article on changes in nursing students' out-of-college relationships. As a lecturer in the university and a personal tutor for some of the students who took part in the research, Howard points out the unequal power aspects which specifically revolved around his contact with them in and out of the classroom, his grading of their assignments and his completing end-of-course summaries on which employers' references would be based. To address these issues, Howard used BPS guidelines, carried out his research after all coursework was marked and got approval from the local research ethics committee.

Of course, pedagogical action research does not always involves students; sometimes, as in my own research, it involves fellow lecturers as illustrated in case study 3.

Case study 3: Factors that influence new university lecturers' beliefs about learning and teaching

In this study I was keen to find out what effect taking the Postgraduate Certificate in Learning and Teaching in Higher Education would have on relatively new lecturers' pedagogical beliefs and values. Thirty current PGCLTHE participants were emailed to ask if they would be willing to take part in a questionnaire and interview study. In the event ten agreed. They were interviewed by a research assistant who transcribed the results and gave them to me anonymised. I then presented the findings at a conference and the results were also disseminated at Liverpool Hope University at the annual Pedagogical Action Research symposium, so while anonymity was maintained, confidentiality was not. One particular respondent did give me cause for concern as much of his interview expressed his bitterness about being on a short-term contract and having to leave at the end of the year. The personal dilemma I faced: should I present his account unedited in my research findings with its explicit criticism of a department within my university or should I leave it out altogether thus compromising my research findings?

In this case study, the effects of being a researcher who is also a colleague were mitigated somewhat by using a research assistant to carry out the interviews; nevertheless the fact remains that I am closely involved with the PGCLTHE, including moderating the marking of their module portfolios and, although anonymised, it was fairly easy from the context of the interview transcripts to be able to identify most, if not all, of the participants. This problem of 'insider research' has been discussed by Clegg (2000: 436):

> Insider research involves particular ethical dilemmas. The author of this article at the time the assignments were written was course leader for an Advanced Professional Diploma, but has since stepped down from that role and has completed the course herself. As a writer and interpreter she was therefore both insider and latterly positioned primarily as a researcher. Access to reflective practice statements was negotiated recognising the extreme sensitivity of the relationships between the actors.

The dilemma about the angry and hurt participant I dealt with by presenting an 'edited' version which left out some of the more direct criticisms. Looking back at this decision, I do not feel entirely comfortable that what I did was right; it protected the department and the institution but diluted the 'lived experience' of one of the participants. It also did not take account of my responsibility to the university in terms of feeding back the findings and making useful recommendations as has been suggested by Beale (2004) who says this is incumbent on the researcher whether or not the institution has commissioned the research. There is a related difficulty which is exacerbated in research which involves more than one institution where there may be issues of power and rivalry (Bell and Taylor, 2005).

(Norton and Aiyegbayo, 2005)

Conclusions and reflections

Writing this chapter has been a salutary exercise. I have always passionately believed in pedagogical research to improve the quality of learning and teaching and taken, I thought, good care to abide by ethical principles, but as the case studies show, I have not always dealt with these in an exemplary manner. Reading the literature such as it is, and looking to see how other researchers have generally neglected ethical issues, has made me think a lot harder about this. I still believe that it is the responsibility of the individual to 'think ethically', but in doing that I think some general principles and guidelines are helpful. I particularly like those which are derived from the medical practitioners' code of 'firstly do no harm'. It is too easy to be carried away with thinking about the benefits of improving practice in a genuine zeal to help improve students' learning or encourage fellow teachers to reflect on their own teaching to modify it, without thinking through the costs of participation.

As I said at the start of this chapter, I have no answers, but writing it has made me think again about the usefulness of ethical codes and guidelines and how if researchers work in an institution where there is no ethics committee, at the very least having one's research proposal scrutinised by a critical colleague is a starting point for ethical practice.

References

Beale, D. (2004) 'Ethics in applied research and teaching', in Illingworth, S. (2004) 'Approaches to ethics in higher education: teaching ethics across the curriculum'. Available online at www.prs-ltsn.leeds.ac.uk/ethics/documents/ethics_across_curriculum. pdf (accessed 23 October 2005), pp. 30–35.

Bell, E. and Taylor, S. (2005) 'Joining the club: the ideology of quality and business school badging', *Studies in Higher Education*, 30(3): 239–256.

Blake, B. (2005) 'Addressing ethical issues: a user's guide', Exchange, p. 24. Available online at www.heacademy.ac.uk/documents/ Exchange_Issue_1.pdf (accessed 10 July 2005).

Canadian Society for Teaching and Learning in Higher Education (2000) *Ethical principles in university teaching* (authors: Murray, H., Gillese, E., Lennon, M., Mercer, P and Robinson, M.). Available online at www.umanitoba.ca /academic_ support/uts/stlhe/ethical.html (accessed 22 October 2005).

Clegg, S. (2000) 'Knowing through reflective practice in higher education', *Educational Action Research*, 8(3): 435–450.

Evans, C.J., Kirby, J.R. and Fabrigar, L.R. (2003) 'Approaches to learning, need for cognition, and strategic flexibility among university students', *British Journal of Educational Psychology*, 73(4): 507–528.

Gordon, G., D'Andrea, V., Gosling, G. and Stefani, L. (2003) 'Building capacity for change: research on the scholarship of teaching', report to HEFCE available online at www.hefce.ac.uk/pubs/rdreports/2003/rd02_03/rd02_03.doc (accessed 9 October 2005).

Howard, D. (2002) 'Changes in nursing students' out of college relationships arising from the Diploma of Higher Education in Nursing', *Active Learning in Higher Education*, 3(1): 68–87.

Illingworth, S. (2004) 'Approaches to ethics in higher education: teaching ethics across the curriculum'. Available online at www.prs-ltsn.leeds.ac.uk/ethics/documents/ethics_ across_curriculum.pdf (accessed 23 October 2005).

Keith-Spiegel, P. and Carr, K. (1996) 'Annotated bibliography: ethical issues in teaching and academic life'. Society for the Teaching of Psychology (APA Division 2), Office of Teaching Resources in Psychology (OTRP). Available online at www.lemoyne. edu/OTRP/otrpresources/otrp_eth-teach.html (accessed 13 October 2005).

Kirkwood, A. and Price, l. (2005) 'Learners and learning in the twenty first century: what do we know about students' attitudes towards and experiences of information and communication technologies that will help us design courses?', *Studies in Higher Education*, 30(3): 257–264.

Meyer, J.H.F. (2004) 'An introduction to the RoLI', *Innovations in Education and Teaching International* (Special Issue: *Metalearning in Higher Education*), 41(4): 491–497.

Norton, L.S. (1997) 'The effects of tutor feedback on student motivation in essay writing', seminar paper presented at the SEDA Spring Conference on Encouraging Student Motivation, University of Plymouth, 8–10 April 1997.

Norton, L and Aiyegbayo, O. (2005) 'Becoming an excellent teacher: factors that influence new university lecturers' beliefs about learning and teaching', paper presented at the 5th International Conference on the Scholarship of Teaching and Learning (SoTL), London, UK, 12–13 May 2005.

Norton, L. S and Norton, J.C.W. (2001) 'Essay feedback: how can it help students improve their academic writing?' ERIC abstract No. ED454530.

Norton, L.S. and Norton, J.C.W. (2005) 'Predicting which students might be academically at risk in higher education', paper presented at the 11th Conference of EARLI, Nicosia, Cyprus 23–26 August 2005.

Norton, L., Owens, T. and Clark, L. (2004) 'Encouraging metalearning in first year undergraduates through reflective discussion and writing', *Innovations in Education and Teaching International*, 41(4): 423–441.

Poole, G. and MacLean, M. (2005) 'Ethical considerations for research in higher education', Working Paper No.1 of the University of British Columbia Institute for the Scholarship of Teaching and Learning. Available online at: www.tag.ubc.ca/about/ institute/Working%20Paper%20ISoTL1.pdf (accessed 22 October 2005).

Chapter 13

Concluding reflections

New challenges for ethical inquiry in the context of a changing world

Susan Groundwater-Smith and Anne Campbell

Practitioner inquiry in a global world

This book has been first and foremost one that has asked us, as those engaged in one form of practitioner research or another, 'How can we best conduct ourselves in ways that do justice to our practice and our profession?'. Variously, we have been asked to consider such issues as: fairness; relationships; thoughts and habits; participation and representation; and, inevitably, power. We have been confronted by complex dilemmas that require us to employ a kind of reflexive intelligence (that is, an intelligence that not only reflects upon phenomena, but also critically examines where and how our beliefs about those phenomena have come about) when unravelling them and weighing them up. There is a recognition throughout the chapters that practitioner research is contingent upon the contexts in which it is undertaken; that what may be appropriate in one setting may require a different resolution in another.

We are not here arguing that we swim in a sticky morass of relativism, but rather that we are sensitive to the dynamics of a given time and place when considering ethical issues. For example, confronting people with very limited literacy skills with official, indeed officious, letters requiring 'informed consent' could itself be seen as an unethical practice in that there is scant regard for the dignity of those being assailed by the bureaucratic demands. While chapters have not specifically considered the ethics of conducting cross-cultural research or inquiry in indigenous settings, it is worth referring to such a context to make the point. Robinson-Pant (2005: 98) discusses research in Maori communities in New Zealand, where 'respect is a term consistently used by indigenous people to underscore the significance of relationships and humanity'. Negotiating the terms of an inquiry in such a community might be very different to that where the researcher is dealing with powerful policy-makers who have the means and resources to manipulate and dissemble; to choose to accept or reject research evidence. For example, Baroness Estelle Morris in her opening address to the 2006 British Educational Research Association Annual Conference, and speaking as a former education secretary, noted that government policy is informed first and foremost by values and ideology rather than a rational analysis of available evidence. Parity of esteem between the practitioner–researcher and those with whom she may be engaged is always a critical variable.

The world of the practitioner–researcher is a changing one. It is one governed by converging information and communication technologies, a matter to which this chapter will return later. It is also one where boundaries and barriers are on the move. It has become commonplace to talk and write of globalisation. However, in the area of practitioner inquiry it has clear implications. As a case in point, we shall briefly turn to the Bologna agreement and beyond it to the Erasmus Mundus programme. In 1999 some 29 European countries as far afield as the United Kingdom, Iceland and Poland agreed to adopt a system whereby their tertiary degrees at the undergraduate and graduate levels were more aligned one with the other. A system of credits was to be put into place that would enable greater student mobility and access for both students, teachers, researchers and administrative staff to a range of opportunities and services.

Compatible with the agreement was the creation of Erasmus, a programme to encourage transnational cooperation between universities targeted at higher education institutions and their students and staff in all member states of the European Union then 25, the three countries of the European Economic Area and the three candidate countries being assessed for admission to the EU. In turn, the Erasmus Mundus programme has broadened to encourage participation from a wide range of students, teachers and researchers from countries all over the world. In its own words:

> Erasmus Mundus is a new global scheme providing a distinctly 'European' offer in higher education. It seeks, primarily, to enhance the quality and attractiveness of European higher education world-wide. Secondly, Erasmus Mundus Masters Courses and scholarships will provide a framework to promote valuable exchange and dialogue between cultures. By supporting the international mobility of scholars and students, Erasmus Mundus intends to prepare its European and non-European participants for life in a global, knowledge-based society.
>
> (Erasmus Mundus, 2001)

For the academic year, 2006–2007, 741 students from 92 countries and 231 scholarship holders from 45 countries were participating in the programme. Many of these graduate students are those who are undertaking master's level courses in education and who will, as part of their studies, be investigating practice in their own settings, many of which may be in the developing world. They may well find themselves enmeshed in regulatory frameworks that are unfamiliar to them, particularly in the area of ethical inquiry. While Bridges (2006: 15) writes of adaptive preference, justice and identity in relation to wider participation in higher education within a country, namely England, his notion of adaptive preference is one worth considering here.

The notion of adaptive preference is a pivotal one in liberal economic and social theory and, by extension, I shall suggest in moral theory. At its simplest it reflects the observation that in choosing what they will do, how they will spend their time or resources or what kind of life they will lead, people are affected by or take into account, for example, what they can afford, the likely responses of others to their choice, and the values and practices which shape them and the communities in which they live.

How then will a practitioner–researcher proceed, investigating practice within the constraints of a higher degree programme in another country? What happens to the notion of critique as espoused by a number of writers in this book, coming as they do from a number of different national settings? Returning for a moment to Robinson-Pant's (2005: 112) account of cross-cultural perspectives in educational inquiry, she quotes a student making a point during a seminar discussion: 'Students in the group felt that supervisors needed to acknowledge more the tensions of coming from another culture and political context and that in many countries, to be critical at all is "very risky"'.

This issue was recently brought home by Salleh (2006: 518) in a discussion around practitioner inquiry in Singapore education. It is argued in the article, that was first presented as a paper at the International Practitioner Research/Collaborative Action Research Network Conference held in Utrecht in 2005, that there are very real cultural constraints placed upon teachers participating in an action learning project in an environment that is unaccustomed to risk-taking – where the operational mantra is 'do it right the first time'. This tension is an almost unbearable one in the light of Kemmis's (2006: 474) concern for practitioner–researchers to 'tell unwelcome truths'.

Practitioner inquiry has grown and matured over the past 50 years. They are years remarkable for the rate and depth of social, economic and technological change. When the very ground is shifting under our feet, it is hard to hold onto some of the most fundamental of ethical principles. We cannot afford to remain hidebound. We need to be able to respond sensitively to new circumstances but we must also be clear about the consequences of actions that we take as they impact on others. This requires of us a capacity to imagine what it is to be the *other*. In Harper Lee's novel *To Kill a Mockingbird*, the central character, Atticus, advises his children to learn the simple trick of getting along with 'all kinds of folks' by climbing into their skin – to exercise what we would now name as empathic intelligence.

Arnold (2005: 20) describes empathic intelligence in these terms:

Empathic intelligence is not the same as emotional intelligence or cognitive intelligence, because it is essentially concerned with the dynamic between thinking and feeling and the ways in which each contributes to the making of meaning. The word dynamic is important because it highlights the psychic energy generated when one mobilises both thought and feeling in understanding experience.

She sees it as a capacity to be intersubjectively engaged with the 'other'; to have a commitment to the well-being of the 'other'; and to be intelligently caring and professionally expert. Arnold draws extensively on the work of the American educational philosopher, Martha Nussbaum (1997: 9), who argues for three capacities for the cultivation of humanity in today's complex world:

- the critical examination of oneself
- an ability to see beyond the local and to perceive the self as being bound to humanity by ties of recognition and concern; and
- a capacity to employ the narrative imagination by being able to step into the shoes of others.

If we aspire to have practitioner inquiry based upon ethical principles, these precepts would seem to provide a touchstone from which to operate. By adopting them we are engaging in the kind of practical reasoning advocated with such passion by Kemmis (2006).

Practitioner inquiry in a digital world

Just as the world is changing in response to global economic and social forces it is also responding to burgeoning digital forces. The convergence of digital technologies and the establishing of virtual networks have led to new modes of communication, dissemination and publication, all of which have ethical consequences for the practitioner–researcher. Consider the discussion in relation to one of the case studies cited in the student voice chapter (Chapter 9) where it was argued:

> It is interesting to reflect upon issues related to informed consent when data is being gathered unobtrusively such as was the case in Independent Girls' School where the postings on the bullying website on the school intranet were made available for the research. Tavani and Moor (2001: 6) in their discussion regarding privacy protection in the context of web-based technologies suggest that the concept of privacy is 'best defined in terms of restricted access, not control … it is fundamentally about protection from intrusion and information gathering by others'. Students were posting their responses anonymously in a password-protected environment. The site's webmaster was able to monitor responses through his knowledge of student passwords and intervened only when some example of the school's etiquette code was transgressed, such as naming a student rather than the behaviour that caused alarm. None of this information was available to the school-based practitioner–researchers or the researcher-in-residence. All the same, this is an area where we have to exercise caution. As Tavani and Moor (2001: 7) observe, the individual flow of information cannot be controlled, but individual protection can. The web is something of a blurred area in this respect. 'In general, diverse private and public situations can be imbedded and overlap each other in complex ways.'

Or take the possibility of practitioners working collegially in a digital setting that leaves traces of what has been said by whom to whom. Imagine for a moment a group of teachers in a 'chat-room', a digitally mediated networked community, exchanging developing insights about a feature of their practice. A number of practitioner groups are now exploring the efficacy of establishing communities of practice that share and interrogate knowledge in a distributed fashion through internet-based networking technologies.

The benefits could be seen to be the potential for developing multiple perspectives when the learning community is a distributed one in contrast to a school-based group that may be already relatively fixed in its ideas. The online community, for example, may allow teachers from a variety of schools to 'chat' across disparate backgrounds. The medium allows for anonymity; one doesn't have to be always asking for advice from people in the local setting. The chat-room may provide support for people who are experiencing different dilemmas. As well, there could be clear benefits in relation to bringing together people who may otherwise be isolated in more remote communities. A group can be formed from a wide array of teachers and experiences.

Kimble *et al.* (2001: 221) have researched 'virtual' communities of practice in the context of business enterprise in a global environment. They argued that there are two kinds of knowledge that can be built: 'hard' knowledge, knowledge that is more formalised and structured; and 'soft' knowledge, 'the more subtle, implicit and not so easily articulated knowledge'. It is the latter that would most likely be of principle interest to practitioner–researchers.

Interestingly, in a later web-based paper Kimble and Hildreth (2004: 6) warned of the dangers of individualism *within* the organisation when the movement is from the 'co-located physical world' to the 'geographically distributed virtual world'. They suggest that workers may form weak ties within the workplace when they develop strong ties outside it. This caution is unlikely to apply to practice-based settings where practitioners are so embedded in the life of the practice; but nonetheless, it is one worth noting.

One of the central ethical concerns of research that draws upon digital sources is the matter of identity – how might it be protected, why should it be protected, who knows that it is being accessed and to what purpose? Naive users of chat-rooms may not have even considered how accessible their ruminations might be. The American Association for the Advancement of Science (AAAS) identifies such ethical concerns as:

> the ability of the researcher to anonymously or pseudonymously record inter-actions on a site without the knowledge of the participants. [The problematics are associated with] the complexities of obtaining informed consent, the over-rated expectation, if not the illusion of privacy in cyber-space, and the blurred distinction between public and private domains.
>
> (AAAS, 2002)

While it is unlikely to happen in collegial practitioner–research settings, it is worth observing that 'lurking' researchers could see an opportunity to study individuals and groups within a naturalistic setting without the presence of an intrusive researcher (Nosek *et al.* 2002: 174).

Of course, identity is not only constructed through text. Another source of ethical concern for practitioner–researchers in a digital world is the use of images. The capacities of digital image-making builds by the month; not only are digital cameras ubiquitous but many of today's mobile phones have a capability to capture both still and moving images, not to mention the covert images caught by CCTV cameras in every location. The irony is that there is little control over images collected for security purposes, whereas those employed for research purposes are subject to greater and greater regulation. This is especially the case when it comes to collecting images of children.

Razvi (2006: 1) has pointed out that in the United States, university institutional review boards (IRBs) are 'extremely wary of ethics of visual data because of the potential to harm study participants'. This is certainly true also in countries such as Australia and the United Kingdom. Furthermore, in the instance of practitioner research in schools, systems themselves have edicts regarding the use of images of children, how and where they may be used.

At the same time that restrictions are being put into place, the power of the visual image in practitioner inquiry is being explored. Turning back for a moment to the study conducted at Independent Girls' School quoted earlier in this chapter and discussed at length in Chapter 9, the culmination of the bullying study was the development of a digital narrative constructed by the students themselves; this was only possible because the school was not a government school and where parental permission for the images to be used was considered sufficient.

So what are digital narratives and why are we seeing them employed more and more as a tool in practitioner inquiry? Kimble *et al.* (2001) found that 'story telling' is critical as a form for the storage, organisation and interpretation of knowledge of practice. The digital narrative is not only a medium for illustrating a case, but also can become one that can be a source for debate and discussion of a particular innovation or intervention. It is a method for linking still images and narrative together to create a short, evocative and informative multimedia work that incorporates still imagery, movement, voice and subject into an easily accessible form.

For example, digital narratives have become a tool used extensively by museums to enable visitors to develop their own understandings and explanations for collections (Mulholland and Collins, 2002). One of the authors of this paper has recently been working with the Australian Museum where the audience researchers, designers and education officers were engaged in a collaborative inquiry to investigate young people's perceptions of intended changes to major exhibitions (Groundwater-Smith, 2006); the latter is a work in progress with no publications to date. Similarly, she was the facilitator of an investigation conducted by a series of schools to examine uses of technology in robotics, web design, radio communication and satellite mapping. In each case digital narratives have been developed with the intention of publishing them on the worldwide web.

In these instances the digital narrative was designed and produced as the result of engagement of both the practitioner–researchers and the young people involved in the programmes; such mutuality itself raises ethical issues. Lin (2006: 1) argues, 'Being allowed to reflect on their activities, to present their own views of the data and to interact with the researchers, creating and enhancing such mutuality between researchers and respondents opens up a profoundly democratic way of conducting and validating research'. It is then important to observe principled forms of negotiation – what will be included, how it will be represented, how will the engagement be legitimised? All of these are significant questions. However, in the context of this discussion, the most important of the questions will be 'What will be the consequences of making this multimedia digital narrative available in such a public space as the net?'.

Another aspect of dealing with the digital world is its capacity to yield up information at any time and in any place, providing of course that one has access to the technology and the capacity to use it. This chapter, for example, was drafted in a remote area in New South Wales on a laptop computer with a modem link that enabled the user to access her university library, one that subscribes to a wide array of electronic journals, as well as the search engine capabilities of Google™ and a range of radio podcasts if she wished to use them. It was then sent electronically to Liverpool in England for the co-author to refine and develop. All over the world such electronic transactions are occurring – blogs and journals are proliferating; MySpace™ and YouTube™ are becoming sites where ideas are generated and exchanged. Copyright and ownership are themselves now contested. The ethics of intellectual property have barely yet been addressed.

Conclusion

This final chapter has raised more questions than it has answered. It has suggested that there are new moral and ethical challenges to be faced in a globalised, digital world. Obstacles, confusions and dangers can either be acknowledged and well-judged responses developed, that will themselves remain provisional and contingent, or we can remain blind to them and unsuspectingly be tripped up.

Of course our era is not the only one to have been marked by rapid change and social uncertainty. Consider the context in which Dewey organised his propositions regarding ethics and human behaviour. The Stanford Encyclopedia of Philosophy (2005: 8) points out:

> Rapid social changes that were taking place in his lifetime required new institutions, as traditional customs and laws proved themselves unable to cope with such issues as mass immigration, class conflict, the Great Depression, the demands of women for greater independence and the threats

to democracy posed by fascism and communism ... He [Dewey] stressed the importance of improving methods of moral inquiry over advocating particular moral conclusions, given that the latter are always subject to revision in the light of new evidence.

We too believe that the issues and challenges required to behave ethically as practitioner–researchers require of us continuing attention and vigilance in ways that contribute to good and well-lived lives.

References

AAAS (American Association for the Advancement of Science) (2002), 'Ethical and legal aspects of human subjects in Cyberspace'. Available online at www. aaas.org/spp/dspp/sfrl/projects/intres/main.htm (accessed 1 December 2006).

Arnold, R. (2005) *Empathic Intelligence*, Sydney: University of New South Wales Press.

Bridges, D. (2006) 'Adaptive preference, justice and identity in the context of widening participation in higher education', *Ethics and Education*, 1(1): 15–28.

Erasmus Mundus (2001) http://ec.europea.eu/education/programmes/mundus/index_en. html1#2 (accessed on 7 December 2006).

Groundwater-Smith, S. (2006) 'Millennials in museums: consulting Australian adolescents when designing for learning', Invitational address presented to the Museum Directors' Forum, National Museum of History, Taipei 21–22 October 2006.

Kemmis, S. (2006) 'Participatory action research and the public sphere', *Educational Action Research*, 14(4): 459–476.

Kimble, C. and Hildreth, P. (2004) 'Communities of practice: going one step too far?'. Available online at www.aim2004.int-evry.fr/pdf/Aim04_Kimble_Hidreth.pdf (accessed 20 September 2005).

Kimble, C., Hildreth, P. and Wright, P. (2001) 'Communities of practice going virtual', in Y. Malhotra (ed.) *Knowledge Management and Business Model Innovation*, London: Idea Group Publishing, pp. 220–234.

Lin, Yu-Wei (2006) 'Mutuality between researchers and respondents in virtual ethnography', paper presented to the Virtual Ethnography Workshop, Amsterdam, 27–29 September 2006.

Mulholland, P. and Collins, T. (2002) 'Using digital narratives to support the collaborative learning and exploration of cultural heritage', presented at the International Workshop on 2–6 September.

Nussbaum, M. (1997) *Cultivating Humanity: A Classical Defence of Reform in Liberal Education*, Cambridge, Mass: Harvard University Press.

Nosek, A., Mahzarin, R. and Greenwald, A. (2002) 'eResearch: ethics, security, design and control in psychological research on the Internet', *Journal of Social Issues*, 58(1): 161–176.

Razvi, M. (2006) 'Image-based research: ethics of photographic evidence in qualitative research', presented at the Midwest Research-to-Practice Conference in Adult, Continuing, and Community Education, University of Missouri-St Louis, MO, October 4–6.

Robinson-Pant, A. (2005) *Cross-Cultural Perspectives on Educational Research*, Maidenhead: Open University Press.

Salleh, H. (2006) 'Action research in Singapore education – constraints and sustainability', *Educational Action Research*, 14(4): 513–524.

Stanford Encyclopedia of Philosophy (2005) 'Dewey's Moral Philosophy'. Available online at http://plato.stanford.edu/entries/dewey-moral/ (first published 20 January 2005; accessed 20 December 2006).

Tavani, H. and Moor, J. (2001) 'Privacy protection, control of information, and privacy-enhancing technologies', *Computers and Society*, 31(1): 6–11.

Index